MW00806157

THE JAM WERE THE

Initially derided by New Wavers for being uncool suburbanites, Paul Weller, Bruce Foxton and Rick Buckler unexpectedly proceeded to fulfil every promise ever made by punk as they took social protest and cultural authenticity to the top of the charts.

The three-piece from Woking, Surrey racked up 18 hits, among them the timeless likes of In the City, Down in the Tube Station at Midnight, Going Underground and Town Called Malice. Their classic albums included *Setting Sons* and *Sound Affects*. Yet their musical excellence was only the half of it: they prided themselves on remaining accessible to their fans, disdaining Americanisation and spurning commercial compromise. Although it was a blow to their army of followers, their split at the end of 1982 was hailed as the perfect illustration of their integrity: a bowing out at the top, regardless of financial temptation.

Their story, though, was more complicated and sometimes less honourable than how it appeared from the outside, with the group's vaunted values contrasted by private recrimination and duplicity.

Sean Egan has spoken to a raft of insiders to provide the definitive Jam biography. Via access to recording producers, music label staff and all three members of the Jam, he has uncovered the full truth about a remarkable band.

Love With A Passion Called Hate: The Inside Story of the Jam

First published in 2018 by Askill Publishing
© 2018 Sean Egan
ISBN: 978-0-9545750-9-0

Back cover photograph: Derek D'Souza

WITH A PASSION
CALLED

THE INSIDE STORY OF THE JAM

SEAN EGAN

ASKILL
PUBLISHING

INTRODUCTION

The Jam were runts who became kings. By outflanking the numerous detractors amongst their peers, they fulfilled every promise – spiritual, political and musical – that the punk movement ever made.

In Clash single '(White Man) in Hammersmith Palais', Joe Strummer sneered that the Jam thought it funny 'Turning rebellion into money.' He was by no means alone in articulating misgivings about the band. The Jam came from uncool suburbia; they skirted conformism by censoring the profanities on their records to facilitate peak-time radio play; they were happy to promote their product on the despised *Top of the Pops*; they contradicted punk's anti-nostalgia principles via retro mod suits and R&B cover jobs... The foremost indictment of the Jam for their critics, though, was that frontman, guitarist, chief songwriter and main spokesman Paul Weller more than once indicated that he was not on the same implicitly leftist or anarchistic page as all the other new wavers. Not only did Weller tell a fanzine, 'We'll be voting Conservative at the next election,' but the Jam's July 1977 single 'All Around the World' overtly repudiated the intoxicatingly berserk final word of the Sex Pistols' 'Anarchy in the U.K.' by stiffly commenting, 'What's the use in saying "destroy"?'

Having successfully negotiated such opprobrium, in the run-up to their third album the Jam were on the point of losing their record label. Bruce Foxton formed a fearsome rhythm section with drummer Rick Buckler. However, with Polydor Records having rejected their latest songs, the Jam bassist could be found publicly mulling over running a bed & breakfast in the event of the band foundering. The victory that the Jam proceeded to pluck from the jaws of defeat cannot, therefore, be underestimated.

By 1979, with their point having been made about the rock aristocracy's decadence and self-indulgent virtuosity, UK punks sought to incorporate into the music's ethos more melodic sounds and higher production values. The Jam transpired to beat everyone to it. Their 1978 album *All Mod Cons* audaciously mixed the spirit of punk with the sonics of power pop. Moreover, its rave reviews and chart success suggested anything but an ensemble recently in danger of washing up on the shores of B&B management. Meanwhile, the bottomlessly malicious proletarian vengeance fantasy 'Mr Clean' indicated that Weller was shedding his conservative opinions.

Following *All Mod Cons*, the Jam assumed an air of greatness. Their 1979 album *Setting Sons* was a powerful examination of a dilapidated, class-bound Britain. Fine melodies and sweeping production ensured that its sad timbre didn't prevent the record also being stirring. It span off the single 'The Eton Rifles', a smouldering depiction of class warfare that improbably became a top-three single. Even more improbably, early the next year 'Going Underground', the group's scorching hard-rock denunciation of nuclear militarism, sailed to the top of the UK singles chart.

Sound Affects (1980) was less thematically ambitious than *Setting Sons* but once again solid in quality. It contained the band's second number one single, 'Start!' The song examined the Jam's relationship with their fans and saw Weller rejoicing that other people felt as fervently about social issues as he did – or, as he put it, 'Knowing that someone in this life loves with a passion called hate.'

Moreover, the Jam's art by this point had a dimension that other graduates of the class of '77 unwisely disdained for fear of being accused of going soft. Their catalogue is speckled with moving love songs like 'English Rose', 'Liza Radley', 'Monday', 'But I'm Different Now' and 'Happy Together'. That these compositions, like the rest of the Jam's canon, were sung not in phoney Americanese but in an English, working-class accent proved that sentiment didn't have to mean the sacrifice of punk integrity.

And what of the fortunes of the Sex Pistols and the Clash, the onetime top dogs of punk who had once ridiculed them? The former had successively lost musical director Glen Matlock and lyrical fulcrum Johnny Rotten, with the band's remnants participating in a pseudo-autobiographical movie whose tawdry and exploitative nature was as reprehensible as the artistic crimes of any rock aristo. The Clash had descended into a self-parody who treated with neglect and disdain the country that had once inspired them to write the great songs that were now coming increasingly rarely from their pens.

That the Jam were now not just the best but the most beloved musical ensemble in the land seemed to be officially confirmed in early 1982 by double-A sided single 'Town Called Malice'/'Precious'. Not only did it sail to the number-one spot, but it saw the three-piece granted the symbolic accolade of being the first act to be allowed to perform two tracks back-to-back on *Top of the Pops* for more than a decade-and-a-half. The Jam were not preaching to the converted, but bringing social commentary to the masses. Reporters were now beating a path to Paul Weller's door to seek out his thoughts on matters both musical and non-musical, as befitting an artist who had the aura of Spokesman for a Generation.

And then it was – unthinkably – over. In July 1982, Weller met with Foxton and Buckler and told them he had decided to leave the group, thus effectively bringing down the curtain on the Jam's career. It was a dissolution perceived as the final proof of the band's integrity, a noble falling on their swords in preference to the way the likes of the Rolling Stones and the Who insisted on keeping their money-making operations on the road long past the point where they had anything worthwhile left to say. Buckler and Foxton felt less magnanimous about the decision, partly because the reasons Weller gave them for the split differed from the ones he proffered the media. Nonetheless, that the split turned out to be permanent preserved the Jam in amber, leaving as far as the wider

3

world was concerned their integrity and their legacy forever unsullied.

This book tells the story of the Jam's short but remarkable career. There have been previous Jam biographies. All have their merits but all lack distance, being the product of Jam personnel, fans, friends or colleagues. Here is the first comprehensive and impartial Jam overview, celebrating them for their qualities, but where appropriate highlighting suspect motives and questionable conduct. Drawing upon exclusive interviews with all three Jam members, as well as with the people responsible for helping make and market their records, *Love with a Passion Called Hate* thoroughly and honestly examines the story of a unique band.

A SORT OF NOWHERE PLACE

Like all of the Jam, Paul Weller hails from, as he once termed it, 'a sort of nowhere place.'

Twenty-six miles south-west of London, the town of Woking in the county of Surrey is noteworthy for an ethnic diversity unusual for a 'dormitory' town: it contains the first mosque to be built in Britain. Otherwise, Woking is a classic suburb in the sense that its very quietude is blissful for older people but stultifying for the young. Rick Buckler observed to *Surrey Life* magazine in May 2012, 'We couldn't wait to get out of Woking, and to escape everything that it had, or didn't have. You leave Woking, you go somewhere else … The horizons were fairly limited … there were never any exciting activities.'

Like all of the Jam, too, Weller attended Sheerwater County Secondary School. The first difference in his circumstances compared to those of the other members of the Jam comes from the fact that Weller wasn't afflicted by parents who were prone to a variant of the lecture famously delivered to John Lennon by his guardian, his aunt Mimi: 'The guitar's all very well, John, but you'll never make a living out of it.' His father John and mother Ann encouraged Weller's musical dreams. In 1977, Weller would state in Jam song 'The Modern World' that even at school he felt quite sure that one day he would be on top. Was that confidence the direct result of his ambitions being thus buoyed? 'Yeah, definitely,' says Weller. 'Absolutely. Very, very lucky to have me mum and me dad, because they were both really supportive. A lot of people I know, their parents were dismissive of it all, were discouraging, but my parents were total opposite. But then they both liked music, 'specially me mum. They weren't musical themselves, but they both loved rock 'n' roll. Neither of them were academic. My mum was a cleaner, my dad worked [in] building, so it's not like they were gonna say to me, "You're gonna go to college son, or university." They weren't options.'

The Wellers' unambiguous support of their son's ambitions, though, had its downside. John Weller famously told journalist Paolo Hewitt, 'If it was a choice between Paul getting a guitar or something or paying the bill, we'd get the guitar.' This is, of course, on one level an admirable and refreshing change from the usual parental bewilderment. On another, it suggests a slightly disturbing level of indulgence. Weller's childhood was not materially privileged: his home for the first eighteen years of his life did not originally have an indoor toilet, a bathroom or hot water and he never had a foreign childhood holiday. Yet he was undeniably spiritually pampered. 'He was always quite spoilt,' founder Jam member Steve Brookes told Weller biographer John Reed. '…his parents doted on him and when things didn't go his way, he would stamp and shout and break things.' In 2017, Weller himself was mature enough to admit to Simon Goddard of *Q* that his teenage self was, 'Arrogant, overly serious and quite spoilt as well. By the time I was 18, although I wasn't a fucking superstar or anything, nevertheless I was making my living playing music and didn't really have a boss as such. I was very hot-headed and probably difficult to deal with.'

While having been spoilt is apparent in one aspect of his personality, peculiarly it is contradicted by another. Despite his pampered childhood, Weller's personality is inordinately intense and displeased. 'I'm never really happy wherever I am,' he admitted to Mike Stand of *Smash Hits* in 1980. 'I never see life as being steady. I've always been uncertain. I've never felt I could sit back and relax – there's just too much going on.' This wasn't a passing phase of youth. Eighteen years later, he was telling Paul Lester of *Uncut*, '…all my friends say I'm a rude, miserable bastard. They can't all be wrong.' That Weller knows that there is no justification for this mindset is partly down to the fact that he saw how troubled was the home life of his Jam co-founder. Weller admitted, 'I don't know why I'm like that … I've never had any real big traumas. Never anything that say Steve Brookes went through with his parents…' One could play psychoanalyst about Weller's pugnaciousness and depressiveness. A child to whom the word 'no' is rarely articulated must grow up with a subconscious assumption that the world should run along the lines he wishes. As that is not an objective which any human being can achieve – and as that grievance can't even be publicly aired because it's clearly unreasonable – it might very well come out in displays of arbitrary fury or melancholy.

All of this, though, is not the same as suggesting that Weller is a bad person. The very love with which he was inordinately showered has left him with considerable attributes. For instance, he is by all accounts an indiscriminately loving father to his eight children by four partners. He is also renowned for acts of great financial generosity to friends and family. The social conscience he has displayed both in song and life could also be said to be a symptom of a good heart.

Weller came to love music even more than his parents did, although he was quite selective. He told Lester, 'A lot of my attitude was based on Mod. I was never into rock bands.' Musically, Weller nailed his colours to the masts of Sixties pop, black or white, and was converted to the merits of rock only two decades into his recording career. 'Little Richard and Chuck Berry and Fats Domino,' he says. 'That's the real rock 'n' roll for me. Not that I don't like the Stones. I love the Stones. Rock 'n' roll is the first sort of music I ever heard, me mum and dad playing Elvis records and Little Richard records when I was a wee kid. They used to win jive competitions. I can remember going round the working men's club and they'd be up jiving. So that was always there. Me and Brooksey, and the Jam as well when we first started out, we would play all rock 'n' roll covers, mainly because they had three chords and they were dead simple to learn. Where does rock 'n' roll stop and rock start? Out of the two I prefer rock 'n' roll because it's exactly what it said: it has the roll as well, it's got that swing to it. So it depends what you define as rock. If it's like a lot of the Seventies rock, I fucking hated that and I still hate it now. I didn't hear any swing or any blackness in it at all. It was just widdly-diddley fucking tossers. Histrionic crap. If you're talking about the original black rock 'n' roll, that's what I really dug.'

Being born in 1958 – on May 25, to be precise – Weller began maturing around the same time popular music did. At the forefront of pop's development, of course, was the Beatles, always his biggest love. In 1995, he told Lisa Verrico of *The Guardian*, 'As a small kid, they were the first group to make me sit up and take notice of their songs. I guess I really started to check them out in '63 or '64. I was six years old … I became a total Beatles fanatic. I loved everything about them – their clothes, their music and, when I was a little older, their attitude.' He remained enraptured by them as their music evolved into phantasmagorical fare like 'Strawberry Fields Forever'. In 2009, he observed to *Mojo* of the latter track, 'I can remember the wonderment it filled me with as a kid and it still does after all these years – the soundscape it creates in my mind which I can never put my finger on and never want to.'

Another band who would have an enduring effect on Weller was the Small Faces, power-pop merchants turned psychedelic soulsters. One of his first musical memories is seeing the group perform their 1967 single 'Tin Soldier' on television. 'They were the most complete band,' he told John Hellier of Small Faces fanzine *The Darlings of Wapping Wharf Launderette*. 'They had a great look but that alone is no good if you can't play … The music, well that was just fantastic.' Weller would in the Jam's latter days take advantage of the fact that he actually looked a little like the band's frontman Steve Marriott, teasing his hair into an approximation of the Small Faces' singular style (off-centre parting, ears uncovered). In 2007 Weller chose 'Tin Soldier' as his favourite piece of music when he appeared on radio programme *Desert Island Discs*.

In late 1974, Weller belatedly discovered the charms of another Sixties group when he encountered the Who's signature song 'My Generation' on the soundtrack to the David Essex movie *Stardust*. His adoption not long afterwards of the mod fashion style was intertwined with his exposure to the band's 1973 concept album *Quadrophenia*, which explored the world of the Who's Sixties mod fanbase.

By the early Eighties, Weller was citing the Kinks' Ray Davies as his all-time favourite songwriter, although that might have been partly due to the fact that he was now seeing the world through the nationalistic prism of UK punk. In 1982, he told Chris Salewicz of *The Face*, 'He was the only person writing in that way at the time – writing about basic, ordinary life. And it's very pure English language that he uses – there are never any Americanisms in it.'

While the soundtrack to Weller's pre-teens was second to none, the Seventies and teendom – which arrived for him roughly simultaneously – saw a downturn. 'The early Seventies started off alright with Bolan, Bowie and aspects of the glam thing,' he says. 'Then it just descended into nothing, really. There wasn't anything that meant anything to me, anyway. A lot of my mates got into Philadelphia music and disco and stuff, but I didn't think there was anything happening. Just all those American stadium-rock bands. In England, there was nothing happening.' Weller describes British rhythm 'n' blues combo Dr Feelgood as 'the first band that made any sense to me in the Seventies.' He elucidates, 'When I heard *Down by the Jetty*: "Great, just something I can fucking understand and get into." And seeing Wilko Johnson. He was the first guitar hero of the Seventies for me – kind of led the way for me.'

At the age of twelve, Weller was given an electric guitar as a Christmas present. That it was soon neglected seems to have been partly the consequence of his parents not understanding that it required an amplifier. However, he eventually dusted it off, obtained an amp and began the process of discovering chords and tunings. The Wellers also had a piano under their stairs and Paul became reasonably proficient on keys as a consequence.

For a while, Weller's musical development went-hand-in-hand with that of a boy whose name has not gone down in rock history: Steve Brookes. A Sheerwater pupil a day younger than him, Brookes was so close to Weller that for a while he escaped his troubled home life by moving into Weller's house and sleeping on his bedroom floor. Weller taught Brookes some chords and insisted that they would escape the rat race together by becoming stars. The pair had lessons from the proprietor of the area's music shop and an older boy at school.

Weller, though, found he wasn't merely a guitarist. 'Some people are naturally songwriters,' he says. 'I remember [the] first three chords that I ever learned, I started to write my own song. It was probably shit, but that doesn't matter. I just got it straightaway in my head. As soon as we learnt new chords, we'd write a song around it. It was always the first thing in our minds to be songwriters and to write our own material.'

Originally, the pair pursued their professional aspirations as a duo. 'It was me and Brooksey's vision as two fourteen-year-olds,' muses Weller. Their debut was a lunchtime performance in the semi-soundproofed music room at Sheerwater County Secondary. Sometime in late-1972, John Weller secured them a turn in Woking's Albion public house. The pair's set was hardly momentous – a selection of around eight Sixties covers dominated by Beatles numbers – but many were the people, including his own parents, who were surprised that Weller found the gumption to perform in front of an audience at all. Weller's personality was the diametric opposite of that of his gregarious father. 'Very, very shy,' Weller describes his character at the time. "Til I got on stage. Lots of performers are like that. Very quiet, humble people until they get on stage and it all fucking comes out.' Even when the Jam achieved vast success, Weller was afflicted by stage fright and would routinely vomit before gigs.

Despite their ventures as a duo, Brookes and Weller knew that the group format was the most likely road to stardom. The fact that there were few musicians their age in Woking, however, posed an obstacle to assembling a band. They found one solution by persuading Dave Waller, a poetry-loving contemporary, to shell out £18 so that he could join the set-up on rhythm guitar. That Weller at this juncture switched to bass is, one suspects, partly a consequence of his hero-worship of Paul McCartney.

Worship of rock culture in general meant that, during this period, Weller went in and out of a short drug phase involving tabs, spliffs, pills and even shoe polish. 'But by the time I was 16, I'd given them up anyway,' he told Paolo Hewitt in 1980. 'I don't see there's any answers in drugs at all, actually. I think I'm lucky in the sense that I discovered that at an early age...' Weller would have a later, mid-life-crisis drug period, but the final line-up of the Jam – although more than partial to a drink – would never be a drugs band, and they are highly unusual for rock artists of the era for having no busts against their name.

Soon the rehearsals in Weller's bedroom and the local working men's club were augmented by Neil 'Bomber' Harris on drums. The group found a permanent berth in Sheerwater's music room, where the indulgence shown them by their music teacher merits John Avery a footnote in rock 'n' roll history.

The group's name is said to have come from Nicky, Weller's 4½-years-younger sister. Weller's mother told Paolo Hewitt that Nicky said at breakfast one day, 'We've had the [sic] Bread, we've had the Marmalade, so let's have the Jam.' However, Buckler told another Jam biographer, Alex Ogg, 'I think it was just because we were jamming at Sheerwater School. I don't think anyone turned around and said, we're the Jam.'

Bucker told Ogg that, however derived, he thought the name 'horrible' but that the group 'couldn't think of anything better.' In truth, it was always a poor choice. Firstly, it was banal. Secondly, it was awkward, without rhythm. Not insignificantly, in the band's early days of success, media presenters would often be found not using the definite article in their introductions. Thirdly, it was sort of stupid in as much as it would indeed put some people in mind not of music but a preserve. Fourthly, it assumed connotations unhealthy for its time and the Jam's direction: improvised, extended musicianship – jamming – was verboten under punk's anti-self-indulgence credo. As with so many band names, however, all these drawbacks ultimately became immaterial as people got so used to it that they ceased to think about it. In the end, the only connotations it possessed were what it reminded people of about the band's music, which meant that it reminded most people of high quality.

Despite the Jam's heady achievement of winning the Best Group of Instrumentalists category at the May 1973 Sheerwater Community Association talent contest, Harris decided to leave the group. The Jam acquired a permanent drummer in Summer '73 with the arrival of Rick Buckler, born December 6, 1955 and raised near Woking town centre. Buckler was one of three brothers. Buckler told *Q* in 2015 that he and Weller, 'sort of knew each other at school. Anybody who was interested in music used to hang around the music room and swap albums.'

After dropping out of school halfway through 'A'-Levels, Buckler worked at a succession of jobs – warehouseman, fishmonger, draughtsman – before settling into electronics quality control. Weller, as well as being acquainted with Buckler from the school music room, was possibly cognisant of a trio Buckler had played in with his twin brother. Buckler was invited by John Weller to a Jam rehearsal, following which his first gig with the group was at Sheerwater Youth Club in May 1974.

A fact little known during the Jam's existence – and indeed even today – is that Buckler's first name is actually Paul. He adopted the diminutive of his middle name to avoid the confusion arising from two people in the same group possessing a first name in common. Yet Weller was not actually named as Paul on his birth certificate but rather John – his mother is said to have given the hospital that name in a delirium – even if he has always been called Paul by his family. There is symbolism to be plucked from that convoluted scenario for anyone who cares to note that, despite the Jam forever insisting the group was a democracy, Weller was always its focal point, lead singer, chief songwriter and – by extension – meal ticket. It should also be noted that, in the early days, the band's name was 'Paul Weller and the Jam'.

Buckler's father, Bill, was an employee of the vast organisation that was the General Post Office, starting as a postman and eventually becoming a telephone engineer. Mother Primrose was a housewife. They were the archetypal parents who looked askance at the idea of popular music as a means of earning a living. Not only did Buckler never have drumming lessons, he was never allowed a drum kit in his home. He would write in his autobiography, 'Asking my mum if I could practise drums at home would have been like asking her if I could play football in the living room amongst the family china.' He picked up his skills purely from rehearsals, gigs and hitting his drum sticks on the end of his bed. From these almost comically constricted beginnings, he became one of the finest drummers of his generation.

By the end of 1973, the slightly comical Tweedledum-Tweedledee quality to the Jam's roll call (Waller-Weller) was no more. According to whom you believe, Dave Waller's departure was a jump or a push. Few dispute, though, that his guitar work was not particularly good. However, according to some, his aggressively leftist mentality bequeathed the Jam a legacy of a belief in songs reflecting working-class culture.

In May 1974, Waller's place was taken by one Bruce Foxton. Foxton was born on September 1, 1955 at Albert Drive, Sheerwater, where he was raised. Like Weller's, his parents were London émigrés. His father Henry was mainly a painter and decorator, while his housewife mother Helen did a variety of part-time jobs. He had two older brothers. Foxton was at the time of joining the group a printing apprentice – and a guitarist. 'I joined the Jam as a second rhythm guitarist,' he explains.

Within a couple of months of Foxton joining, Weller had taken his earliest opportunity to leave school, aged sixteen. Although habitually slapdash in his schoolwork, he appears to have concentrated on what his ambitions dictated it would be wise to: his two Certificates of Secondary Education (a version of 'O'-Levels for the less academically able) were in English and Music. He told Paolo Hewitt, 'Yeah I was pretty useless, but I was fairly good at English, which involves poetry and that. I wrote a poem for my CSE in English rather than do an essay.'

Weller would come to be perceived, like Bruce Springsteen, as a songwriter who understood the life of the working man. Like Springsteen too, he has never been a working man himself. Weller had a window-cleaning round with Brookes for a short spell and on odd occasions helped his dad on building sites. However, by the time of his departure from academic pursuits, his nascent talent was already bringing £15 per week into the household – around £140 in today's money. He had certainly by 1978 ceased having working-class income, prospects or mentality.

As with all bands who are just starting out, the Jam's early live work was a story of quasi-grovelling for semi-embarrassing gigs in unprepossessing venues in front of unreceptive audiences. Now, though, they began just perceptibly to move up in the world. It wasn't just youth clubs, community centres and British Legions that were indulging their aspirations anymore: they had built up sufficient chops and respect to be able to stake regular berths at Woking's Michael's club. Even better, they began to go on forays to exotic climes like Aldershot and Basingstoke.

Their growing abilities were of course part of the reason for this rise, but there was another significant factor. John Weller was indefatigable in championing his charges. A band being managed by one of the member's fathers is a potentially tricky situation. However, this never seems to have been an issue with Jam personnel. Buckler dismisses the suggestion that Weller Jr's colleagues feared his father would favour him in arguments. 'Because we all had the same goal and the same direction, there weren't really any arguments of any great note,' he says. 'It was all pretty much we know what we're doing, we know what the direction is we want to take and we were fairly unified on that.' Weller actually views his father's management as crucial to the band's success. 'We probably wouldn't have got it together without him,' he says. 'Maybe I would have still been a musician, but I don't know if us as a band would have gone on. We'd have probably had a punch-up and split up. He was a kind of emollient.'

LONDON CALLING

Despite their fanning out into Hampshire, the Jam's patch remained essentially their home county for half a decade. Eventually, this meant that the gratification generated by the fact of regular work was replaced by a feeling both of being on a treadmill and compromising their musical visions. 'We reached a brick wall,' reflects Weller. 'We played every fucking shithole – pub, workmen's club, social club. We played anywhere: weddings, fucking bar mitzvahs, whatever, and we did that for a good five years probably. And then after a while you kind of run out of it. I was always hoping and wondering when we could get to play to people of our own age, which we weren't doing in Woking. We were playing social clubs. Obviously, it's families and old people.'

'We always had to play a lot of cover numbers, like the old Chuck Berry numbers and Beatles numbers and Kinks things and what have you,' recalls Buckler. 'So we didn't really get a lot of chance to play our own music.' Says Foxton, 'It was inevitable that we outgrew the social club, working man's club shows, because we wanted to play more R&B and break away. If you're doing working men's clubs you have to play slow ballads. Nothing wrong with that, but you had to play something for all the family.' The turning point came as 1975 melded into 1976 and the band began to procure more and more gigs in the country's capital, where they had first played in November 1974. Buckler: 'It was great to move into London to find young bands doing their own music to their own audiences for a change. That really did give us a shot in the arm. The money was definitely a lot less to play at a London club then than it was to play in some of the working men's clubs round our own area, but it was something that we just felt we had to do.'

Not that the desire to play more hard-edged sounds was the sole motivating factor for their forays to the 'Smoke'. Notes Foxton, 'That's where the music industry was, and to get a label or anybody interested along, they're not going to come down to the Woking Working Men's Club, they'll come to the Fulham Greyhound or the Marquees of this world. That's mainly why we wanted to get up into town.'

Many visitors to London complain that the wonders of the capital are offset by the abrasiveness of its denizens. Asked the difference between people in Woking compared to those in London, Foxton laughingly says, 'They might give you a little bit more time of day, I suppose. Everything in London is so rushed and pretty frantic. They're just concerned about what they're doing, haven't got much time for you.' Weller, though, experienced no disillusion about London. He had been enchanted by it from a young age. Although Woking is less than an hour's drive away, and despite the fact that his father grew up there, for Paul Weller the capital was almost mythical. Steve Brookes has recalled that on his visits Weller would take a tape recorder with him to capture the city's supposedly bustling glamour. Little seems to have changed. 'Home for me now is London,' Weller states, almost anxiously. 'It has been since I was eighteen. I still love Woking. Not necessarily what it's become, but obviously my roots are all there, that's where I grew up as a kid and my formative years and all my friends and family, etc. London is my home, man. It has been for many, many years.'

On those early London dates, the fascination Weller had held for several years with the Sixties mod movement culminated in the Jam adopting a stage uniform of smart suits and pointed-toed, two-tone shoes. 'Paul was into the clothing,' says Foxton. 'He was too young to be an original mod. My middle brother was an original mod. I saw him with the Lambretta going off down the local ballroom to listen to Motown and was quite envious. Paul discovered it for the first time during the Jam days. It was a good way to go. I loved the clothes and it suited the band. I loved the whole idea. For me, not having really lived that mod era, it was fantastic to have a go at it the second time round.' Buckler: 'We wanted to look like we felt we sounded. We wanted to be sort of sharp and on the button. That look really just fitted in with our own psyche of it. But Paul was into the Marriott look and the haircuts and all of that sort of thing, more so than myself and Bruce.'

It was certainly an improvement on their previous image, the sort of shoulder-length-haired, kipper-tied affair that one now only sees in TV shows mocking the fashion excesses of the Seventies. However, while photographs of the Jam in mod suits demonstrate that they did indeed look good, the image also created problems. One was that in the context of the Seventies it was nonsensical. 'Mod' is an abbreviation of 'modernism'. In the post-austerity Sixties, the sharp-cut suits and short but well-maintained hair of the movement were indeed achingly up-to-date – as was its embrace of obscure R&B and soul music in a very white culture – but what Weller and his colleagues were now engaging in was a modernist revival, intrinsically a contradiction. Moreover, smart suits did not chime with the now more widely-held belief that rock 'n' roll was synonymous with informality. Additionally, when the Jam attached themselves to punk, their retention of their suits amidst a movement that favoured the sartorially confrontational marked them out in some eyes as imposters. And then there was the fact that dressing retro reinforced the prejudices of many Londoners who viewed people from suburbs like Woking as laughably behind the times.

Nonetheless, the look was maintained by the Jam right through to late 1977.

John Weller's diplomatic skills were not quite sufficient to prevent one particular 'punch-up,' if that is how the July 1975 departure of founder member Steve Brookes can be termed. Brookes decided to go solo because he was burdened by a full-time job, distracted by a serious romantic relationship, increasingly suspicious of Weller's mod obsessions and engaged with Weller in what he later described as a 'struggle for dominance.'

'I was pretty gutted really, because I lost me best mate in some ways,' says Weller. Gutted enough, in fact, to make Brookes a non-person. Although he speaks fondly of him now, for a period Weller refused to acknowledge the existence of his one-time closest friend. Brookes would ultimately not be the last Jam member Weller would erase from his life.

Interestingly, Weller being the last man standing from the Brookes-Waller-Weller axis had never been the most likely outcome. Buckler has noted that Brookes was a far more proficient guitarist than Weller. Meanwhile, Dave Waller's forceful personality may not have been to everyone's taste, but was more appropriate for a rock group than Weller's taciturnity-cum-awkwardness, while Waller's reported comment when hearing Elton John's 1973 single 'Saturday Night's Alright for Fighting' that the Jam should be writing similar songs about working-class culture is extraordinary punk prescience.

For a short period after Brookes' departure, the Jam went through the tedium of auditioning and recruiting people who didn't work out. 'We tried a keyboard player, there was another rhythm guitarist at one point,' recalls Buckler. He adds, though, 'We always seemed to bounce back as the trio.' Says Foxton, 'It found its own feet in the end ... After doing numerous auditions and for whatever reason not getting on with the guy that was auditioning or his playing wasn't what we wanted or whatever, we had a re-jig ... We just got fed up with auditioning and thought, "Well, let's give it a go with the three of us" ... Paul was playing bass at that time, when there was four of us, so we switched over, because Paul found it more comfortable to play rhythm/lead guitar ... Paul showed me a couple of bass lines and I took it from there,

19

so it just come about naturally in the end.' Weller (who has said Foxton wasn't a strong enough rhythm guitarist to fulfil that role) avers, 'Sometimes you need a component to leave for the other parts to become something else, and that's exactly what happened. When Steve Brookes left, it left me free to be the frontman and also the main songwriter. Our sound really came from that. We just *worked* as a three-piece.'

The three-piece, though, was not a common set-up. Trios are not unknown in popular music, of course, but the very fact that they are far less common than the lead guitar/rhythm guitar/bass/drums set-up demonstrates the belief – or anxiety – that fewer than four members results in overly-sparse soundscapes. The only way for a three-piece to compensate for holes in its collective sound is industry. The Jam became a power trio, if less in the virtuoso-oriented vein of Cream and the Jimi Hendrix Experience and more in the hyperactive approach of the Who and Dr Feelgood (effectively three-pieces because their singers didn't play an instrument). 'It does make you play harder,' says Foxton. Concurs Buckler, 'There was nowhere to hide in a trio. You can't just stop playing. All three of you have to put in a hundred per cent.' Buckler adds, 'Because of this thing of being a three-piece, we all contributed as much as possible. There's a lot of melody lines that come out of Bruce's bass, for instance.'

Although Weller can acknowledge that the three-man Jam was a sonic improvement even despite losing his best friend, the changeover meant that there was one sort of dynamic within the group that, from his point of view, was a loss. 'I was closer to Steve,' says Weller. He says of Foxton and Buckler, 'There was three or four years' difference in our ages and I think it makes a big difference. When I was sixteen or seventeen, Bruce was 21 and he had a proper job and he had a car and he had a girlfriend. It was like: wow, he's a grown-up.'

Weller was now in a group with people with whom he did not

much socialise. Rock groups, of course, don't primarily select personnel on the principle of whether they are, or will become, personally close. If a band is lucky, the personnel will like, or at least be able to tolerate, each other. Sometimes, though, the situation created is a dysfunctional family involving a complicated mesh of obligation and resented interdependence. While it wouldn't be true to say that the Jam disliked one another, the fact that they were now comprised of people who were essentially just colleagues quite possibly doomed them from the outset to a relatively short life.

Such issues, though, are pushed to the back of the mind when a band is carving out a trail to the holy grail of stardom. This might be said to especially apply to Weller, to whom music was much more than a calling. He recollects of this period, 'Even at that time, I had quite romantic notions of what a band should be and how important music is and rock 'n' roll is. I took it further than just enjoying the music. I thought it was a cultural force as well. I was obsessed with it. It was everything to me.' Unencumbered by thoughts of what their new set-up might mean for their longevity, the three-piece Jam continued their efforts to Make It.

RIDING A REVOLUTION

Playing in the capital had given the Jam the musical freedom to play 'Most R&R Maximum R&B' (their gig poster strapline, adapted from an old Who billing). However, there was a difference between playing music well and being part of the vanguard of a new movement. Notes Weller, 'I was waiting for the revolution to happen and then in 1976 when I saw the Pistols – I saw them at the Lyceum at an all-nighter – I realised the revolution was about to begin and I fucking wanted some of it.'

The Sex Pistols' gig on July 9, 1976 at the Lyceum Ballroom in the Strand in London's West End was their 35th live performance. During the eight months since their November 1975 debut, the London quartet had indeed been the unlikely instigators of a revolution. Although a group of musicians barely out of their teens, boasting no virtuoso players and fronted by a singer who could be both disquieting and discordant, they inspired almost religious fervour. At their debut gig, a member of the headlining act – Stuart Goddard, later known as Adam Ant – became the first in what would be a long line of musicians to abruptly decide to ditch his unexpectedly dated-seeming musical set-up in order to emulate their approach. Not long afterwards, Joe Strummer, frontman of R&B revivalists the 101'ers, decided to break with his colleagues to form a band in the Pistols' image. Said group would become known as the Clash. The origins of the Damned were more gradual, but they coalesced from the same pool of edgy London musicians as the Clash. The aggregate effect of such conversions, formations and affectations was a movement predicated on musical minimalism, stage confrontationalism, grotesque clothing styles and the replacement of the traditional respect for predecessors with studied contempt. The movement was given the name 'punk rock'. As this movement's initially inchoate credo became codified, it adopted a concern with addressing social issues in song lyrics, cropping hair short in repudiation of a hippie ideal that was considered to have failed, and disdaining the pseudo-Americanisms which had so long enveloped British post-Elvis popular music.

'They were just the antithesis of everything else that was happening musically,' says Weller of the Pistols. 'It was only like a year after the Feelgoods seeing the Pistols. You have to see this in historical context: just to see a band who had short hair, played three-minute songs, violent and aggressive, hating the audience, or that kind of vibe. When you're that age (I was seventeen when I see 'em), it's everything you want really. It's everything I was missing from all the other shit that was around. I don't subscribe to the whole Year-Zero bullshit – that's just a press thing; I never remember that happening really – but all the people that we liked from the Sixties had morphed into something totally alien. The whole rock star thing didn't mean nothing after a while. It was vacuous. Everyone read into punk what they wanted to read into it. For me, it was the clarion call. Seeing the Pistols was the call to arms: it was like, now it's our time. We were all too young to be part of the Sixties.' Weller was also impressed by the Clash. He told Hewitt, 'What they said in interviews was so different, no group had ever fucking said it before. They just showed up the music business for what it was … The whole separation of stars and their audience. I had never thought of those things before.'

Foxton recalls, 'Seeing the Pistols gave Paul a real musical direction. He wanted to write along those lines. When he came to us with the first few songs, it was fantastic. It was like, "Yeah, this is what we want to do." We broke into the London pub circuit aiming to play more rock 'n' roll songs, but we still needed some sort of firm direction. We were influenced by the Feelgoods etc., as you can hear on the early songs, but the Pistols did change his way of thinking and writing.' Buckler recalls Weller's songs, pre-punk, being 'very sort of Beatle-esque writing, love songs and that sort of thing.' He says that the Sex Pistols 'certainly opened up Paul's eyes to the possibility of subject matter.'

Buckler, though, feels that Weller's new writing style didn't completely transform the group. 'We didn't really have to make much change,' he insists. 'We still wore the suits. We were still playing hard, fast rock 'n' roll.' Weller semi-confirms this when he says of punk, 'I took what I wanted from it, really. I read into it what I saw in it, and maybe that's not the same as what the Clash thought or the Pistols thought. I saw it as a cultural revolution for our generation because it had been a very, very barren time before that and if nothing else punk brought kids out of the bedrooms and back into the dancehalls and the clubs. People making their own clothes, people doing fanzines, people forming bands. Whatever it may have been, it was quite a creative time. It only lasted from '76 to '77. Once you saw people walking around in punk uniforms... Walk down to Chelsea down the King's Road, '78 maybe, and seeing all these fucking idiots with Mohicans and leather jackets all drinking cider and off their bollocks on either smack or sulphate. I didn't really think it was about that. I thought it could have been a real working-class revolution, personally. But maybe that's 'cos I read too much into it, which is a fault of mine, or a blessing.'

Buckler admits of the punk scene, 'We did feel a little bit on the fringe of it.' While the Jam were undoubtedly considered part of the punk movement in a way that, say, the Stranglers were not, at the same time they laboured under an outsider status. The reasons were various. Despite their set being increasingly comprised of originals, and despite the disdain punks were expressing for any older musician (the fabled Year-Zero mentality to which Weller refers and which he is almost alone in claiming punk never adhered to), the Jam still played covers of songs from bygone years. Surrounded by people enthusiastically partaking of amphetamine sulphate, they publicly disavowed drugs. They rejected punk's penchant for ripped-shirts and bizarre body ornamentation, continuing to play their fiery music in decorous collar-and-tie. It all suggested people who didn't quite get it, like a wimp at the school disco dressed to impress in his dad's Sunday best. Mark Perry, editor of punk bible *Sniffin' Glue*, told Weller biographer John Reed his feelings about the Jam: 'I just thought it was ridiculous that these guys dressing in suits and having all the mod-ish moves tried to latch into punk ... they seemed opposite to what punk was supposed to be about. During punk, we put aside what we'd liked before. I was into Zappa and Little Feat, but the idea was to forget what you'd known before...' The Jam's presumptuous or phoney aura was hardly leavened over the next couple of years by provocative comments that Weller proceeded to make in the music press.

For Weller, the first and foremost reason for the Jam being the runts of the punk litter, at least amongst fellow musicians, was the fact that they came from Woking. He told *Mojo*'s Phil Sutcliffe in 2004, 'The Jam were never seen as hip. We were three little hicks from hicktown. We were never part of that trendy art school social world. We were very much outsiders.' The Jam's sin wasn't simply the fact that they were non-Londoners. Being a punk band from up north like Manchester's Buzzcocks or County Durham's Penetration had its own punk credibility oriented around the lack of privilege in the 'regions'. Nor did hailing from the South Coast cause the Adverts to be looked on with scorn. The Jam's problem was that they came from far away, but nor far enough. That they hailed from green-fringed suburbia automatically made them less cool than products of urban squalor, but, more than that, they were like Londoners – accents, mindsets – but a risibly less cool variant. No doubt also playing a part in the perception amongst the capital's punks of the Jam as prats is the sort of shock articulated by Foxton above at the brusqueness of Londoners. The Jam had fallen prey to the mentality revealed by the Sex Pistols in their song 'Satellite', which sneered at its out-of-towner subject for living in

25

what Johnny Rotten dismissively labelled a 'satellite of London.'

The disdain in which the Jam were held would mould their attitude, their songs and their career. While Weller hated not being a city boy, and was quite ferocious in saying so, he was taken aback when his criticisms of his hinterland were repeated back to him by the punk musicians whose credo and art he so admired. Particularly dispiriting must have been the suggestion that his band's origins were an actual disqualification to membership of the scene. In more than one of the songs he wrote in the wake of first seeing the Sex Pistols, Weller pleaded his case to not be excluded because of his roots.

For his part, Foxton says he never felt that the band would have had more of a cachet if they'd actually hailed from the capital. 'I thought it was first and foremost about the music,' he reasons. 'It wasn't just London bands playing in London, was it?' Certainly it has to be said that the Jam were readily accepted by punk crowds, who were visibly less obsessed than punk musicians with credibility and more preoccupied with a good show, something few disputed that the Jam provided. As the band began noticing familiar faces in the audiences at their London gigs, they realised they were building not just a following, but a hip and devoted following. Weller later said, 'Even when it was only 400 people, those 400 were a really powerful force.'

PROVIDENCE AND A RECORD DEAL

The next step upwards for the Jam was a record deal. John Weller hadn't been backward in coming forward in this regard, having tried to interest EMI in his charges as far back as early 1975. Perhaps it was a good thing that, despite some interest, the overture went nowhere: it's difficult to envisage a long career for what was then an unremarkable covers band had the behemoth label signed them at that point. Two years on, the Jam were a far more interesting proposition.

The Jam acquired their first music-press coverage in October 1976 by staging an alfresco, impromptu London mini-concert. Explains Weller, 'We played in Soho Market. Just simply plugged into a stall holder's socket and started playing on the street. The Clash [turned] up to see us. I think there was a mutual interest in what we were doing.' In 1980, John Weller told Phil Sutcliffe of *Sounds*, 'I got to know this stallholder and asked him if we could use his electricity. We plugged in a three-pin and played off the back of a lorry. Chas De Whalley and Jonh Ingham were there and Caroline Coon took some snaps.'

The write-ups by the music journalists John Weller spoke of in that quote naturally provided the band a handy spotlight. Before long, independent label Chiswick Records were sniffing around. The Jam camp, though, kept their heads. They were wise to do so, for a minnow like Chiswick was hardly likely to be the only option when every label in the land was currently desperate to nab its own punk act. This was not just because of the usual penchant for record companies to follow the latest trend, but because at the time the punk philosophy which dictated that established rock acts were creatively bankrupt sell-outs genuinely seemed like it threatened the future of any musician over thirty. In such a febrile atmosphere, it was unlikely that new wavers as patently talented as the Jam would not attract the interest of a major.

Despite this, the Jam were undoubtedly the beneficiaries of

providence. It related to the frustrations experienced by one Chris Parry, a Polydor Artists & Repertoire manager whose prescient belief in punk had been heartbreakingly and repeatedly frustrated.

New Zealand-raised Parry says his function within Polydor Records was, 'a junior A&R man.' However, he also says, 'I was 27, with a beard. I looked a bit like Cat Stevens. I was a decade above [punks].' Although outrageously elderly, Parry was one of punk's early champions. He was alerted to the Sex Pistols by his managing director Freddy Hine. Parry recalls, 'He was concerned about Slade and the Osmonds all fading away and I was saying to him, "Well, clearly time moves on. There's new bands out there. We've just got to find some for the label." Freddie had a friend that owned the 100 Club and [he] said, "Look, I've just had this band down here. I've never seen fans like it. This is weird. I remember the Stones coming down here. It's like that sort of thing. They've got their own fans and they don't look like anybody else. You should check it out." So I went down to the 100 Club and saw the Sex Pistols. I loved what I saw.' Was what he saw the future? 'Yeah, totally. Got it in one.'

Parry championed both the Pistols and the Clash in the face of record-company hostility and bewilderment. Sex Pistols manager Malcolm McLaren paid him a visit and accidentally left behind a cassette featuring his charges' music. Parry: 'Everyone was quite interested about this character that came into the A&R department. I gave my head of promotions the tape. He came marching up the next morning and said, "If you think I'm gonna fucking promote this shit you have another fucking think coming."' When Parry took his boss Jim Cook to see the Clash play in Chelsea, he recalls, 'We were at the back and some arsehole ligged a bottle of beer. It shimmed past Joe Strummer's head – if it had got him right in the forehead it probably would have killed him – and it hit the back of the wall. Joe stopped. He put his guitar down and he was so furious. He saw a long-haired fucker that happened to be my boss and he just thought that's where it came from. I went "Joe, Joe, Joe, it wasn't him, it was behind us." Then we got out of the building after the set and Jim Cook just said, "If you think you're gonna sign them, you can think again."'

It was perhaps this sort of hostility from the gatekeepers of the music industry that led McLaren to make a remarkable overture to Parry. 'There was a moment when [Clash manager] Bernie Rhodes and Malcolm McLaren actually realised that they were just knocking against doors that weren't opening,' recalls Parry. 'There was a lot of competition on the street between the Sex Pistols and the Clash in the sense of how they saw themselves. It was [a] love-hate thing. It was like a football league with two teams: who was gonna be number one, who was gonna be number two. Malcom said, "Why don't you just sign both of us? Because at least we can get on to the next phase." Christ knows what he had in mind to follow, but he was serious. I had a conversation with Bernie about that and Bernie was pretty okay. Bernie was frustrated as well.'

However, Parry says, 'I wanted the Pistols. The Pistols were my band. I liked the Clash, I just found that there was a bit about the Clash that was just a bit retro. There's a bit of R&B in the Clash. I just thought they were jumping on someone else's bandwagon.' Accordingly, Parry recommended a contract be drawn up for McLaren's mob. 'I thought we'd signed the Sex Pistols,' he says. 'I thought we'd wrapped up the Sex Pistols on a Friday and that's the very Friday that EMI signed them. Malcolm was very duplicitous because him and his lawyer worked two labels at the same time. We were the foil label, now I know. Malcolm didn't really want to do Polydor. Malcolm really wanted to go to EMI. He wanted to go to the heart of the music business in Britain and shake it up. He needed to be where the Beatles were ... They were in the studio. They were recording, I thought for us, that weekend. I phone Malcolm on the Sunday to see how recording was going. He said, "I'm sorry Chris, late Friday night we signed to EMI." We couldn't stop them. We could kick them out of the studio, which was what my bosses decided to do, and they got a very bad feeling about punk from that moment on. Corporately, it wasn't a good story anymore because they felt they'd been fucked over.' Parry, though, felt even worse than his superiors: 'I was in tears about the Sex Pistols. I was in bits.'

Parry opted for the Clash as consolation prize. 'Clash were unsigned when they went on that ill-fated tour with the Sex Pistols,' says Parry. 'I put the Clash in our A&R studio in Stratford Place, where Polydor was headquartered. We had 'Janie Jones', 'White Riot'. We had the album, really, unlike McLaren's tape, which was four tracks. I played it to my head of A&R. There was less angst about it. It was all pretty good to go, and Bernie was quite happy because Malcolm had this EMI deal and Bernie now just wanted to get a deal, get going. By this time, Stiff Records [had] put out the first punk discs so everyone was getting a bit panicky.' In fact, famously the Clash signed to CBS Records for an advance of £100,000 in January 1977. Some reports say that a taxi cab was diverted at the last minute toward CBS when the band members were in the act of traveling to append their signatures to Polydor paper. Parry and his employers had been 'fucked over' again.

However, Parry was already beginning to learn something about perseverance and philosophicalness courtesy of Jonh Ingham, the misspelt music journalist who was one of the early print champions of punk. 'His advice to me when the Sex Pistols went to EMI was "Don't worry, Chris. Just sign the Clash. Sex Pistols are great, they're going to break through and they're going to make a lot of noise, but the Clash will be the longer-term bet. You'll be better with the Clash."' Although Parry wasn't able in the end to deploy this philosophical reasoning to acquire his second choice, it became even more relevant with the act he *was* able to sign. 'I did remember that. I remembered that it's not necessarily the ones that break through into new ground, it's the ones that crowd round behind them that often do the best. And so was to be the case. I did well out of remembering that as I went through life.'

That Parry turned his attention to the Jam was a consequence of the recommendation of one of the group's increasingly large band of followers. 'I was hanging around all the punk kids,' he says. 'I was buying beers because I had an expense account. There were a few people I kind of liked and one of the guys that was always there was Shane McGowan.' McGowan would later find fame as frontman and main songwriter of the Pogues, but was then a humble fanzine editor. 'Shane was there early on in the punk movement. A likeable guy. I was in Chelsea Town Hall, the Clash were playing and the Clash had signed to CBS. I came up to the show anyway. Shane said, "Don't worry, Chris. I know it's really hard for you, but there's another good band coming up. There's a band called the Jam, they're planning the Marquee Saturday night. They'll be worth you checking them out."'

Parry says he had not heard of the Jam before. He also insists he saw them in the last week of 1976. 'In December beyond Christmas, before New Year.' However, the only documented Jam date at the Marquee on a Saturday in this period seems to be January 22, 1977. Either way, he says, 'They were the under-card. No one gives a shit who you are really, and the Marquee on Saturday night was not a particularly good club. It's amateur night really. But they played really well … Roland Rennie, who was an A&R guy at Polydor, said, "The thing about a successful band, there's something about them, something that separates them from everybody else," and Paul Weller did that for me. I just felt that he had something about him in his voice. He munched his syllables somewhat, but there was something about him.' Him having been slightly sceptical of the Clash for their backwards-glances, Parry might be expected to have been put off by the even more pronounced throwback elements of the Jam, but Parry reasons, 'The sound was retro to some extent but was updated to be fresh in itself. Just gave me the sense that this will work.' He additionally says, 'I happen to like the Who a lot. The very early Who records. I also like the very first Kinks records. So I liked that R&B edge, English-style with a bit of fashion. It didn't weird me out that there were these kids wearing slightly sharp suits being a bit kind of mod. And I had some personal friends who were truly mods, but older … They weren't perceived as phonies. I think a lot of that's down to Paul's personality as well. If Paul was a phoney, then so was Joe Strummer, really. Once that punk idea with the Pistols at the head of it broke through the breeches, it was open season for anybody that could pretend to be whatever they wanted to be. Which is what a movement is about, really.'

Parry spoke to the band that first night. 'I went backstage, met John. They didn't know that I was going to turn up.' For once, he found that being a representative of Polydor Records worked to his advantage. 'That was like a ding-dong for all of them, particularly Paul, because that was the label that records the Who. That was very fortunate. For all the hardship I had with Malcolm and Bernie and the Pistols and Clash, this was a walk in the park when it came to actually having to deal with people because Paul was more than interested to be signing to Polydor.' He notes, 'Paul was the clear leader. He was the one that was most interested. He was the one that was talking to me. The others deferred to him, definitely. I think trios are the DNA of a band. If you get a great trio, you get the best band. But a triangle has something at the head.'

When Parry went for a drink with Weller at West End watering hole the Lamb & Flag, he was even further impressed by him. 'He was quite clear about his sense of destiny. He said, "I am going to be a leader of my generation." He was quite clear about that. I believed him. He wasn't trying to impress me. He was actually telling me.' Not that he found Weller to be self-assured in a context outside of his musical talents. 'He came from the 'burbs of London and from a working-class environment. Good family, but solid working class, kind of limited. He wasn't totally confident. He wanted to break out and go beyond what would normally be expected of him.'

Although Parry wasn't so hasty as to offer them a deal before he'd arranged a demo session, by February 15, 1977 the Jam were Polydor recording artists. Weller later told Paolo Hewitt that he had never felt guilty about choosing Polydor at a time when it was unfashionable for bands to sign to a major label, reasoning, 'I thought it was the only way we could be ever heard everywhere.' Of Chiswick he said, 'They obviously offered a lot smaller financial deal, but we just felt it wasn't even the finance actually, because we only signed to Polydor for a fairly small sum of money anyway … we just wanted everyone to hear our records.' Indeed. the Jam were initially offered nothing like the £100,000 advance and long-term commitment CBS provided to the Clash, a deal which, considering punk's guttersnipe ambience, seemed incongruous to some and even to one person – Mark Perry – 'The day punk died.'

That Parry was able to directly offer the Jam a deal was due to him laying down the law to Polydor: 'After the Clash thing fell apart, I just went, "I can't be dealing with you guys. I cannot involve you in the process of signing a band because by the time you get off your arse and see it, talk about it, think about it, it's all gone. So just give me a fucking budget and I can at least sign something half-decent." And they gave me a budget. They gave me six thousand pounds and six per cent. It was a piss-taking budget, but that's what I signed the Jam to.' The four-year, four-album deal with a royalty rate escalating by one per cent each year was, Parry says, 'about a cheap a contract as you could get away with.' He adds, 'I told Jim Cook, "If we have hits, I'm going to get this band a decent fucking lawyer and they're going to come in and get a proper deal. Just so you know."'

Parry was better than his word. By April, impressed by the group's first single, Polydor had raised the Jam's royalty rate to a generous 13%. Explains Parry, 'I got a lawyer called John Cohen. I said, "John, got this band. The manager is naïve but I'm sure you can look after him. They're signed to Polydor. You can't break it. The deal is shit. Just go there and negotiate in good faith and get them a better deal." And he did. He doubled the royalty.'

In signing even the first, meagre deal, John Weller was moving into somewhat unfamiliar territory. This fact was underlined by him having to explain to Parry that he couldn't accept the six grand in the form of a cheque: neither he nor any of the Jam had bank accounts. 'Cash,' Parry amusedly recalls of the way the deal was sealed. 'John got it from the bank next door down Oxford Street, Lloyds.' Yet despite his amateur-town aura, there seems to have been no question of dispensing with Weller Sr's services in favour of somebody whose knowledge of the music business might extend beyond arranging gigs in public houses and working men's clubs. 'Basically he acted the way he needed to,' shrugs John Weller's son. 'I thought he done brilliantly. He learnt as he went on, like we all did. I don't know if it would have worked without him. He was the fourth member. We came as a team. We'd brought this thing up from nothing and my old man especially put a lot of time and effort into it.' Paul Weller's viewpoint, of course, is not exactly impartial, but Buckler's perspective on the matter is indistinguishable from his. 'He'd done a lot of work for us in the early days,' says the drummer. 'There was a couple of tricky moments when the record company wanted to replace him with a professional manager, because obviously they were there putting their hands in their pockets for us and they really wanted our advances or whatever spent correctly. There was concern over John's capability. It was more from the business end that there was problems, but I think John did at least take advice from the right people, the right publishers, agents, lawyers, etc.'

'He was very rootsy,' says future Jam and Style Council producer Peter Wilson of John Weller. 'He was a great hero of Paul, and Paul was his best friend. He had immense respect for him. There were some sniggers about John in the record company, about his working-class approach. He was very unsophisticated. He wasn't a smart lawyer or accountant or record company smoothie. He just was fighting the corner for his band.' Offers Parry, 'I really respect the Weller family. For all the things I might pull my hair out [over] in terms of professionalism and everything else, in the end of the day they looked after each other like a good, working-class family would. Paul I think understood fully the shortcomings of his father in some respect as he got more sophisticated, but John was there for them. He was unsophisticated, he was visceral to some extent where he knew where he could be visceral, trying to learn, struggling. If you can imagine, this family, they were playing the Marquee on a Saturday night and then within three months they were entering the charts. It was the weirdest shit."

When in 1980 Phil Sutcliffe secured a rare John Weller interview, the latter told him, 'I started picking a lot of people's brains: take six opinions, apply your own intuition and then hope for the best was my method. When I think about it the only chance I took was with Paul's life, not mine, because I never had nothing going for me anyway ... The worst thing I went through was feeling left out – no, 'inadequate' is the word – when we were discussing longer-term plans. I didn't understand the politics as well as the figures and that. But Chris and Martin Hopewell from the Cowbell agency helped me on that ... I'd spent my whole life in debt and hassles and I said to myself there was no way I was going to drop a group of 18-year-olds in the shit ... The artistic side is left to the band because I haven't got a clue, the politics we talk about between us and the finances are left to me. They know if the Jam has four bob we get a shilling each.'

AN AMBIGUOUS ENTRÉE

'It could have been seriously tits-up,' Parry admits of his decision to demo the Jam before signing them. However, he felt that the chances of Polydor being gazumped as they had with the Pistols and the Clash were remote: 'Paul's love of the Who put me in safe hands.'

'We did two sessions,' Parry reveals. 'The first session was me working with the band just making sure they were able to record, just tighten up a few things, giving them some ideas ... We went to a studio just round the back of Wardour Street. I did two or three tracks with them... In being an ex-drummer, I know Rick Buckler was trying to be too smooth without the ability to keep time, so I worked with him to try and simplify his style and tighten it up. Rick was a very good drummer. He just was trying to be something he wasn't. I helped him a lot on keeping his gunpowder dry during a song. Make a few chops where's it's needed to push the guitars, but keep time. That's one thing he didn't do very well at the beginning. He learnt that very quickly. It took me three years or four years of drumming to understand that.'

Satisfied with the first session, Parry arranged a second. 'We did the second session at Polydor, the same as we did the Clash. I bought [in] another engineer called Vic Smith and cut twelve songs or something like that and that was great.'

Vic Smith's experience went back to the late Sixties and included working as engineer or producer for such luminaries as Cat Stevens, Joe Cocker, the Rolling Stones and Black Sabbath. Around halfway through his four-year, five-album association with the Jam, he would decide he wanted to be credited as Vic Coppersmith-Heaven. For the sake of convenience, this latter name is the one by which he will be consistently referred to in this text. Parry: 'I'd worked with him. I kind of knew what I saw and I just thought it was a good experiment, just see if they got on and see how it worked. It was clear to me that I was going to have to organise and make sure that Jam records got made and made well. I thought it was a good way of stepping back and seeing if this engineer was any good and would the Jam like him and what came out of it. I came in at the end of the evening and picked up the tape. I didn't see the band that day. I wasn't interested. I knew what they were capable of. I was very impressed. I loved it.' What was on the tape? 'Pretty much the whole album, except 'Away from the Numbers'. That came later.'

'I was an engineer at Polydor Studios around the mid-Seventies, mixing anything from TV adverts to solo artist records, and bands that were being considered by Polydor to sign,' recalls Coppersmith-Heaven. 'One day I was told by the A&R department that three bands were coming in for demo sessions that they would like me to record – the Clash, the Jam and Billy Idol. These sessions took place, and Polydor asked me which band I'd most like to work with. It was very difficult at the time to choose as they all had exciting elements to their music and sound.' Shortly after the sessions, Coppersmith-Heaven went to see the Jam play a gig at the Half Moon in Putney. 'It was loud, thrashing, intense,' he recalls. 'They had a very sharp visual appearance and a positive attitude, and their songs were very interesting, with good arrangements, lyrics with social statements, and it was very much music of the time. So I chose the Jam to work with out of the three. I only hoped that the A&R department of Polydor would agree with my personal choice, as I'd had a similar experience as part of an engineering team at Decca Records in the Sixties when the Beatles were turned down by the company, before they were signed by EMI after doing their amazing demo session for Decca. However, Chris Parry was as enthusiastic as I was with the band, and he got the Jam signed.'

Regards shaping the Jam's recorded sound, Coppersmith-Heaven notes, 'It wasn't really a production challenge, it was more of an engineering challenge to capture the Jam's live set on tape.

The songs needed little change.' He asserts that he didn't feel the fact that he was older posed any sort of problem. 'As we know now, the music has moved generations since we recorded it. Yes, there was an age difference between us at the time, and we might have had different interests, but when you're together developing an art, age is not a constricting factor.'

With the Jam having successfully negotiated Polydor's hoops, Parry was in no doubt which song he wanted to release as their entrée. 'At the beginning, all I wanted to do was get 'In The City' recorded and sounding like an exciting record of its time. We recorded that in the same room at Stratford Place. This was the third session. I'd realised this was the Jam's first record, it had to be. It was the right one. We recorded it and then we spent an awful lot of time mixing it to try and get that sense of the bounce and the urgency and the slightly heart-pumping adrenalin feel that was inherent in the song. I think it's alright. I think we got it off as best we could. It's a good record. That was my first record that I ever produced as an individual.'

Except, of course, that the producer's credit was shared, as it would be on all Jam records up to and including third album *All Mod Cons*. Were he and Coppersmith-Heaven equal partners? 'Probably a bit more than equal because I was the A&R guy, I was representing the company, so I was putting Vic to task. I didn't know much about the engineering, to be fair. I'd been in the recording studio in New Zealand with the band I was in and all this, but this was slightly outside of my field. But I still knew what a good record sounded like. I couldn't do it myself. I wasn't an engineer. Vic had learnt his craft. He was able to produce what I had in my head.' Parry says of his professional relationship with Coppersmith-Heaven, 'He had a monkey on his back.' How does he think Coppersmith-Heaven felt about that? 'This was challenging on lots of levels. He'd never found a band to record as young as the Jam and was excited by it and that was all being brought to him because of me and I had a sense of what they needed to sound like, and a lot of it was just not quite in his comfort zone. I was challenging him without knowing the process, so it was kind of weird. We had some interesting discussions, but at the end of the day I didn't piss him off to say, "I'm walking out" and he didn't piss me off enough to say, "I'm firing you."'

'There was no real division of labour,' is Coppersmith-Heaven's recollection. 'I was more the engineer/producer, whereas Chris was enthusing the performance, waving his hands at Paul, Rick and Bruce, gesticulating with encouragement, a bit like a classical conductor would do.' Coppersmith-Heaven also says that he doesn't recollect the single being recorded before the LP. 'A single doesn't really materialise until you complete the recorded track,' he says, 'but while recording the album, 'In the City' became an outstanding musical statement.' He was impressed by the song's 'intensity of performance and an anti-establishment sentiment in the lyrics, with ideas about the feeling of their generation. It had the power needed to be the first musical statement of the band.'

'It was very fast,' Foxton recalls of the recording of the Jam's debut album. 'We were young and just on a real high to have a record label sign you. It was done at Stratford Place in the West End, off Oxford Street. Polydor had their own studio there. It took, like, ten days to record, because obviously it was pretty much our live set, so once we got the individual sounds it was very fast. Just very exciting. A whole new world was opening up.' 'You could say that we'd been rehearsing for that album for five years,' says Buckler. 'It was a matter of choosing the best material that we did live. The Jam were always predominantly a live band, so we didn't go into the studio thinking of creating things.' Indeed, despite the quick turnaround, during this recording process the band were still fulfilling live commitments. However, the Jam were already discovering the possibilities studio work afforded them to expand their sound. Recalls Coppersmith-Heaven, 'We were always looking for alternative acoustic spaces to record which Polydor Studios did not offer. So we extended our recording to the bathroom, toilets and lifts, which sometimes gave the guitars and vocals a lift in sound.'

The sleeve prepared for the release of the 'In the City' single was designed by Polydor's in-house art director, Bill Smith. Very rarely has someone had such a longstanding influence on the look of an artist's product. Although Smith would go freelance toward the end of the following year, he continued to design the Jam's record sleeves for almost the entirety of their career, missing out only on the last album and final clutch of singles. During his tenure, he also devised the group's tour posters, press advertisements and merchandise.

'I heard about the Jam pretty much as soon as they were about to be signed,' Smith recalls. 'Chris Parry came in and said to me, "You should maybe go and see them live and see what you think and start thinking about what we can do with them." I saw them in the Red Cow or somewhere like that and I thought they were pretty amazing. Obviously, there was quite a big thing going on at the time about punk, so I was really keen to try and work with a band within that ilk. When I saw them, they had an attitude of punk, but obviously weren't really a punk band as such because they could play their instruments, Paul Weller could sing and they had some good songs and a good look to go with it all. I'd actually seen the Pistols and the Clash before I saw the Jam. The Jam had, not quite a Beatle-ish uniform, but a look that was pretty much their own, so that really started me off on what I was going to do with them ... Basically, I was in right from the get-go, so it was a perfect opportunity to work in tandem with a band as they grew and they developed.'

Smith first met the band when Parry booked them in for the Stratford Place demos. He recalls, 'They were basically a young band trying to establish themselves and there was an attitude that comes when you're young and you're starting on the road to what you hope is going to be success, so there's a certain arrogance and self-awareness.' In terms of ideas for visuals at least, Smith didn't get the impression of the Jam being a democracy: 'Paul was the spokesman of the band and the other guys basically let him get on with it ... Paul's always had a very, very good eye and a look and a feel for what he wanted. So we would have quite long conversations.' Smith states that the Jam, not Polydor, always had final approval on their record sleeves.

Smith is now conscious of the fact that he was working in something of a golden age for record-sleeve designers. The era had passed wherein artists and record companies were cavalier about dressing their product, while the diminution of his craft brought about by small CD cases, and its later near-annihilation by downloads and streaming, was part of an unimaginable future. Every one of the Jam's 45 rpm releases, for instance, came housed in an illustrated sleeve, or 'picture bag' in the vernacular. 'The picture bag was a punk thing,' says Smith. 'The record companies before then would not necessarily put every single into a picture bag. They would go into a standard Polydor bag with the hole in the middle and you could read the label on the disc itself. Picture bags became standard during '76 and '77. It was partly value for money, but also partly a way of getting across what the band was doing. [It was the] very early stages of promo videos and all that sort of thing. Most of the time the only visuals that a fan had were from either an album sleeve or a single bag.'

Smith recalls of his Jam work, 'The very first picture and studio session we did was for *In the City*, the album, and then the 'In the City' single came from that.' The common factor on single and album sleeve was a tiled background upon which was aerosoled the band's name. Explains Smith, 'The basic idea for the album was the band had just done a gig, maybe were running along the road and were either escaping from someone or were trying to get away from fans. They'd managed to get themselves into a toilet and, while they were there, they thought, "Oh, we'll leave our name before we go."' As he did with all his sleeves, Smith art-directed the photo session, in this case supervising the work of snapper Martyn Goddard. Smith: 'We built a tiled wall in the studio and set up all the lights and everything. [We] got the band in place – they put their suits on and had a bit of hair and make-up done – put them against the wall, lined everything up and shot a couple of Polaroids to make sure the lighting's okay. They stood away, I went up and sprayed the logo with black spray paint and then sat the band back in front of it and literally took two rolls of film, one black-and-white and one colour, and that was it.' In other words, he got right the first time lettering destined to become immortal.

'It was a matter of, whatever the logo had turned out like, that was going to be the logo,' says Smith. 'I had in my mind how I wanted the logo to look, but I'd not really practised it or written [it] down anywhere. I had an idea that I wanted "The" to be smaller, "Jam" to be big and the "m" to come underneath so it would be a bit like an underline, and I just sort of did it. Once and for all – that was it. I then recreated it a couple of times for backdrops at concerts, so they had it quite big on some white sheeting, but the tiled wall was literally the first time I did it.' While the group-pose shot was held over for the cover of the first album, replaced by dynamic live photographs, the lettering's perfection made it a must for the Jam's entrée to the wider world. (The example of it seen on the front skin of Buckler's bass drum on the back of the 'In the City' single might suggest the logo was already in circulation, but this was in fact overlaid in post-production.) The lettering's tone of urban decay and disaffection chimed perfectly with the spirit of punk. Moreover, so striking and distinctive was its mixture of scruffy (the fuzziness and unevenness that comes from writing with an aerosol can) and stylish (a miraculous overarching symmetricality) that it quickly became the group's official logo, reproduced on millions of record sleeves, advertisements, badges and magazine spreads. Although by the end of 1978 it had been succeeded on the record sleeves by other designs, it was the spray-painted version of the logo that became iconic – not least because it was so easy to emulate for anybody with access to a spray can and a bare wall.

Seeing his work staring back at him as it fanned out into the culture was, Smith says, 'fantastic for me as the designer but even more fantastic for the band because suddenly there was something that literally everybody recognised and knew immediately who that band was and what they stood for.' The downside was that he earned nothing for this additional usage. 'I did ask for a royalty but, of course, at the time I did it all I was actually employed by Polydor Records. The copyright law is slightly different these days. Polydor pretty much owned the rights to all of the imagery for their releases, unless you were a major, major band – the Who or whatever – and you could say, "I want to employ my own people because I want to then be able to use all the stuff for merchandising."' Did this rankle with him? 'It didn't at the time but it does now, because even now people don't know that I did the Jam logo or that I did all of those sleeves for the band.'

Its rather ironic that Smith had such a long relationship with the Jam, because such was the impact of the logo that, in a way, it would have hardly mattered if he never did anything else for them. As Smith says, 'I hit the nail on the head straightaway, I suppose.'

Debut releases are always wrapped up in significance, but in the context of punk, band entrées had to be more than good records representative of an artist's sound and abilities – they also had to be manifestos. 'In the City' fitted that bill well. Or possibly too well:

despite the disc lasting a mere two minutes, eighteen seconds, its lyric was packed with almost too many statements to assimilate.

The first thing it declared was Paul Weller's love of the Who. Weller took the title of 'In the City' from the Keith Moon/John Entwistle-written B-side to said ensemble's 1966 single 'I'm a Boy'. It has also been postulated that he lifted part of the melody of same, but if he did it's only discernible to musicologists. Via a reference to Liddle Towers, the record also demonstrated Weller's embrace of punk's spirit of social protest. A man who died in 1976 after claiming he had been assaulted in custody by police officers, Towers – and the fact that none of his alleged tormentors were ever brought to justice – was a Seventies *cause célèbre*. The Angelic Upstarts, Dave Goodman and the Tom Robinson Band all released songs about his case. Although Weller refers to Towers only fleetingly and elliptically – stating that he hears that in the city men in uniform now have the right to kill a man – this would not be the last time Towers cropped up in the Jam songbook. Something else the record emphasised was Weller's fixation with the virtues purportedly inherent in the state of youth. His lyric extols the 'young idea', exalts the golden faces of the under-25 and insists that it's the kids who know where it's at.

Another of 'In The City''s multiple motifs is London, and the wonders thereof. The very phrase "in the city" is an outsider's way of referring to the capital. The hatred Weller articulated in interview and song of the sleepiness and parochialism of his hometown might be understandable, but his perception of London as a gleaming citadel is the richest irony when so many punk bands who actually hailed from the capital viewed it as anything but. The line, 'It's so grey in London town' from the Clash's 1977 track 'Remote Control' summed up the fact that, for many working-class Londoners, the capital's greater level of activity and higher number of entertainment outlets were hardly compensation for its enclosed, dreary vistas and spiritual coldness.

The second-class status of Weller and his suburbanite cohorts informs the lyric's final element. It's a component that makes this a peculiarly ambivalent anthem. Weller's fury in 'In the City' is not primarily directed at the government, the straights, the 'system' or any of the other traditional targets of punk discontent. Rather, it is punks themselves with whom Weller is angry. Weller complains that the thousand things he wants to say to an unidentified city-dweller always go unarticulated because, when he does open his mouth, this unidentified 'you' makes him look a fool, an expression of vulnerability where one would least expect to find it.

Considering all of the above, 'In the City' could be viewed as not manifesto-like at all, but rather a stream of consciousness and an inchoate expression of grievance. However, its breathless urgency, snarling passion and defiant tone gave the recording the aura of a classic punk fist-clencher and it was accepted as such.

As well as broadly fulfilling the remit of a manifesto, 'In the City' fitted the bill as public introduction, right down to band members being given an individual showcase. First to be thus presented is Weller, who opens the record with characteristic slashing, trebly guitar as he plays the memorable, staccato riff. Said riff is then taken up by Foxton's bobbing bass. Then it's the turn of Buckler to make an entrance, exploding onto the soundscape with brittle, hyperactive drumming. The three then proceed to demonstrate this group's remarkable tightness and power via a breakneck, incendiary performance.

As he would throughout the Jam's recording career, Foxton provides vocal harmonies and responses with a smooth timbre that pleasingly complements Weller's deeper, harsher tones. Weller's spat, intense vocals, incidentally, are still betraying signs of the fake American accent used by British bands before the localised social commentary of punk made it seem inappropriate-cum-phoney.

When Weller decided to dismiss the over-25s, he did so

knowing full well that the dismissal was a hostage to fortune. Lurking at the back of the mind of every Who fan was the fact that in 1965's 'My Generation' their heroes had avowed, 'Hope I die before I get old.' Both Foxton and Buckler say they felt no qualms about the 'In the City' lyric at the time. 'We didn't think about that,' says Buckler. 'We weren't planning our pension or our future. We were just living it as it stood.' However, when the two played the song when performing with the group From the Jam in the mid-Noughties, the inherent irony wasn't lost on Foxton. 'I'm singing "The kids under 25" and I'm nearly 52,' he says. He could at least justify the contradiction on the grounds that the considerably older Who vocalist Roger Daltrey was *still* belting out 'My Generation'.

'In the City' was released on April 29, 1977. The group's loyal fanbase and the interest generated by press coverage ensured that the record started working its way up the UK singles chart. Accordingly, the Jam were asked to perform it on *Top of the Pops*. They accepted the invitation. Acquiescing to appear on the BBC chart-rundown television show was another black mark for detractors who didn't consider them authentic punk. Many young people disdained the programme for its old-time showbusiness ambience, unhip presenters, tacky dance troupes and insistence on miming in preference to live performance. Moreover, what the acts lip-synced to was not even technically their records but hastily re-recorded versions necessitated by prevailing trade-union rules. An additional grievance was the disproportionate power of the show: as the only regular pop-oriented programme in a country with just three TV channels, this terminally cheesy proposition was in the preposterous position of being able to make or break records and artists. The Sex Pistols would not assent to the indignity of visiting its studio. However, while the Pistols at least consented to the show screening their promotional films, the Clash made it a career-long point of honour to not only refuse to appear on *Top of the Pops* but to even decline to sully their hands in a proxy fashion via provision of their videos.

Weller, however, says there was no question of joining the ranks of the *Top of the Pops* refuseniks. 'What was the option?' he reasons. 'To see Pan's People dancing to 'Bankrobber'? How fucking sad was that? Legs & Co, sorry. I'm showing me age there.' He is referring to the notorious moment in 1980 when the Clash's solemn reggae about a man who 'loved to steal your money' was gyrated to by the programme's resident pulchritudinous dance act while dressed in leotards striped to resemble the shirt of a cartoon burglar. The scene was completed by bandana masks, hurled money and a sign reading, 'This is a stick-up.' 'I'd been watching *Top of the Pops* since I was knee-high to a whatever,' says Weller. 'Religiously, every Thursday night since the Sixties, so for me to be on that show was like being on the front cover of the *NME* or something. There's a thing that you've grown up and lived with and you've dreamt of doing. It was fucking naff, because you had lots of other shit on it as well, but it was better to see us on it than some other tossers. We did the Bolan show [*Marc*] as well. We were just happy to be on TV. Fuckin' 'ell – you're eighteen and you're on national TV.'

The recollection of others suggests that the Jam were not as enthusiastic about *Top of the Pops* as Weller insists. 'There wasn't a big argument, as I remember, but it was discussed,' says Parry of the notion of punkishly declining the show's invitation. 'John steamrolled it: "You're going to do *Top of the Pops*." That's when he kicked in as a bit of a manager. He was having none of it. There were some things about John that's really good and some things really terrible, but basically he was all for the up.' Dennis Munday – the Jam's product manager at Polydor from mid-1978 – says he found the Jam no more enthusiastic than other punk groups about doing the show. 'They saw it as a bit selling out,' he says. 'I always argued this with Paul. I said, "I'd rather see you on than some crappy pop band. If it keeps a crappy pop band off of *Top of the*

Pops, great."' Certainly, Weller's lack of enthusiasm for miming was consistently evident in the Jam's *Top of the Pops* appearances. As Munday notes, 'The chewing gum and the lip-synch wasn't very good.'

Needless to say, the Jam featuring on *Top of the Pops* helped the ascent of 'In the City', which ultimately peaked at number 40. Their appearance on the show was significant for more than the obvious reason. The Sex Pistols and the Clash were at this point ignored by most radio programmers, the former on grounds of morality, the latter for reasons of non-commerciality. A Pistols promo would not feature on *Top of the Pops* until July '77, when third single 'Pretty Vacant' gave the censors no grounds for prohibition. Meanwhile, the likes of the Adverts, the Boomtown Rats and the Stranglers were yet to make their debuts on the show. That it was the first new wave record to feature on *Top of the Pops* meant that, for many members of the British public, 'In the City' was their first experience of the genre and therefore helped shape their perception of the movement and its music. If this can be posited as a form of triumph for the Jam over their sneering punk peers, that triumph was completed in October when the masters were to be found stealing from the apprentices: the riff of 'Holidays in the Sun', the new single from the movement's hallowed figureheads the Sex Pistols, owed a clear debt to that of 'In the City'.

Around this time, Parry was offered the chance to become even more deeply involved in the Jam's career when John Weller offered him a co-management role. Recalls Parry, 'John came to me – we were playing in Hastings on the Pier – and he said, "Well I hope you're not just going to leave us like this." I said, "Well, John, I work for Polydor. I'm going to go and find another band." He said, "Well, I want you to stay involved." So we did a publishing deal. I went to see a guy called Bryan Morrison. We formed a company called And Son and signed the Jam publishing. I said, "Well, that locks me in John, I'm involved with you now." (He didn't understand how the publishing worked.) I was co-producing their records, I was driving the whole project through and I could do that, [but] he was still saying, "But you might leave me." I said, "Look John, if you want me to be involved in management, this band's taking off, I could leave the company and manage the band with you possibly. Talk to your lawyer and then we'll discuss that. I'm not sure if I want to do it, I'm not sure if it's good for you." Eventually, his lawyer came up with the contract, but I wasn't sure I wanted it. I felt that I had more to do, but I thought at least it gives them the sense of confidence. As it happens, within a few months he found his feet. He wasn't that keen [for me] to get involved in the management and I wasn't that sure anyway and that contract never, ever was exercised.' Is he now kicking himself over that? 'No, not at all. I thought it was the right thing to do. Getting involved with the Jam's ongoings [was] never going to be my cup of tea.'

PUNKS WILL BE PUNKS

In the City, the album, was released on May 20th.

Despite the band's smart suits and ties, the front cover managed to convey the menace that – rightly or wrongly – the general public had come to associate with punk. This was the combined result of the bleakness of the monochrome design, the urban-squalor conjured by the aerosoled name, the subway-redolent tiled background and the group's unsmiling demeanour. Curiously, it's the equable-by-nature Buckler – wearing rectangular shades and caught in a louche pose – who in particular looks like someone you'd cross the street to avoid. Offsetting the powerful front cover was a back cover that was somewhat clumsy. It featured a distressed version of the aerosol logo, falling across which were three menacing shadows. Smith's aim was to convey, 'an even older wall or someone had come in and said, "I don't like that logo" and started smashing it about.' Unfortunately – as with the same effect strived for on the back of the precursor single – it's embarrassingly obvious that the method Smith elected to use was to glue fresh tiles over parts of the band's name. All Jam albums would feature the record's lyrics on their inner sleeves. On this occasion, though, the policy is only partially adhered to. In a design reminiscent of William Burroughs' cut-up technique refracted through Jamie Reid's ransom-note designs for the Sex Pistols, ribbons of paper featuring typed stray lines from different songs are placed across the white-tile background motif.

The album's twelve tracks were split evenly between the two vinyl sides. Bar two cover versions, all are written by Weller. Only four of the songs exceed three minutes, almost certainly a function of the fact that punks pointedly disdained the self-indulgently protracted song-lengths that had become fashionable in rock in recent years.

Although the album also contains the traditional rhythm & blues patterns and themes to be expected of Weller's I-took-what-

I-wanted-from-it attitude, opener 'Art School' is pure punk, from the retained 'One-two-free-four!' count-in to the feedback climax. A libertarian anthem, it exhorts listeners to do whatever they feel like doing, and to do so as quickly as possible lest time runs out on them. It invokes the British-rock art school tradition whereby young hopefuls destined for guitar-slinging stardom learnt their chops while drawing their grants and dodging their coursework. The fact that Weller – unlike Clapton/Davies/Richards/Townshend – wasn't from this tradition is not the point: he is essentially asserting that the punk movement is the 'new' version of art school. That said, the metaphor is a little cloudy and doesn't stand up to too much scrutiny. This under-developed quality is true of quite a lot of early Jam lyrics, the consequence of the fact that Weller had still not quite turned nineteen when the Jam's first records were released. Such sloppiness, though, often became irrelevant in the frenetic context of punk, which tended to distract the listeners' attention from lyrical flaws as it swept them up in the excitement of blurred tempos and hypnotic riffs. Such is the case with 'Art School', which pumps along very agreeably, helped in no small measure by Buckler's adroit use of his ride cymbal and Weller's dagger-sharp axe-work.

'Art School' would never have been written without punk. The sonic blitzkrieg of the following track, 'I've Changed My Address', is certainly punk, but lyric-wise it's a pre-punk throwback. Its well-trodden rock motifs include Weller addressing an ex-lover as 'baby' and repudiating romantic commitment in a US accent ('Never could see what was in this matrimony thang').

Although such sentiments are a rock 'n' roll tradition, so is, paradoxically, them often sitting alongside yearnings for true love. Witness 'Takin' My Love', the B-side of the 'In the City' single and penultimate track on side two of this album. Because it's a tribute to Dr Feelgood, it too is amusingly pseudo-American ('Daddy's little cat's gonna rock all day'). This time, though, Weller is not trying to push a partner away but celebrating his closeness to his 'pretty baby.' Unfortunately, the music to this much more good-natured track is boring.

'Slow Down', album track three, is the Jam's version of a song by Fifties R&B artist Larry Williams. Never as high-profile as peers like Little Richard and Chuck Berry, Williams was just as talented, as proven by the fact that several of his compositions are well-known via covers by titans like the Beatles and the Rolling Stones. As well as 'Slow Down', they include 'Bony Moronie', 'Short Fat Fannie', 'Dizzy Miss Lizzy', 'Bad Boy' and 'She Said Yeah'. 'Slow Down' has, curiously, always tended to lose something in translation. A plea for a second chance to a woman whose romantic attention has wandered elsewhere, Williams' original was a thumping uptempo affair enhanced, like much of his material, by a jumping sax solo. In the hands of even masters like the Beatles, though, it was thin and plodding. The Jam do no better, their retooling of the song as grimy punk proving tedious rather than refreshing. The fact that Weller gauchely gets the lyric wrong (what does he think 'If you want our love the best' means?) doesn't help.

The lumpen is followed by the sublime. It's easy on one level to mock the philosophising of 'I Got By In Time'. However, nostalgia and reflective longing is no less a component of childhood than adulthood, so it's not unreasonable for eighteen-year-old Weller to get ruminative about the emotional turmoil created by the passage of life and the course of relationships. Weller's lyric has a real pathos as he laments in turn the loss of a lover, a male friend and once-cherished ideals. The song is given even greater power by the fact that the known biographical information suggests that the verse about the friend from whom Weller was once 'inseparable' is Jam co-founder Steve Brookes. Lines like 'All the bonds you make between you can be broken any time you want' are granted an additional melancholy by being framed within a lilting tune and breathless punk-soul arrangement. One is tempted to consider Weller's singing over-intense – until such time as his voice quite movingly cracks with emotion.

'Away from the Numbers' – at four minutes-plus, easily the longest track – is shot through with a similar melancholy, albeit one bolted to defiance. Weller states his determination to break free from a conventional life and to not be a 'number'. It's possible that the terminology is appropriated from Sixties mods, who used it to disparage younger mods who sought to follow the trail they'd blazed. (In much the same spirit, Weller's musical generation would soon be lamenting 'part-time punks'.) 'This link's breaking away from the chain' is an early example of how Weller could alternate the type of gaucheness and confused rhetoric heard in 'Art School' with nigh-exquisite turns of phrase. The billowing, mid-tempo musical backing is not quite as heart-rending as that of 'I Got By In Time', but has passages that come close.

The side closes weakly with 'Batman Theme'. Neal Hefti's driving but jingle-like title tune to the Sixties TV spoof of the Caped Crusader – also recorded by the Who around a decade previously – staked its claim for a place in the tracklisting by dint of being a song familiar from Jam encores. However, after the lyrical sensitivity and sonic nous of the previous two tracks it comes across as juvenile and buffoonish, something compounded by the passionlessness of its vocal delivery.

'In the City' kicked off vinyl side two. It was followed by probably the apotheosis of Weller's adoration of said city. As with the title track, the homage to the capital in 'Sounds from the Street' is shot through with both a celebration of the spirit of punk and an insistence that the composer's suburban roots shouldn't be held against him. Weller exults in the strains of street life, especially young musicians rehearsing and performing. He puts a patriotic spin on this feeling, but one made distinct from the quasi-jingoism of the Clash's 'I'm So Bored with the U.S.A.' by its innocence: he asserts that he doesn't care that the US kids have access to the sea (by which he seems to mean oceans) because the young in Britain have got the streets (by which he seems to mean the punk scene happening on those streets). Once again, it's tempting to state in the face of such naiveté that allowance should be made for the fact that Weller is only eighteen, but once again such excuses prove unnecessary in light of his knack for a melody so sweet and affecting that it either gives legitimacy to his fumbling philosophising or makes it immaterial.

The sweet sonics even make the listener not dwell much on the changes in tone that curiously undermine the general serenity of the lyric. In the song's bridge, Weller acknowledges that London punks consider him a fraud because he's from Woking. 'But my heart's in the city, where it belongs,' he protests. In the final verse he abruptly rejects the idea of punk as a social force, sneering that it's never going to change a thing, then turning his ire on an unknown target to whom he asserts that he's at least doing more than they are by trying to be true. Such mercurialism may accurately reflect the nuances of human thought but in the context of an anthem – usually the province of one-dimensional assertions – it's all rather strange.

'Non-Stop Dancing' is utterly untouched by punk, being as it is a stomper whose lyric pays tribute to the Seventies all-nighters at which Sixties soul records were played to enthusiasts who danced to them into the early hours in a style partway between artistic and athletic. Although the phenomenon is mainly associated with Wigan (hence the term Northern Soul), Woking had its own all-nighter scene. You wouldn't know Weller was from Surrey, though, from his drawled Americanese. For all his superior songwriting skills, Weller was really the only non-virtuoso musician in the Jam. (Buckler's carefully stated appraisal of his musical abilities is, 'He is quite a competent guitar player.') You wouldn't know that, either, from his extended, swift-picking here.

A showboating guitar solo might have been another black mark for the purist punks, but such is the excitement generated by this track's coiled-spring tightness and pitiless pace that nobody else cared.

'Time for Truth' is the most overtly political song on the album, but is very different to most punk diatribes. That Britain was governed during its ascension by a Labour administration inevitably meant that punk's social critiques were more complicated than a 'left is right, right is wrong' standpoint (although that didn't stop the Tom Robinson Band using exactly that mantra). The widespread public antipathy to trade unions caused by the era's endless strikes also played a part in blurring the usual political battle-lines. 'Time for Truth', though, doesn't merely ignore the abstract threat of Margaret Thatcher's hard-right government-in-waiting in favour of here-and-now grievances, but seems to posit society under threat from the left. Against its brisk, staccato soundscape it lambasts one 'Uncle Jimmy', clearly Labour Prime Minister James Callaghan, who had visited Weller's hometown at the end of 1976. Weller tells this 'red balloon' that he should 'fuck off' and complains that he and his cohorts have turned Britain's great empire into manure. He mocks Callaghan for a luxurious lifestyle divorced from a reality in which uniformed killers roam the streets. One might suggest that it's rather unfair to place the responsibility for the death of Liddle Towers – to which this is clearly a reference – on the shoulders of Callaghan. However, Callaghan – a notoriously censorious and authoritarian politician – was also a onetime parliamentary adviser to the Police Federation, the trade union for British police officers that was extremely robust in defending its members against claims of misconduct. Was Weller aware of Callaghan's ties to the police, and the conflict of interest this arguably created? Probably not, but he has somehow stumbled into making a valid point that many punks less keen on criticising the Labour Party would never have.

Following 'Takin' my Love', the album concludes with 'Bricks and Mortar'. This song explores the fact that Stanley Road – the Woking street on which Weller was raised and after which he later named a solo album – had been profoundly changed in recent years, losing half its length and several of its houses, the latter in preference for office blocks. Weller wonders in his lyric if, in light of the country's homelessness problem, this demonstrates the right priorities. He also condemns the fact of building sites lying fallow for months after the JCBs have packed up – a common phenomenon in the Seventies when, with land not at such a premium, things moved slowly in the construction trade. Weller seems to be complaining of a lack of a central planning that his red-baiting elsewhere would logically suggest is anathema to him, but the song comes more from the heart than the brain. He was experiencing unusually early what eventually happens to everyone, namely the altering of the landscape of one's youth in a way that feels like an outrage rather than just a function of time and tide. On this occasion, the naiveté isn't redeemed by the music, which is mediocre, lacking momentum and in possession of a gratingly tuneless instrumental section.

Parry was pleased by the album. He reflects, "In the City' stood out, 'Away from the Numbers' stood out [as] where he went, and a lot of the other stuff was cool. It was good. It was an entertaining record. I'd give it 91 of a hundred. And it sold consistently.'

In the City reached number 20, remaining in the UK album chart for eighteen weeks. It was clear that the work was a powerful entrée, even to those who had reservations about the multiple clues it outrageously betrayed of love for music which pre-dated punk. The album possessed a relentless energy, at least half a dozen of its twelve cuts were very-good-to-classic and its title track created an instant punk anthem destined to sit beside the likes of the Damned's 'New Rose', the Sex Pistols' 'Anarchy in the UK', the Clash's 'White Riot' and X Ray Spex's 'Oh Bondage Up Yours!'

Even its instances of naiveté weren't necessarily a demerit. As Barry Cain memorably noted in his *Record Mirror* review, 'It's been a long time since albums actually reflected pre-20 delusions and this one does.' In the '76/'77 punk goldrush, record companies ended up signing sundry acts of no particular talent. *In the City* emphatically proved that the Jam were not in that category but had become recording artists through merit.

Only one person would seem to have been left unhappy by *In the City*: Paul Weller himself. In the documentary released to tie in with the 2015 *About the Young Idea* Jam exhibition, he said, '…we were kind of at the mercy of the producer really, because what the fuck do we know? … I remember being disappointed with it. I didn't feel it was our sound, 'cos Vic would always get us to track stuff up … Which I guess in some ways did become what people think of [as] the Jam Sound.' It's not uncommon for musicians to be shocked at the way the exigencies and conventions of studio recording somehow contrive to turn their songs into a polished, layered, compressed, slightly antiseptic version of their 'natural' sound. However, Weller's feelings are remarkable for the way they seem to, right from the outset and despite their long relationship with him, pave the way for the Jam's eventual rupture with Coppersmith-Heaven.

When the Jam took receipt of *In the City*, they rang the offices of Stiff Records in the hope of exchanging copies of it for *Dammed Damned Damned*, the three-time eponymous debut LP widely considered the first UK punk album. The Damned's response was typically mischievous. 'They said that they were going to send us a copy of their album with something disgusting in it,' recalls Foxton. 'So we thought, "Okay, well we'll get in first," and we sent our album full of crap, basically. And they sent their one just with jam smeared all over it, so it was really embarrassing.'

Such scatological shenanigans can be dismissed with a bemused 'punks-will-be-punks' attitude. Another altercation with a top punk ensemble had more serous ramifications. On May 7, the Jam set off as support on the Clash's White Riot UK tour. It was an impressive bill, but the jaunt ended in rancour within three days. In 2017, Clash roadie Barry 'Baker' Auguste told Pat Gilbert of *Mojo*, 'The Jam left because they thought they should be headlining the show... we all thought they were a mockery. Weller's dad would come into the dressing room and start bossing everyone around. In the end, he said they wanted more money. But Joe in particular felt they weren't right for the tour.' Clash friend Robin Banks told the same journalist a different story: 'It was Bernie [Rhodes] stirring it up. We liked them as individuals, especially Weller. But Bernie kept saying, "The Jam are going to be bigger than The Clash," winding everyone up. He didn't want them on the tour and we were quite happy with it.' The Jam walked off the tour, denying themselves both appearance money and promotion for their long-playing debut. Foxton downplays the affair. 'It was only an incident in terms of the big machine kicks in, the record companies kick in and the Clash's manager, there was an argument over lights on a bill,' he says. 'We weren't getting the full use of lights, but I don't think it was anything to do with Joe [Strummer] and Mick Jones and that.' He insists there was no rancour between the bands: 'We hung out with them here and there. I wouldn't say we were best of friends, but I don't think we didn't get on ... Where has that come from?' Weller says, 'I liked the Clash and I loved Joe. He was really sweet to us when we were starting out. Mick was always sweet and I always liked Mick.'

Nobody would know from these comments that the White Riot tour incident marked the start of a long-term prickliness between the two groups and more than a smidgeon of competitiveness. Weller insists, 'I didn't feel any rivalry. What we did was completely different to what the Clash did.' Not quite. Once the Sex Pistols ceased to be movement leaders by virtue of splitting up, it became apparent that the Jam and the Clash were the main candidates to take over as the standard-bearers of punk. They came to be viewed by the public as two sides of the same coin as they each dexterously helped to broaden the soundscapes of punk while striving not to lose its spiritual values. This, though, produced no feeling of common purpose between them. The public mutual sniping that took place over the following few years certainly fit the description of rivalry – and not a friendly one.

Part of the problem for the antipathy was a serious misgiving about Weller amongst punks, one encapsulated by a telegram the Clash sent the Jam following the latter's White Riot-tour walkout . According to press reports, it read, 'Maggie [Thatcher] wants you all round for target practice tonight.' However, the telegram reproduced in the Foxton/Buckler book *The Jam: Our Story* read, 'Congratulations on victory on Merseyside and Manchester. Maggie will be proud of you[.] See you in Southafrica [sic] for gun practwce [sic].' Whatever the wording, the telegram was a reference to recent public comments made by Weller, comments which reinforced suspicions aroused by 'Time for Truth' that Weller's political philosophy was hostile to not simply the current government (which even most Labour voters would concede was massively flawed) but to leftism itself. In the May 12, 1977 issue of *Sniffin' Glue*, Weller said, 'All this "change the world" thing is becoming a bit too trendy ... We'll be voting Conservative at the next election.' He told another punk fanzine, *48 Thrills*, 'We'd like to see change. I don't think people realise how close we are to a police state. The Labour government will want everything state-owned soon. It's getting to be like 1984 already.' The Union Jacks in which the Jam draped their stage gear were easily explained as yet another adoption of a motif of Weller's beloved Who, but when he told the *New Musical Express* in its May 7 issue that he admired the hard work of the Queen, whom he called the country's 'best diplomat,' it seemed to confirm Weller as a patriotic-cum-nationalistic conformist. The press release for the Jam's debut album declared the band's 'strong and loyal conviction for Queen and Country,' adding, 'Anarchy in the UK holds no sway for the Jam.' Any suspicion that this was merely a variant of the calculated defiance of expectation standard amongst rock musicians would seem to be disproven by the fact that the Jam played on bills at two events which celebrated the Silver Jubilee, and were only prevented from appearing on more because of local-council suspicion of punk acts.

Of course, nobody ever wrote down a list of punk rules (at least not until the edicts mockingly proffered by Malcolm McLaren in the 1980 Sex Pistols movie biography *The Great Rock 'n' Roll Swindle*). Moreover, punk could legitimately be asserted to be not so much political as anti-political (the message essentially articulated in the Pistols' 'Pretty Vacant'). However, it was clearly the case that most adherents of punk embraced libertarianism, confrontationalism and concern for the economically and socially underprivileged, none of which are usually considered the main principles held dear by conservatives. Meanwhile, the glee taken by the entire punk movement from the Sex Pistols' anti-royalist diatribe 'God Save the Queen' – released at the end of the month in which he expressed admiration for the woman currently celebrating twenty-five years on the throne – put Weller and punk in diametric opposition.

'I think it was just to wind up relevant people,' Foxton says of Weller's comments. 'I don't think he intended to vote Conservative ever. I think it was just a dig basically, and to get a reaction, which it did. But we were young and still naive there as well. I'm sure there's a lot of the lyrics that Paul wrote that he would cringe over now.' He adds, 'It didn't do any harm in the end, did it?' 'I think that was Paul trying to wind somebody up,' Buckler echoes. 'For my part, I wasn't really that interested in politics as such because it just all seemed such a mess. There was a lot of discontent at that time. I think it was just a way of saying, "I'll do whatever I like and it doesn't matter what the public opinion is or what you may think." I barely remember the incident. It wasn't something that was in the forefront of our minds.' For Buckler, music and formal politics 'don't really mix,' whatever the stripe of the party. He avers, 'You can't become political as a songwriter because it takes away your freedoms. It means that you are suddenly weighted one way or another in people's view, and I think that was probably the biggest mistake that was made. It's a bit of a dangerous thing to do, 'cos it does take away your impartialness, your freedom if you like, especially as a songwriter.'

In later years, Weller would explain away his comments by variously claiming that he was goaded by a mischievous PR into making them, that he was getting revenge on the London punks who looked down on him, that he was trying to carve out a distinct image for the Jam or simply that he was joking. The disingenuousness of all those explanations is matched by what he says now. 'I don't think I was old enough to vote anyway at that time,' he offers, apparently unaware of the fact that by the time of the 'next election', of which he had provocatively spoken, he was three years over the legal voting age.

Chris Parry certainly doesn't buy into the idea that Weller was simply trying to shock. 'I know his politics changed, but I think he genuinely felt – like a lot of people – that Britain was just chugging to a kind of a dead end,' he says. 'There was the three-day week, the endless union guys just coming out and saying how it's going to be, fucking rubbish piled on the streets. It was just, what the fuck was this country doing? The Pistols said, "Well, everything's fucked and we're gonna be anarchists." I think Paul was a bit more considered. I didn't have a long conversation with him, wasn't going to get into politics with him particularly, but he was for that sense of when Britain was good, or Britain had a sense of pride and position. It was deemed as conservative and I know he got seriously dobbed about it, but if you really were looking at Britain at this time, there was a huge amount of damage being done by the unions. These people just had their shock troops. Anybody they didn't like, they'd just turn up at the factory gate and close it down. When Paul [said] "I'm going to vote Tory," he was reflecting how a lot of people felt. It was completely different from where the punk movement might have been, but that was that kind of small-c conservative. That sense of, "Well, hang on Britain's fucked, we need to change this." And it was more fundamental than just the politics.'

Weller publicly supported the Labour Party under the leaderships of Michael Foot (1980-1983), Neil Kinnock (1983-1992) and Jeremy Corbyn (2015 onwards). So strong did his anti-Tory convictions become that in the Eighties he cancelled a planned recording session with the singer Lulu after finding out about her Thatcherite leanings. His lyrics were always anti-authoritarian, but became increasingly collectivist throughout the Jam's career and on into the Style Council's, before losing any political content whatsoever during the solo career he embarked on in 1992. Only Weller will ever know if his apparent ideological shift was an unprincipled caving-in to peer pressure or a sincere reaction to the Thatcherite era inaugurated in Britain in May 1979.

To ensure proper promotion of *In the City*, the Jam turned to an agency to arrange their own UK tour, which began on June 7, a week after the album entered the charts. The three-dozen dates climaxed with a gig at Hammersmith Odeon. It was a symbolic stepping stone. Seating 3,500, the London venue would have been deemed unacceptably un-punk only a few months before, but shows at such places were made inevitable as punk acts both grew more popular and transpired to be as susceptible to the desire to gain economic well-being as any previous generation of musicians.

Parry recalls that, three weeks before the Hammersmith show,

'Tickets were beginning to slack. This was a big jump forward. This was three thousand people or whatever and we had to fill it. Paul played 'All Around The World' one night after the show. I said, "That's a great song, Paul. I want to record that. I want to record that *now*. It's a hit." He said, "Are you sure?" And so on Saturday, they had a couple of days off, we went down to Bond Street where Chappell Recording Studio [was]. Vic and I were there and the band rocked in. They could record for that day only and they recorded 'All Around the World'.' Parry's co-producer was also impressed by the song. "All Around the World' was an explosion of ideas,' enthuses Coppersmith-Heaven.

Weller has credited Parry with improving the arrangement of the track. 'It was a very simple change,' says Parry. 'It just had a few more extra beats on it. They had a half-bar, a couple of extra bits. We just tightened it up, basically, nothing special. It flowed well and they recorded it and they left. We had a couple of tracks in the can. We could add the B-sides. They got back on tour and we got it out in ten days. We got it out that week before and the ticket sales just rocketed because all of a sudden there's a new Jam track out. I love that sort of stuff. The spontaneity of working with the band and organically just growing this thing. It was very exciting, and we got a great record out of it. It was hurried, it's not a great production, but if you think about it, Paul wrote it on the road, played it on the road, I heard it, we wrapped it up and we put it onto the market before they came to London. That put them into a whole different ballgame. They were now a very serious group.'

VERY LOCAL HEROES

'All Around the World', released on July 15, 1977, entered the singles chart the day before the Hammersmith Odeon concert. It was the first standalone Jam single, but by no means the last.

'We were all kids who'd grown up in the '60s when singles weren't just advertisements for albums like they are today,' Weller later told Simon Goddard. 'We were into the whole thing of doing non-album singles, good B-sides, putting everything into three-and-a-half-minutes.' That the rock aristocracy had lost interest in the single was a standard punk grievance. However, the Jam were alone amongst their peers in continuing to release tracks exclusive to the single format even as their contemporaries drifted toward the regular industry practice of employing the 45 rpm format as a promotional tool for the 33⅓ rpm format. The majority of the Jam's sixteen official UK singles were not to be found on their albums. It's arguably easier to be generous with original B-sides – they could even be viewed as a cynical way of enticing fans to buy an A-side they already, or will, own on album – but it's still impressive that twelve of the Jam's sixteen B-sides (or alternative sides of double-As) were exclusive, and that figure doesn't even include the additional B-sides on special-edition singles.

On the colour picture sleeve of 'All Around the World', the band seem to be almost defiantly displaying their retro hinterland as they preen in front of their logo in suits and spats. That the back cover bore a credit for their hairdresser (Schumi, since you ask) would have earned them another black mark with the purists. It was also a reminder that although all three Jam members had in recent years shortened their once shoulder-skimming hair (albeit in Weller's case probably more because of mod's imperatives than punk's), Foxton would always sport a coiffure that was a little too long and styled for the comfort of those on flare-and-platform alert. Bill Smith says that it was Weller's idea to pose in suits. Contrary to the wide assumption that the band's clobber always came from men's clothing chain Burton, Smith reveals, 'He would quite often have the suits specially made by old tailors in and around Carnaby Street.' And the hairdresser's credit? 'If it rubbed people up the wrong way, I think that was probably partly the reason for doing it.' This was all as nothing, however, to the heresies that could be read into the lyrics on both sides of the record.

The flipside of the single was Bruce Foxton's writing debut. Fine bassist though Foxton is, it has to be said that 'Carnaby Street' exhibits the same faults as the rest of his slim Jam songbook, being musically clunky and lyrically gauche. Adding to those shortcomings for punks, however, was its nostalgia. 'Not what it used to be!' is the refrain of a song that lambasts the decline of the London thoroughfare that became famous in the Sixties for polka-dotted, candy-striped boutiques patronised by men in military jackets and women in mini-skirts. The bassist denounces the street in its present state as a mockery and exhorts kids not to resign themselves to its loss of the zeitgeist but to bring back its glory. Today, this seems too minor a thing about which to be so vexed as to be compelled to write a song. It was not so risible in the context of the times, when new-wave musicians felt their audiences expected them to be angry. Punk purists, however, were more likely to find 'Carnaby Street' risible on the grounds that the stance of any self-respecting punk about such a haunt of the old-guard should be to want to burn it down.

'All Around the World' was a several times worse offender in failing to toe the punk party line. Its verses and choruses call for a youth explosion based around direction, reaction and creation (words Smith made sure to plaster on the back of the sleeve) and a nebulous 'new' for which the composer claims he has been searching across the globe. The song's bridges, however, are just as much a juxtaposition with such sentiments as parts of 'Sounds From the Street' constituted a repudiation of its own overarching message. In the first one, Weller asks 'What's the point in saying destroy?' This is a direct reaction to the ethos of the Sex Pistols, unforgettably articulated in the howled final word of their 'Anarchy in the UK' debut/manifesto/call-to-arms, as well as emblazoned on one of the most famous pieces of clothing designed by Vivienne Westwood, wife of Pistols manager Malcolm McLaren. The second bridge finds Weller stating that what has gone before should not be dismissed because it constitutes a useful foundation for the future. This is an outright repudiation of the year-zero philosophy, as well as No Future, another slogan/stance heard on a Sex Pistols record. These are, of course, perfectly reasonable points. Punk, though, was not about being reasonable. In being a call for moderation, 'All Around the World' was a red rag to those who viewed the Jam as besuited, suburbanite Young Conservatives.

Says Buckler, 'There was a sort of snobbery within the punk world which was totally against what it should have been about. It isn't all about "destroy," anyway. Even the Sex Pistols created some great music. I think more than anything else we were against the establishment, against the way things used to be done. We wanted things to be different.'

Inconveniently for the nay-sayers, 'All Around the World' was a corking track. From its opening 'Oi!' to its anthemic melody to its galvanising call-and-response vocals to its burning guitar work, it's possessed of the very sort of musical vitality that had been dismayingly thin on the ground before the new wave crashed onto the Seventies. The combination of its incendiary sonic power and the mushrooming respect for the band engendered by their debut album propelled it to a chart peak of 13, a remarkable achievement for such a hard-edged record.

October 1977 saw the Jam make their first foray to the United States. Although the second album was now in the can, their mission was to promote the *In the City* LP.

Visiting America was in those days a big deal for Britons. It was only in the previous month that Freddie Laker had made it more than a fantasy for the British working class by introducing the phenomenon of cheap transatlantic air flights. For rock musicians, the US had a particular allure as the birthplace of the music they loved and made their living by. However, the tour was symptomatic of the fact that the Jam and the USA would never really get on.

On the jaunt, accusations of the Jam being suburban and parochial suddenly did not seem to be such a bum rap. Weller was petulant and aggressive even by his standards, and gave an extraordinary quote in which he said he didn't need to leave his hotel room to see the country because he'd seen it in films. Chris Parry accompanied the band on the trip. He recalls, 'They were not internationalists. They were not happy to explore another country, another culture. They were sadly very much products of their environment. They were very, very, very poor tourists ... And that was so sad to me.' This set the tone for the Jam's every Stateside trip.

However, the antipathy went both ways. The band on occasion were met by hostility or puzzlement from audiences and the media, even though some of their dates were at New York's CBGBs, the one venue in the whole of America that would theoretically be automatically simpatico with their sound and attitudes. 'They were saying we were too British,' says Foxton of the American reception. The fact that Polydor USA would later issue as a single the Jam's Motown cover 'Heat Wave' when it had only been recorded to pad out an album certainly gives credence to the idea that their Stateside label had an unimaginative fear that the Jam's Angloisms would be a hard sell.

Whatever the reason, the Jam only ever made inching progress in the States. This was in contrast to their rivals/bookends. Even though the Clash had condemned the nation with 'I'm So Bored with the U.S.A.' (and provocatively opened American gigs with said song), their universal rebel rock proved palatable to American music lovers, who ultimately gave them a multiple platinum-selling album. In 1981, Weller told Chris Salewicz, 'I just don't see the same enthusiasm there. It's so totally different from Europe … it seems that we've just wasted a lot of time there when we could have been playing to a much more positive response to audiences elsewhere … the majority of Americans just want to be entertained, they seem to need to be coaxed in some way into liking us. They don't seem to see much difference between rock 'n' roll and TV entertainment.' Weller questioned the received wisdom that the USA was a market that needed to be cracked. 'Why, after you crack England, are you expected to immediately go and break America? It's a bit of a joke: why not Russia or Red China?'

Foxton notes, 'You can't force it down people's throats was the bottom line. Paul hated being there. I took out of it that it was just an experience to go and see the country and enjoyed my time there.' Buckler recalls, 'We did some things with Blue Öyster Cult and supported them on one of the tours over there. That was a bit of an eye-opener in as much as that big rock-stadium band was alive and well and kicking in the States even though it had pretty much become old hat in the UK. It was a very difficult one to crack, America. It was that decision of either having to leave everything alone and just concentrate on the States for the big prize or to try and play other territories and stick with the UK. We did a fair amount of work in the States, but we never did enough to crack it.' Buckler adds, 'I don't think we really saw ourselves fitting in too well in the States. We didn't see ourselves as a big rock-stadium, all hair- and teeth-type rock band, so it didn't bother us that much. Obviously, it depends how much you give way to the pressures, because any management or record company would want you to do well in the States simply because it's good business.' Surely

Stateside success is every UK band's dream as well? 'Well yes, but under what terms? If you're going to break the States then you've got to do it the American way, which means that you probably have to change what you're doing to suit that particular market. I don't think we felt very happy with doing that. It often gets forgotten, but American musical culture is really completely different from the UK. We've drawn on each other's influences over the last sixty years, which has been fantastic, but it is very much a different cultural way of doing things. The big rock bands still wander around. To us, they would look like dinosaurs. I don't think we wanted to change the Jam in any way just to suit a particular market. We were quite happy doing what we felt best at doing.'

'The problem with America is that you have to play there,' says Dennis Munday. 'You have to do long tours. Paul has never wanted to do that. Touring in England, you can do thirty dates and you've covered the UK. You can't do thirty dates in America and cover it.' He adds, 'It was very difficult for them because, okay, you had the college circuit, but America wasn't ready for punk and wouldn't be until garage came along.'

Says Weller, 'To break America, you've got give up a lot of things, especially in them days. You had to be there six months touring flat out. You had to maybe live there for a year. None of which appealed to me. I can remember some fucking American MD going, "You guys, you gotta get on that bus and go and play everywhere for six months. That's the only way to break America." Even at the time I had a little think-bubble going, "I ain't fucking doing that, mate." I love playing live, but equally I love being at home. So I wasn't prepared to do that really, and I didn't get the vibe from Rick and Bruce either that we'd all be up for that. Also, we never saw it [as the] pinnacle of someone's musical career because you made it in the States. Small Faces never made it in the States. They were one of the greatest fucking bands that ever lived.

That wasn't the priority for me.' Weller adds, 'We were very arrogant as well. We were like, "Well we're big in England, so we don't really give a fuck if we're not big over here." There was a bit of that attitude, which didn't go down very well with the record company, obviously.'

However, Weller says he doesn't agree with the idea that the Jam were simply too English for the US. He insists, 'We would have done it eventually, definitely. Even though we didn't do the slogging-round thing, we did a lot of tours. We used to do at least two tours a year and we had a really good following.' Foxton says, 'Ironically, it was only the last album, *The Gift*, that a slight dent [was made] in terms of sales. Things were just starting to open up for the Jam when we split up.' Weller concurs, pointing out, 'Our last tour in the States, we played in Chicago at the Aragon Ballroom and there was like 8½ thousand people, so it was kind of getting there. It did reach people. Maybe not in huge numbers, but it did reach people.'

Parry is also of the opinion that the Jam could have broken America: 'Absolutely. There's no doubt about it. I mean, the Clash did. And I did it with the Cure. It was easy-peasy if you knew how to work it. But the Jam were tough customers to take out of the country ... There wasn't the attention from the band for that to happen. They were very, very reluctant to travel ... When I left, they had absolutely zero opportunity to go international. They were by definition a local band.' But what of the point of view that the 'local-hero' aura is precisely what ultimately made the Jam so successful in their home country – that UK fans appreciated the fact that, perhaps unlike the Clash, they hadn't forgotten where they came from? 'You can do that and be international as well,' Parry counters. 'Bruce Springsteen does that.'

IT WAS BRUTAL

On October 28, 1977, the Jam released 'The Modern World', their new single and a taster for their second album. Bill Smith's sleeve design was a contrast to the deluxe feel of the previous single, featuring a Jam who looked like they'd been painted by an artist in possession only of a thick-bristled brush and a palette of three colours.

In effect, the single was an EP, for its B-side contained no fewer than three tracks: live versions of soul classics 'Sweet Soul Music' and 'Back in My Arms Again', plus an unlisted fragment of 'Bricks and Mortar'. This might have constituted remarkable value for money, but the generosity was to some extent wasted. At a time either before twelve-inch singles had taken off or CDs were on the market, tripling the contents of a side of seven-inch vinyl led to muffled sound quality.

The sole track on the A-side was, musically at least, excellent. After opening with a fanfare vocal declaration related to the title, it barrels along on a staccato riff, pounding drums and Weller's most snarling vocals to date. The lyric, however, conveys a message that is confused, even nonsensical. In 1979, Weller explained to Harry Doherty of *Melody Maker*, 'That whole song was about all these sorta creeps who said that the Jam were derivative and "not part of the contemporary scene" an' all that shit, so it's just a statement sayin', you know, "We're just as much entrenched in the seventies as anyone else."' It's doesn't come as too much of a surprise that Weller is attacking scribes who have criticised the Jam: he'd already taken such exception to *Sniffin' Glue* cavilling about the time the group took to tune up that he burnt an issue of the fanzine onstage. Unlike 'Get in the Ring', the 1991 song in which Guns N' Roses listed by name journalists against whom the band bore grievances, 'The Modern World' doesn't get specific. In fact, only in the final line when Weller declares, 'I don't give a damn about your review' does it actually become clear at whom his ire is directed. Elsewhere, he could be arguing with a parent, friend, lover or even gas-meter inspector as he denies the charge that he's a fool who knows nothing of the modern world. He complains that he's had this kind of treatment all his life and vouchsafes that he has actually learned to channel hate and pain in furtherance of his ambitions, ones which he had been certain would come true even back in his schooldays. This sort of stuff is guaranteed to strike a chord with anyone who ever harboured teenage 'I'll-show-them' resolutions. However, once an artist starts writing about his own celebrity, he is already moving away from the concerns and realities of ordinary people, and in fact into the same self-absorbed territory that punks held responsible for destroying the integrity of established rock artists. On balance, however, 'The Modern World' was a good record and deserved to go higher than the chart position of 36 it achieved. Moreover, its quality was a good harbinger for its parent LP.

Said LP's imminent arrival had come as some surprise. At this point in history, the standard release schedule was an album per year. The appearance of *This is the Modern World* on November 18, 1977 made it the Jam's second long-player in six months. This would never have been an issue, though, had the record lived up to its precursor single. Unfortunately, it was a stinker.

The problems with *This is the Modern World* start with the cover imagery.

Reveals Bill Smith, 'I wanted to again have an urban aspect but a much more modernist feel to it, which came from both the title and I thought a couple of the songs. I wanted to have a quite oppressive feel.' Unfortunately, the location he picked for the Jam's moody poses was beneath the Westway, an elevated dual carriageway in West London. While the Westway is certainly a valid symbol of urban soullessness and ugliness, it was already well-known as part of the Clash's hinterland. The fact that Clash

72

guitarist Mick Jones had, off and on, lived in his grandmother's flat in a high-rise overlooking the Westway had prompted the music press to dub his group's sound Tower Block Rock. The Clash had also written a fine song about the Westway: boredom anthem 'London's Burning'. Seeming to appropriate another act's mythology couldn't help but make the Jam – who hailed from an area without such concrete-wasteland issues – once again look like yokel pretenders. With bitter irony, Smith wasn't even aware of the Westway's place in Clash lore.

Almost as though to deliberately ratchet up the contempt factor, the jumper Weller is wearing in the cover photo shouts his defiantly non-punk reverence for the past in the shape of nods to the Who. Says Smith, 'Paul had that white sweater and said, "I saw this picture of Pete Townshend with arrows – could we do that?" So I got some gaffer tape and put the arrows on there.' Weller also sported a Who badge.

The back-cover snap of a flailing, in-concert Jam at least was pleasing, capturing what an exciting live proposition the group were at this point. 'That's a fantastic photograph,' says Smith. 'For me, they came alive on stage.' The inner sleeve, meanwhile, was destined to cause neither admiration nor derision but bafflement. Wanting visualisations of some of the lyrical content of the album, Smith commissioned artwork from Conny Jude. Her illustrations were incongruously feminine and whimsical. Moreover, Smith did not seek advice from Jude as to which illustrations related to which songs. Thus did, for instance, the lyric of anti-authoritarian anthem 'The Combine' come to be placed adjacent to a drawing of a high-heeled woman whose stride has opened her dressing gown to reveal her nudity.

Whereas the debut LP was awash in the trebly overtone of Weller's Rickenbackers, this album's music is cleaner and more muscular. It's also often very good. While the record reveals the Jam as having something to say musically, however, it also shows that they have almost nothing to say lyric-wise.

'The Modern World' kicks off the LP, only not in quite the iteration with which the public was already familiar. Here, the 'damn' about which Weller doesn't care regarding bad reviews is replaced by 'two fucks,' thus revealing that he had toned down his curse to make the single radio-friendly.

Revelation of un-punk compromise is followed by cringe-making naiveté. 'London Traffic', the Jam bassist's second compositional outing, laments the hustle, bustle, dirt and filth of the UK capital's car lanes. It's a legitimate enough complaint and was shared by enough people to have resulted a quarter of a century later in a congestion charge designed to reduce the problem. The trouble was, while it may be the natural philosophical province of the Mayor of London in 2003, it sounded forced coming from a happening young musician in 1977. The irrationality of Foxton's argument doesn't help: 'Take the traffic elsewhere' he offers as a solution. Strangely enough, the full-tilt, punchy music that accompanies these inanities is rather good (and ironically would work well as a road anthem). This juxtaposition of admirable music and risible words will be something of a motif of this record.

'Standards' is a piece of anti-authoritarianism which veers between being rousing in its syncopated power and laughable in its vagueness. The reference to 'Winston' fails to resonate because Weller neglects to explain he is talking of Mr Smith from Orwell's *1984*. 'Life from a Window' is the Jam's first foray into softer territory. Weller strums an acoustic guitar and sings rather prettily as he portrays himself sitting atop various high places. However, he is moping about nothing very much, coming out with generalised laments like, 'Sometimes it don't look nice.' In retrospect, though, it's an interesting pointer to an ability to break out of the punk straitjacket, an ability others would prove to lack.

'The Combine' takes its title from a phrase used by one of Ken

Kesey's characters in outsider novel *One Flew Over the Cuckoo's Nest*. However, the song itself is merely the bastard offspring of 'Away from the Numbers'. Weller states that the ties are too strong for him to fulfil his wish to break away from the crowd. It's a welcome acknowledgment – rare in such a self-aggrandising medium as rock – of susceptibility to peer pressure. However, other elements of the lyric are bewildering ('Nobody wants to die, although the crowd say they do'). Once more, the music – especially the snaking, poppy melody – is worthy of better. The side-closing 'Don't Tell Them You're Sane' is Bruce Foxton's take on the same book. In directly exploring the theme of a silent prisoner in a facility for the mentally damaged, it at least has a more comprehensible connection to its putative inspiration. Its qualities end there. It employs the same rationale that the madman has more insight than the people adjudicating on his sanity that was already hoary/meaningless when the Beatles essayed it in 'Fool on the Hill' a decade previously. Musically, the track is a meandering, thrashing chore to sit through.

'In the Street Today', which kicked off side two, is a compositional collaboration between Weller and old Jam member Dave Waller. Its taut instrumentation is galvanising, but it features a lyric – a Waller poem set by Weller – that is almost a parody of punk in its scattershot grievances (the first verse finds the composer lurching between condemnation of football hooligans and fools in high places) and seething inarticulacy ('The kids want some action – and 'oo can fuckin' blame 'em now?')

In 'London Girl' Weller portrays in the second person a young woman who has entered a world of penury by leaving the parental home. The music is mildly rousing but the lyric doesn't quite ring true, even despite the unglamorous realism of the line in which Weller states that the subject has not managed to wash her feet for three weeks. 'I Need You (For Someone)' is the first Jam love song that sounds heartfelt rather than generic. Its devotional tone is not quite touching enough to distract the listener from the conviction that s/he's heard the melody somewhere before.

The melancholy reprieve from nine-to-five drudgery provided by Saturday and Sunday is a subject that can lead to worthy songs – witness The Easybeats' 'Friday on my Mind' and, to a lesser extent, the Clash's '48 Hours'. 'Here Comes the Weekend', however, has no real insights to offer. People stuck in boring trades might have cause to resent advice like 'Do something constructive with your weekend' from a man who had never really had a job in his life. The song is also undermined from the outset by bizarre opening lines in which Weller for some reason invokes the cheapness of life in Zaire. The music is mildly interesting for the fact that, when the band lay off the power-chord dramatics, they proffer sweet melodic touches and delicate arpeggios.

'Tonight at Noon' is another collaboration, but only in the sense that its title and much of its lyric is lifted from Mersey poet Adrian Henri, whose works had been introduced to Weller by Dave Waller. Considering Weller's sometimes awkward lyrics, Henri's deliberately contradictory title can't help but initially seem a linguistic howler by an under-educated kid. Weller co-opts Henri's work to create another love song that stops just short of being something you care if you ever hear again. The Jam round off the album with Wilson Pickett's soul classic 'In the Midnight Hour'. Their rendition is capable, but its quality is made irrelevant by the fact that it's unrelated to everything that precedes it. Such space-fillers would be a feature of all Jam albums from here on.

The notices for *This is the Modern World* were deservedly poor. Chris Brazier of *Melody Maker* summed up the consensus when he said, 'This album only hints at what the Jam are capable of.' The Jam had also delivered another gift to those who viewed them as mercenary, following up their debut LP inordinately quickly as though trying to ride the last remnants of a new wave they suspected was about to recede.

'I think that was down to Chris Parry,' says Weller of the decision to record a quick follow-up. 'He would say, "You guys are into the Sixties bands and they all put two albums out a year back in the day, so you should do that." I don't think it was because [Polydor] thought it was gonna be over. I'm sure they didn't think it was gonna last long, but it was just down to Chris' idea that it would be a cool thing to do, which it fucking wasn't, but there you go.' Buckler and Foxton agree that the quick productivity was the label's idea, but neither of them express a problem with it. Foxton offers, 'Once you get on that treadmill, it's hard to get off. We signed a four- or five-album deal and they said, "Well we need the next album." But I don't think we rushed it.' Buckler actually says, 'We loved the idea. We thought that was great. "Yeah, let's do it."' One of the reasons they might have loved the idea is that – according to Chris Parry – the label offered them 'a shitload of money' to make the record. Dennis Munday has put the more specific value of £20,000 on the advance, over a hundred thousand in today's coinage.

Parry not only disavows responsibility for the rapid arrival of the second album, but remains angry about it to this day. 'It was ridiculous,' he says. 'It was just totally bullshit. You learn your lessons as you go along in life. I should have said to the lawyer, "Whatever deal you do, put a time before the second album can be even thought of."' Of the monetary incentive for the group to go back into the recording studio so soon, he says, 'John, that was a massive kind of financial change for him, and I can understand that, and he just wanted to get that record made. Unfortunately, I wasn't empowered enough to say no. You've got the lawyer. John's becoming more powerful. Paul is already starting to drift back. My communication with Paul was getting lost. I'm not sure whether it's a good or a bad thing because I'm still naïve ... All of a sudden, Jam had gone upstairs. I was downstairs. I went to no meetings. I was just an A&R guy in the corporation and all of a sudden it comes down ... All of these factors come [in]to play and we have a perfect storm which is called the Second Album Syndrome and it's less than one would want. It was a serious struggle. It was tough. I liked some of the songs a lot, but nothing was finished. Nothing was thought through. It was like entering a flat that could have been a wonderful flat and all the contents and all the fittings were shit. It just disappointed. Everyone sees it as substandard and, believe me, it is. We just needed another six months to nine months and Paul to gather his breath and that second record would have kicked arse.'

Coppersmith-Heaven was also unhappy about the situation. He says, 'By the second album, we were already within the record company's rolling machine, and they were demanding an album every year to tie in with touring, so pressure in that sense was building. Unlike the first record, which was a true representation of their live set, the ... songs were now being evolved in the studio with little rehearsal time.' Asked if he thinks the album is underrated, Coppersmith-Heaven simply says, 'No.'

Weller has always been scathing about the album, perhaps the inevitable result of his status as chief songwriter causing most of the critical flak to be directed his way. He flatly told Paul Lester in 1998, 'It was rubbish, half of it ... It was a bit uninspired.' The Jam's rhythm section, however, defend the record. While Buckler admits, 'Two albums within our first year was quite a workload ... We weren't really prepared to record that album,' he also notes, 'I think it's quite nice because [it] reflected that more melodic side of Paul.' Foxton says, '*This is the Modern World* was a good album. There was some good songs on there. 'Life from a Window' goes down a storm.' One good thing can be said of the album: that the Jam refused to make it a carbon-copy of its predecessor. However, both Foxton and Buckler feel that the poor reception to the album was less related to its quality than the very fact that it wasn't categorizable as *In the City* 2. Foxton: 'It was a bit of a change. We'd started to introduce acoustic guitars and a couple of ballads, etc. Maybe it was just a bit radical to add these other instruments so soon.' However, he insists, 'I never looked at it and went, "Oh, it went terribly wrong, that was a big mistake." We were just experimenting, as you do. You've done your first album, which was our live set pretty much, and so you're writing new songs and you think, "Well, we'd like to add a bit of colour here and try an acoustic guitar." I was very happy with the album. We wouldn't have put it out if we weren't.'

It might be suggested that a factor which adds to the impression of flimsiness about *This is the Modern World* is its briefness. Yet while the album runs only to around 31½ minutes, such parsimoniousness was actually par for the course with this band. Albums at that point in history were usually around forty minutes long but, for all the Jam's much vaunted and often justified reputation for providing value for money, not a single one of their six studio LPs attained that length. Moreover, four of them were only a minute or two over the half-hour mark. That this was never particularly noted at the time is down to perception. *In the City*, for instance, was only a minute longer than *This is the Modern World*, but its quality meant that few were left feeling short-changed by it.

The sales of *This is the Modern World* were as underwhelming as its reviews. It climbed no higher than 22 in the charts. While this was only two places lower than its predecessor, its stay in the top forty of just five weeks was thirteen weeks shy of the total *In the City* enjoyed.

The brickbats and poor sales were of course depressing. Remarkably, though, the following twelve months would find the Jam's fortunes sinking much lower and would almost see them squander all their early promise via a permanent split.

At the end of '77, the Jam embarked on a UK tour to promote their second album.

The tour's stop in Leeds led to a hotel fracas with an Australian rugby team. The Jam seem to have been as much sinned against as sinning: Foxton sustained bruised ribs, the Jam had to move to another hotel and Weller's brief appearance in court the next morning on a charge of breach of the peace resulted in a discharge. This amounts to just about the only suggestion of either scandal or conventional rock 'n' roll destruction of the Jam's career, unless Weller's contretemps the following year with Sex Pistols bassist Sid Vicious qualifies. Accounts of the latter incident vary, but the consensus is that it took place at London venue the Speakeasy, that it revolved around the Pistols' recent plagiarism of 'In the City', that Vicious was the instigator and that Weller came off better.

Two of the three tracks on the Jam's first single of 1978 – including the A-side – were written by Bruce Foxton. This surprising development could technically have been proof that the bassist had come on in leaps and bounds as a composer and had secured his new prominence on merit. However, one listen to the record confirmed that Foxton was still nowhere near as skilled a songsmith as Paul Weller. This in turn raised questions about Weller's current motivation and capacities.

'As he got more successful, Bruce was quite comfortable with that,' recalls Parry. However, Parry found that Weller 'struggled' with the same success: 'I'd say to Paul, "What the fuck do you expect? You write great songs, you want to be a spokesman for your generation, well that's what you're going to get, Paul." It manifested itself first with his girlfriend. All of a sudden, "I'm in love and I just want to be with this girl and I've got all these demands upon me and I just want to be me."'

On the In the City tour, Weller met a young woman named Gill Price. The couple shortly moved into a flat together in London. Their relationship apparently was stormy and ultimately ended in rancour, but the fact that for a while Price was good for Weller is demonstrated by him writing several moving songs clearly inspired by the effect she had on his well-being. At first, though, his relationship with her was damaging to his songwriting and hence the Jam.

The process of detachment Parry notes above may have been inevitable, with or without Price. While Weller decamped to the capital, the other two Jam members remained in Woking, not least because they couldn't afford London rents. There also occurred a drifting apart that was essentially necessary. Foxton notes, 'As you become more successful and you spend more time writing, recording, touring, on the road, you see less of each other apart from meeting in the reception to go to your soundcheck and then, "See you half an hour before stage-time." Because you're in each others' pockets so much.' Says Buckler, 'We always found it a very welcome relief simply to be able to walk away from each other when we had the time off. Otherwise you'd have nothing to talk about. We didn't live all the same life. We all had our own friends. So it was nice to have that break.' Parry recalls a gig in December 1978 at Canterbury when his new charges, the Cure, supported the Jam: 'I'd left the Jam by then. Paul was definitely way outside the other two. He had his only little coterie of friends. They were not three together. It struck me then that that was quite a different relationship.'

Aside from romance and band-fragmentation issues, Weller seems to have been shaken by the reception accorded *This is the Modern World*. The panning of his latest batch of songs – the very adventurism of which implied that he was convinced his craft was evolving – must surely have played a part in his productivity proceeding to drop off a cliff. The joy he took in his romantic relationship must have made for quite a remarkable juxtaposition, and one which in turn created the temptation to use his relationship to retreat from the brickbats and hide from his creative responsibilities.

Weller's shaken state of mind seems to have made him susceptible to the notion that the Jam as it was currently constituted was not a viable proposition. Near the end of 1977 Weller asked Glen Matlock if he wanted to join the Jam as rhythm guitarist. Matlock had ceased being musical foil to lyricist Johnny Rotten when he left the Sex Pistols in February '77, but – as Weller knew – had formed a new band, Rich Kids. He was also a bassist. Nonetheless, he was interested. Matlock told John Reed that the overture only foundered when he bumped into Buckler and Foxton at punk venue the Roxy and laughed at their insistence that his joining would necessitate him wearing a mod suit. (Ironically, the Jam had dispensed with the suits by year's end.) After that, Matlock turned the tables and asked Weller if he would join Rich Kids as frontman. He found Weller briefly receptive. One wonders whether the attraction for Weller of working with Matlock – in whichever group – was that the burden of songwriting would no longer be solely on his shoulders.

When – in lieu of new songs from Weller – Foxton stepped up to the breach to enable the Jam to release a disc on March 3, 1978, he provided 'News of the World' and B-side track 'Innocent Man'. The A-side is yet another song in which Foxton is to be found getting aerated about something that might well be objectionable but is hardly a burning issue. If one were to be generous, one could suggest that – as with 'London Traffic' – Foxton has been vindicated by events. However, the bassist is not here condemning anything so extreme as the titular British tabloid newspaper's hacking of a murdered teenager's mobile phone (something that would in 2011 lead to its abrupt demise), but instead common-or-garden salaciousness and intrusiveness. The tune is ordinary, certainly not boasting the best attributes of either punk rock or power pop, which genres are shoutingly invoked at the beginning. The co-opting of the street newspaper vendor's historical sales pitch 'Read all about it!' is simply too banal to constitute an acceptable chorus, not least because the banality is squared by it being unimaginatively bolted to the title of the newspaper in question. Additionally, as is ever the case with his lead vocals, Foxton's delivery is slightly gormless.

That the acoustic guitar riff strummed by Weller in 'Innocent Man' is reminiscent of the Who's 'Baba O'Riley' is somewhat unfortunate in light of the fact that the lick of 'The Modern World' owed something to the same band's 'Pictures of Lily'. However, that's only the start of the problems with a track that – as with 'News of the World' and, come to that, all Foxton's previous compositions – gives the impression of toytown protest and manufactured fury. The subject of the song is not Emmett Till, Angela Davis, Hurricane Carter, Liddle Towers, George Davis or any of the other real-life *cause célèbres* taken up by other rock songwriters. Groan-inducingly, Foxton is simply positing a theoretical victim of judicial injustice. The syncopated chorus might have an emotional power were he talking about an actual case, but probably wouldn't. Foxton invokes the hangman's noose in a country where capital punishment had been outlawed more than a decade previously, and in any case undermines his opposition to it by trilling the contradictory sentiment, 'Instead of him, it should be you.'

Piano provided by Weller bobs just audibly beneath the surface of 'Innocent Man'. Weller's only other significant contribution to this single-cum-EP is the composition of B-side cut 'Aunties and Uncles (Impulsive Youths)'. It's immediately likeable in embracing the idea that rock/punk doesn't have to be all about myth-making and rebel stances, but can encompass domestic notes and everyday trivia. Yet, however charming Weller's bemused cataloguing of family meddling, the track is lyrically and melodically negligible.

The single's sleeve – designed jointly by Bill Smith and Weller – showed the Jam striding down Carnaby Street. Smith concedes that the idea had nothing to do with the contents of the record. He also admits that the record was hardly vintage Jam. 'It would be lovely to only work on music you liked,' he reflects, adding, 'To be honest, I think they were putting out far too much, but I think Polydor were at that time worried that they hadn't signed the right band. They were going to be dropped or who knows what might have happened.' He says that Polydor 'definitely' wanted to get out product before the punk bubble burst: 'They thought it was going to run out of steam.'

That the single climbed to number 27 technically represented a commercial bounce, but the Jam were clearly treading water.

In Spring 1978, Chris Parry organised some Jam studio time intended to provide an idea of what the band currently had to offer pending future formal recording sessions. What it revealed was that the band's creative drought had developed to a potentially terminal state. Weller later told Phil Sutcliffe, 'We'd done about eight tunes, Bruce's and three or four of mine, and they were all piss poor.'

Foxton recalls the period as involving 'pressure.' He says, 'For whatever reason, *Modern World* didn't sell that well and it's like the make-or-break record then. If this doesn't go, we'll be out of a job, basically. We certainly won't have a record company.' That pressure can't have been helped by the unproductiveness of Weller. 'Bruce wrote more songs around that time for the so-called aborted third album because I wasn't writing,' says Weller. 'I didn't have the interest in it, so he stepped in to try to save the day. I don't know if it was a writer's block. I just couldn't be fucked. I'd lost interest in it, and it took a while for it to come back.' Weller remembers this period as one of confusion. 'As long as I can remember, I just dreamt of being in a band, making records, blah blah blah. But I don't think I realised what it entailed. That first album, like most bands' first album, it's just basically your live set, what you've been cooking up for two years or whatever, and then all of a sudden you've done them tunes and now you've got to write another twelve or fourteen. It was a bit like, "I didn't realise it entailed this." So it took me a while to get serious about it and realise this entails a bit more thought and a bit more work.'

Parry, who was absent from the sessions, was as unimpressed as Weller by what he heard. 'They were just demos that were being put forward and they were rubbish,' he says. He recalls the songs numbering 'four or so,' and says, 'I asked them, "Who's wrote these?" Maybe Paul wrote one. Maybe his name was attached to one, but it was mainly Bruce.' For Parry, Foxton was 'a very, very good bass player and a wonderful contributor to the Jam, but he was not destined to be the songwriter.' He adds, 'To be fair to Bruce, he just wanted to make things happen. He just wanted to fill the void. Paul went AWOL … I've no idea why Paul didn't contribute. Knowing artists, I just think he went, "Fuck you lot. You do something and prove what you are capable of. I'm bored with pushing this boat."'

Parry now had a task on his hands. 'My job was simply to get the Jam back on song. Paul was standing off. Bruce was pushing forward with songs, and even Rick Buckler was. It wasn't believable. All of a sudden, within the corporation, the Jam were starting to be, "Well that's okay, we've had a bit of success with them – next." I hated that. All I wanted to do was help the band make something along the lines of when Paul said what he said to me at that pub. I just wanted to make something happen. It wasn't about me. I'd figured out I didn't want to get involved with the management of the Jam. I realised that they were quirky English geezers that didn't really want to travel. I was a New Zealander, I've travelled a long way, I've had a big journey in my life and I wanted to journey on. So they weren't part of what I wanted to do. But I didn't want to leave them in the lurch. And I understood how these record companies were operating. They were terrible. They could sit round the table and say, "This is over" and the Jam were closed down. I wasn't prepared to let that happen. I knew there was no future with the Jam unless Paul stood up and my last stand for them was that nothing – nothing – was going to come into Polydor until Paul stood up. I knew I was going to leave Polydor. I knew where I was going to go, but that was my gift back to the Jam, and if the Jam didn't respond, then fuck 'em.'

A crisis meeting took place at which Parry admits his words were 'quite brutal actually.' He recalls those words as, '"There's no way we're going to make a record where we've got no Paul Weller songs and you, Bruce, are going to be writing the material. These songs are shit."' He adds, 'I just put my foot down. I put a lot of effort and a lot of time into the Jam and I just wanted them to be great. At this point, I've got enough power to say, "No, you're not coming into the studio" ... That third Jam album was not going to be fucked up. They were either going to make a good-to-great album or they're not going to make an album at all. And nobody was going to fuck with me on that. Not Paul, not John, not his fucking lawyer, not Bruce, not Rick, and nobody in my company was going to stop me making that decision. The first time in my life I was a creative gatekeeper, and I loved it.' The Jam camp loved it slightly less. 'They hated me,' Parry recalls of the reaction to his verdict. 'Bruce was as angry as fuck. John wasn't very happy, either.'

Foxton says Parry's words were 'hard to take, particularly when you're young and you just think, "What the fuck do you know?"' Although the exchange was a bombshell, the bassist admits it did the band good in the long run, to say the least. 'It really – mainly Paul – made us go away and think, "Well, okay, got to try harder." It's a bit like your school report: could do better. That was the kick up the arse we all needed. It was our saviour really.' Coppersmith-Heaven is of the same mind. 'It was a very constructive process by Chris to be critical of the songs, which in turn sent Paul back to the drawing board,' he says. 'He was a positive input for the band at that stage.'

Foxton denies that the band were close to a split, but this is rather undermined by the fact that during this period a music paper carried quotes from him which seemed to reveal that he was actively thinking of a life beyond the Jam and even outside music. 'I don't know whether it's going to work out,' he admitted to a *Sounds* scribe. '...when the Jam fall through I ain't gonna join another band ... I wouldn't want to go through all that hustling round the clubs again ... I'd really like to open up a guesthouse or a small hotel. I've seen all these people open up one year with just four or five rooms, the next year it's seven or eight, then the next year they're having an extension built. You can't go wrong.' Foxton now says, 'That's desperation, isn't it? That's something that my mum and dad, bless them, were looking into for years. To get off the treadmill, really. We were looking at a place down in Bournemouth, I seem to recall, a little bed and breakfast. It was in the back of my mind: "Oh sod it, if this ain't working I'll do that then."' Leaving aside the astonishing lack of confidence Foxton was displaying in what continued to be – whatever the group's recent failings – a viable, charting act, the conventionalism and careerism of his vague future plans were easy prey for those who had always considered the Jam unspeakably square.

Like Foxton, Buckler is able to recognise a process of improved focus and industry about the album that became *All Mod Cons*. 'We were under a great deal of pressure to come up with something which was going to do a darn site better than *Modern World* and we went through this thing of re-arranging songs and re-arranging them again,' he recollects. 'I think we all just pulled our socks up, rolled up our sleeves and got stuck in to doing this album the best we could. We had no idea whether it would work or not. We just felt that we had to put a lot of effort into it, as opposed to being cavalier like we were for *Modern World*.'

This process involved abandoning the demo sessions and

granting Weller time to work his way out of his writer's block. During this period, Weller – persistently bothered at his Baker Street flat by what would now be termed a stalker – moved back into his parents' home in Woking. Perhaps this return to the comforting familiarities of childhood is what led to the subsequent revival in his composing skills. Weller told journalist Dave Schulps, 'I wrote the bulk of the songs in a couple of days...'

Parry says that the Jam came back to him with new songs within a month. 'John said, "Paul's writing again." There may have been some more tapes, I'm not sure, but certainly sessions were booked at RAK in St John's Wood and we got cracking. I commissioned the third album to be started. I'm really proud of the fact that I actually closed the door on that and stopped the bullshit, because that was significant in the development of the band. It made the other players realise that Paul was the one that'll drive the creative process.' Weller now says, 'I think it was good in some ways that *Modern World* was a flop because, if nothing else, it propelled me to start getting my shit together and get serious about it, which culminated in *All Mod Cons*, which was our first big hit, if you like.'

Parry adds a curious post-script to this story. 'It probably triggered the end of the band,' he says of his pep-talk/ultimatum. 'It was brutal, it needed to be brutal but, looking back, if it was less brutal maybe it gave room for people like Rick and Bruce to contribute a bit and Paul to relax a bit and maybe they could have been a longer-lived trio.'

APEX OF THE TRIANGLE

It was just after the Parry pep-talk/ultimatum that Polydor made Dennis Munday the Jam's product manager.

Munday explains of the product-manager role, 'You're given an artist roster and your job is to liaise with everyone. You put the records on the release schedule and it's your job to get everything together and do the marketing.' The job also involved – as far as Munday was concerned, anyway – going on the road. 'I went on all the tours from '78,' he says of his work with the Jam. He was also allowed access to the Jam's recording sessions: 'I love it. It gets me out of the office, so I'd spend as much time as I could.' He adds of his studio visits, 'I never interfered [but] if Paul asked me for my opinion, I would say.'

Munday's speciality had previously been jazz, but he says, 'I really did like punk music. The first thing I ever heard was 'New Rose' and that really did turn me on.' Although Munday was enthusiastic about working with the Jam, he says, 'I wasn't quite ready for what was going down, which was the supposed third album. That was quite a shock.' The first Jam meeting he attended crackled with tension deriving from Parry's dismissal of the new material. 'I don't think it was that so much as the way he delivered it,' he muses. 'He basically told Bruce to go back to his day job playing the bass. They took it personally. I mean, he was right in what he said. But it took me back with their attitude towards the company. The meeting was heavy.' He adds, 'I think the problem was they were forced to do the second album too quickly. You should do one album a year.' Did he feel at any point that the group were close to splitting up? 'No. I don't [think] they've ever been close to splitting up, not until the end.'

Munday pronounces of the overall relationship between the Jam and Polydor, 'At that time, and for a long time afterwards, not very good. There was a sort of Us and Them.' The cause of this was, 'The way they were treated. All the punk bands, they were not treated as real groups, for want of a better word. People didn't want punk music, they were hoping it would die quickly. My generation were running the business and it was probably the first time that they'd come across music that they couldn't associate with.'

Munday was pleased to find that he 'got on okay' with the group. It wasn't just his relative youth (late twenties) that made the Jam less suspicious of him. His estuary English meant he sounded like them rather than like a conventional record company exec. He also felt he had, compared to some, advanced man-management skills. 'Something I learnt before I even worked with the Jam is that, when you're dealing with artists, it doesn't always work well to send them away with a flea in their ear. I can't see the point in either humiliating or patronising someone.' Something else that probably helped was the fact that Munday had been an original Sixties mod. Munday reveals of his first sighting of the Jam when he was still the label's jazz A&R manager, 'I was quite taken aback because I walked into the press office and they were sitting there in their black mohairs. It was like looking at myself ten years earlier.'

As the Jam faltered, the Clash were going from strength to strength – and doing so partly by slagging off the Jam.

Following their rapturously received April 1977 eponymous debut album, the Clash had cranked up both their musical kudos and their rebel credentials with 'Complete Control', a single the following September which – to a searing, hard-rock backdrop – denounced their record company for broken promises. '(White Man) In Hammersmith Palais', released in June 1978, was another Clash 45 with something to say. A soaring punk-reggae hybrid, it used a violent incident at a recent London reggae all-nighter as a jumping-off point for a mournful meditation on the state of punk. Joe Strummer's vocal lamented that punk musicians were too busy fighting for a good place under the lighting to be concerned about nurturing the punk movement. One of the targets for his ire was a certain Woking three-piece. It's difficult to interpret his condemnation of people changing their voting preferences as thoughtlessly as they do their overcoats as anything other than an allusion to Weller's recent comments about opting for the Conservatives at the ballot box, especially when Strummer sneers about such type's Burton suits. Strummer proceeds to claim that these people think it's funny 'turning rebellion into money.' That this powerful line was much quoted made it all the more clear that the Clash were in their pomp and the Jam in the mire.

August 18 saw the release of the Jam's first double-A sided single. If it was a harbinger of the band's turning fortunes, it's a fact only evident with hindsight. That one side of the disc featured a cover version betrayed Weller's recent lack of productivity and interest, while the Weller-written obverse has retroactively been cast as a classic primarily because of the esteem in which the album it was subsequently placed on is held.

By dint of receiving most airplay, and probably promotion, 'David Watts' became the de facto A-side and '"A" Bomb in Wardour Street' its flip. 'David Watts' – a Foxton-sung feature of the band's live set – had secured its place on the single in preference to a new Weller song whose title was also a name, 'Billy Hunt'. It was a move with which Munday disagreed: 'I couldn't see the point of going with 'David Watts'. It wasn't the kind of song that was going to break through the top ten. I think 'Billy Hunt' would have sold as many. An industry trick to get a band in the charts is do a cover version. I wasn't particularly for that.' Chris Parry claims responsibility for the choice. 'We were up in Manchester and they were playing 'David Watts' and I liked it,' he says. 'I didn't realise it was a Kinks track. I said, "Let's record it." I thought it should be a single.'

Parry's choice met with some resistance. When it was laid down at the RAK studio owned by Mickie Most – famous record producer and mogul, although chiefly known to the public for his proto-Simon Cowell role in TV talent show *New Faces* – discussion of its potential relative to that of '"A" Bomb in Wardour Street' occasioned an argument. Recalls Parry, 'John's saying, "Fuck it, Paul's not singing on it." There was many arguments about it. I said, "We've got to get a record out and I want to put this one out." And then John said, "Well Mickie's here. Mickie knows what a hit record is." I said, "John, I don't need Mickie. 'David Watts' is what we want to put out, it's a fucking hit." He said, "You might think that, but Mickie is the hits master." And I had to eat humble pie and say, "Mickie, would you mind listening to these two songs and decide which one you would pick?" So we dutifully sat down there, me and John – maybe the band – and Mickie listened to both and said, "That's the hit – 'David Watts'." And John said, "Okay Chris, it's a hit."'

That 'David Watts' originated as a track on the 1967 Kinks album *Something Else* no doubt caused loud groans amongst those who despised the Jam's revivalist tendencies. However, the purism of punk was increasingly lessening its hitherto vice-tight grip. Musical primitivism was losing its novelty and, in any case, was unsustainable in the face of the punk musicians' inevitably advancing technical skills. Meanwhile, it had become difficult to hold punk groups to any particular standard of integrity once the Sex Pistols had been reduced to a trio of its lesser-talented members – Steve Jones, Paul Cook and Sid Vicious – which cynically continued working with Malcolm McLaren in preparing *The Great Rock 'n' Roll Swindle*. Said project span off numerous trashy records notable for being absolutely devoid of the Sex Pistols menace that had once reduced large sections of society to a state of terror. It being the case that the sentiment was increasingly being aired that punk was dead, there was even less reason for the

Jam – always semi-detached from the movement – to tie themselves to its fate.

In one aspect, though, 'David Watts' had punk credibility: its Britishness. Kinks songwriter and frontman Ray Davies had pioneered the English rock song. His unexpected application of a London idiom to a form of music previously considered quintessentially American had yielded many classics. 'David Watts' was one example, albeit a confused one. Some sections of it boast a superb authenticity as they explore every teenage schoolboy's pillow fantasies of being as handy with his fists, as skilled on the football field and as attractive to girls as the coolest kid in the school. However, other verses smirkingly allude to a homosexual scene Davies had recently encountered. References to the titular object of worship being gay, fancy-free and unavailable to admiring females don't gel with the more universal *bildungsroman* passages. Nonetheless, it's an intriguing concoction. The Jam's version is more turbo-charged and stylish than the Kinks' endearingly rinky-dink template, and even adds an extra degree of Englishness in its deployment of an 'Oi!' refrain (possibly prompted by its use to close 'Harry Rag' on the same *Something Else* album). According to Weller, incidentally, little can be read into the fact that Foxton took lead vocals on 'David Watts': it wasn't the right key for Weller's voice.

While technically a new song, '"A" Bomb in Wardour Street' was actually started before the Jam even had a record deal, originating from the point that the group were recording demos to the purpose of persuading Polydor of their potential. 'I booked Polydor on a weekend and that's when the IRA were dropping little bombs into the rubbish bins and the whole area was closed off,' says Parry. 'The session didn't happen because of that ... It was written about that in very early 1977. Or that's when it was formed.' Weller retooled his original ideas to address the increasing level of violence observable at the band's gigs, including at punk club the Vortex in the titular West End road. Despite his skinniness, Weller was handy with his fists, as Foxton found out one day when he found Weller pummelling him about the head after he accidentally broke his bass. As such, one might imagine that Weller wasn't easily intimidated. However, he told the BBC's 2012 *Punk Britannia* series, 'Although the gigs were exciting – not just ours but all the gigs around that time – they were also fucking very scary. It was a very, very violent time.'

The song's music is disjointed, alternating staccato sections with smoother verses. In the lyric, Weller avers that, unchecked, violence will overwhelm the country. This message is robbed of power by what was termed in those days fifth-form poetry ('Where the streets are paved with blood with cataclysmic overtones'). Nonetheless, the song possessed resonance simply by dint of addressing a genuine current concern – the media was as worried by violence around the punk movement as Weller – and was therefore intrinsically superior to Foxton's laughable attempts at topical material on the previous single.

The record – housed in a sleeve with an arrow motif that Bill Smith designed to capture the 'forward motion and action' he felt the Jam represented - climbed to number 25. This was hardly spectacular but, handily for the band's standing with Polydor, it was two places higher than the chart position managed by 'News of the World'.

For most, the proof of the renaissance of Weller as a composer and the Jam as an artistic and commercial force came on October 13 with the release of 'Down in the Tube Station at Midnight'. Yet the song almost didn't get recorded.

'It was just a poem, I didn't have a song,' says Weller. Recalls Coppersmith-Heaven, 'That was a particular instance of the frustration of being in the studio a little too early after the song had been written, meaning we had a lot of work to do to find the instrumentation and arrangement. So at the beginning it wasn't working, and Paul got frustrated, and threw the lyrics in the bin.' It was Coppersmith-Heaven who saved the lyric from the dustcart. Says Weller, 'He would really encourage me: "We could make this into a tune."'

Moreover, it was at Coppersmith-Heaven's insistence that the track trod new musical ground for the Jam. Buckler has revealed that the song was recorded in three sections and then stitched together, the sort of process that the band had always spurned as artificial, as well as presenting problems for live reproduction.

It is another Weller composition about violence, this one written not as a didactic condemnation but a slice of life, one that, despite being in the first-person, possesses an air of detachment. It tells how a commuter is set upon for small change on his journey home on London Transport's underground network. Judging by a reference to them smelling of right-wing meetings, the gang responsible are comprised of skinheads, a revival of the late-Sixties youth cult currently causing concern in the UK because elements of it had a fascistic strain. As the battered man lies helpless, he realises with horror that the gang have taken his keys and that his wife will think their sound in the front door heralds his arrival.

The scenario is very powerful. Unfortunately, the lyric with which Weller fleshes it out is anything but. It's pocked with the sort of phraseology that might have earned Weller a pat on the back in the Sheerwater poetry classes in which he stood out, but in the context of a commercially-released creation by a grown adult is simply embarrassing: the misuse of the word 'glazed'; the description of the station steps as being 'partially naked'; the assertion that taking a train ticket is analogous to pulling out a plum; the bizarre, meaningless statement that the narrator's life 'took a look and drowned me in its own existence.' Moreover, the lines about commuters going home to people who will love them forever carries a distasteful whiff of contempt for the narrator.

Then there is the little remarked-upon fact that midnight seems a rather late hour for a commuter to be travelling, especially in an era when the tube network closed down overnight.

The reason little attention has been paid over the years to how feeble is Weller's lyric is the sheer excellence of the music that backs it. The record starts with the whooshing sound of a tube train before the arrival of the type of stuttering, razor-edged guitar work that would become a Jam trademark. Foxton's bass pulsates sublimely. Weller's lyric may be trite, but the headlong nature of the melody on which it rides gives it a suspense. Additionally, Weller renders the story in an appropriately small and vulnerable voice. The song's title line is hauntingly shadowed by high-pitched quasi-wailing from Foxton. By the closing section, Weller is virtually prattling as his vocal speeds up to match music that has excitingly gone into double-time.

No less admirable is the record's Britishness. This juncture marked the point at which Weller began to insist on the validity of exploring his own culture. Perhaps not coincidentally, around this time the last vestiges of a pseudo-American accent drained from his singing style. This may not sound a profound development, but in those days musicians were afraid that singing in anything other than a US voice could close off commercial avenues, particularly beyond the limited field of punk. The sense of authenticity and integrity this potential self-sacrifice created only added to the Jam's esteem over the following years.

The single's sleeve featured a literal design. Smith: 'We did it down in the tube station, [although] not at midnight.' Smith set up the shot at Bond Street station with photographer Martyn Goddard, then went up to fetch the band, who stood poised until a train could be heard rumbling along the tracks. 'We took a few shots and then moved off again. We had to do it very, very quickly – we didn't get any authority.'

While the sleeve again featured the aerosoled Jam logo, the

record's title was spelt out in the jagged lettering once familiar from the product of Immediate Records, latter-day home of Weller's beloved Small Faces. Smith searched font foundries in vain for the typeface but was doomed to come up short because it had never been made commercially available after being designed for Immediate by Sean Kenny. Smith spent a day or so working with tracing paper, black ink and blow-ups to create those letters in the song title not liftable from old Small Faces sleeves.

On the reverse of the picture bag was a headshot of a young Keith Moon. No explanation was necessary as to its inclusion, nor the presence on the record's B-side of 'So Sad About Us', a cover of a track from the 1966 Who album *A Quick One*. The previous month, Moon – whose hyperactive drumming prowess and larger-than-life personality had played such a big part in making the Who icons for millions, including Weller – had died of an overdose of a prescribed anti-alcoholism drug. He was just 32. Working on the back-cover design was doubly eerie for Smith. By coincidence, he had recently designed the jacket of the Who LP *Who Are You*. Famously, it featured a Who photograph taken at Shepperton Studios in which Moon is sitting in a chair bearing the legend 'Not to be taken away', a fact now turned from mildly amusing to poignant. The Jam's tribute is perhaps beyond the bounds of criticism, but for what it's worth their version of 'So Sad About Us' is respectable but doesn't quite possess the aching melancholy of the Who's gem of an original.

The B-side contained a second track, the Foxton-written 'The Night'. The bassist wisely steers clear of social commentary on this anthemic celebration of seaside-set hedonism, even if there is a strain of 'Friday-on-my-Mind' proletarian desperation. The instrumentation is as high-grade as that on the A-side, while the tempo is so breathless as to pack in everything Foxton needs to say in well under two minutes before an abrupt, echoing close. The lyric doesn't yield anything remotely worth quoting, but the whole concoction is Foxton's best creation yet. Foxton's one-third share of the record's publishing royalties (Weller and Pete Townshend copping the rest) would have been fairly healthy: the disc climbed to number 15.

According to Buckler, the selection of 'Tube Station' for A-side status was almost a matter of whimsy. 'It was always very difficult for us to choose which ones we were going to put out as singles,' he says. 'When we actually looked at the list of songs available, I think 'Tube Station' was at the bottom of the list, so we said, "Right we'll do that, we'll release that then." Rather than our most likely candidate.' Was it always a three-way decision like that? 'Not always. Sometimes things were written specifically and you think, "Well, this has got to be the single without question" ... Sometimes [Weller] might have said, "Look I really want this to be a single" and we'd go, "Yeah, okay." It was no big deal over that. Most of the time we worked really well together with this sort of stuff ... We'd obviously chat about it. We'd often seek advice from other people and say, "Well, which one would you fancy listening to?"'

For his part, Radio 1's Tony Blackburn was not impressed by 'Down in The Tube Station at Midnight'. The DJ known for his perennial jollity and decidedly mainstream tastes publicly complained, 'It's disgusting the way punks sing about violence. Why can't they sing about trees and flowers?' Weller felt compelled to ring the station and point out on air that the song was anti-violence.

The trouble was, Weller wasn't a particularly good advocate for himself, in either this incident or any other. A later appearance by him on Radio 1's record-review panel show Roundtable provided an example of how painful his non-performing public appearances could be. When the show's host prompted him into anecdote by invoking the time the Jam man had phoned the station to defend 'Tube Station', Weller could offer in response only, 'That's right,' with an agonising silence then descending between him and his interlocuter. All of the Jam were often comedically monosyllabic and unexcitable, as though living up to the confession of the narrator of 'David Watts', 'I'm just a dull and simple lad.' The Jam weren't even able to inject some character into their interactions with the media via the braggadocio that usually comes so naturally to rockers. Weller by all accounts – including his – was an egomaniac on the quiet, but little of his confidence in his art revealed itself in his public utterances.

It provided an interesting contrast with the Clash, and one that was not readily explainable. The three core members of that latter ensemble – Strummer, Jones and bassist Paul Simonon – were gregarious people despite all having troubled backgrounds. The morose Jam members, conversely, all came from perfectly happy and stable homes.

The rich, layered but still gritty new Jam music revealed by their latest single had demonstrated new dimensions to the Jam's sound. Parry: 'Vic and Paul, they'd settled on this idea that Paul could build another layer of music that wasn't necessarily going to be replicated in the same way live. Something like 'Down in the Tube Station at Midnight' – the two guitars in harmony, that kind of idea.' Parry also admits, 'Nothing to do with me. I was planning the next tour. I was coming into the studio in the afternoons [and] early evenings and I was listening to the tapes.'

Hitherto, Buckler reveals, Weller had 'always felt very uncomfortable' with overdubbing. The drummer reasons, 'We always had the feeling that there was people out there who could make great albums, and when you went to see them live it just didn't happen because they'd put so much effort into the sound recording that they simply could not carry it off. That was a bit of a fear from us. Our strength was being a live band. It wasn't until *All Mod Cons* and we started working with Vic Smith that Paul started to feel a bit more at ease with doing some of the guitar overdubs.' Says Weller, 'It's got some great qualities about being a powerhouse three-piece, but it was limiting as well. It's also frustrating sometimes, 'cos you can't play four or five parts.' Of overdubbing, he says, 'It was nice to be able to do that – all those harmony guitars and stuff. It made it the icing on the cake.'

That Parry had chosen to exercise only a nominal co-producer's role across the summer of '78 had a perhaps inevitable consequence: he made the band wonder why they needed him. 'Tube Station' was the first – but by no means last – Jam record on which Vic Coppersmith-Heaven received sole producer credit. Coppersmith-Heaven recalls that it was he who decided on RAK as the venue to record the album, liking its 'beautiful wood panelling that gave the Jam's recordings a live, natural sound.' However live and natural, however, this sound needed much work. 'All the Jam's new songs were in their earliest basic form, and all were fairly unrehearsed,' Coppersmith-Heaven says. 'We were arranging and recording in the studio at the same time. When the band started playing those arrangements, they also had to develop the intensity that they would have at a live set as if they had been playing the song for years. This would take time, and it meant there was to be a lot of interaction between the producer and the band. At that time, Chris was also very busy with his A&R position at Polydor offices, so he would jump from the office to the studio and back again.' After recording a clutch of tracks in this way, Coppersmith-Heaven told the group that the situation wasn't tenable. 'It was disruptive and we were losing the creative flow. So I asked the band to choose one producer they'd like to work with.'

Parry recalls that the choice the Jam made was as much to do with his brutal words previously as anything else. 'As that session progressed, John turned up at some point mid-stream and said, "Look, there's a problem, and the problem [is] you, Chris, turning up at the studio and talking about the music because actually Vic and the band know what record they want to put out and they're fucked off with you because of what you did." I went, "Okay, I'll go down there" and had a meeting.' Parry discovered that there was one person who actually didn't have a problem with him, and in fact tried to manipulate his continued presence. 'Paul gave me a get-out clause,' he reveals. 'He said, "Can you play another instrument, Chris? Like, can you do keyboards?" It was kind of interesting ... He was just trying to find a place for me to be. Paul wanted me to hang in ... I said, "No, I can't play keyboards." He said, "Oh, okay. Well, they don't really want you to be around." They were on a roll and Paul had the songs and I think Vic had had enough of me, which is fair enough, and Bruce and Rick, I'd fucked them off. So it was fine. I said, "Look guys, I won't come to the studio anymore, but I am your A&R manager, I am your boss in that sense. I have to get the tapes. So I'll turn up every night and Vic'll give me a tape and let me know what you're doing and then I'll make it work with Polydor because we're a team." So I just [fell] back to that position. It was okay. I was a bit upset, but not massively.'

While the Jam were happy with their new producer situation, the same could not be said of Polydor. If the label had had its way, the Jam would have got a different producer entirely. 'They were never happy with Vic,' Munday says of Polydor. 'I got on okay with him, but he was a prickly character ... Not with the band, just personality-wise ... He just pissed people off ... It didn't bother me, because he did a good job ... but it certainly bothered my boss.' Polydor suggested to an unimpressed Munday that Coppersmith-Heaven be replaced by Stranglers producer Martin Rushent. 'I knew Martin and he was the wrong person for them, his personality,' says Munday. 'It wouldn't have worked.' This would be far from the last time that Polydor tried to oust Coppersmith-Heaven.

'I didn't get many compliments from the label, just rumours about being replaced,' says Coppersmith-Heaven. 'The record company weren't that connected to the band ... just to their potential record sales, and they would of course be looking to get into new markets. They probably should have spent more time marketing the records we made than trying to change producers. This went on for almost three years.'

Parry, meanwhile, was moving on. By the autumn of 1978, he was guiding the fortunes of the Cure at his own label, Fiction Records. 'What I decided is I wasn't going to run the long term with the Jam,' he says. 'I knew that they were not going to be a true international band. I wanted a band that was going to go around the world. I wanted to sell big shows. I wanted to be huge ... So when they got their glory moments and all that stuff, I was gone. I was quite instrumental in bringing them on and when I left it was a good time for me to leave. It was a very comfortable relationship, really. We did a lot of things together. We had a fantastic experience together, and all within three years. I was learning and they were learning. It was great ... I had a brilliant position with the Jam on publishing and management, but I just gave it all away. Do I regret that? Not at all.'

Parry's departure meant that Munday shortly had an additional job with the Jam. 'When Chris left, I had to do A&R as well,' says Munday. 'They got a new A&R manager in and the band wouldn't work with him.'

The Jam's new ease with exploiting the possibilities afforded by the recording studio were fully apparent come November 3, 1978 when their third album was released.

Before s/he got to the music, the first thing the purchaser noticed about *All Mod Cons* was what a sumptuous package it constituted. It was a riot of colour, especially an inner sleeve scattered with pictures of pop-culture miscellanea, from Airfix paint tubs to military insignia to postcards to matchbooks to travel clocks to old records. Notes Smith, 'That montage on the inner bag was literally

Paul's list of favourite things. Some of them are his and some I gathered together.' All of this was to the purpose of giving expression to two crazes of Weller's, mod and pop-art. The latter rather nebulous Sixties concept involved – in that decade's fashionable spirit of irreverence – melding media ephemera with classical art techniques. Pop-art even extended to the record's labels, which featured red-white-and-blue concentric circles, a nod to the fact that – in quintessential pop-art style – the Royal Air Force national insignia (aka the roundel) had long been co-opted as a badge of identification by the mod movement. The album title itself punned on the estate-agent abbreviation for 'All Modern Conveniences'.

On the front cover, the Jam were to be seen – sporting their new unmatching, smart-casual look – in a Wardour Street photo studio chosen for its bareness. On the back, the same space hosted their instruments in place of their bodies, with a radio in the foreground supposedly playing the music made by said instruments. Both album title and artist name were rendered in the Immediate Records font. Smith never felt from this point that the Jam had an official emblem. Were the group not conscious of the enhanced merchandising opportunities that might result from a permanent logo? 'No, definitely not.' The credits featured a thank-you to 'the Southend Kids for conversation' – a reference to recorded discourse from everyday youth that was belatedly dropped from the album. This was the first sleeve where the list of credits Smith was given to incorporate in his design stated the producer's name to be 'Vic Coppersmith-Heaven'. Referring to the machinations by Polydor to oust the former Vic Smith as Jam producer, Bill Smith drolly offers, 'Maybe he just changed his name and thought the record company might think it was someone different.'

'All Mod Cons', which opens the album, finds Weller inveighing against a parasitical figure who, judging by a reference to artistic freedom, is a record-company executive. Weller avers that when he and his colleagues are skint once more, 'You'll drop us like hot bricks.' The song is so brief – 1:20 – that it almost seems a device to give the album a title track, even though the title is unrelated to the lyric. The track is, though, representative of *All Mod Cons*: superficially attractive in its sprightliness and brightness, but ultimately empty.

'To Be Someone (Didn't We Have a Nice Time)' introduces another of the album's motifs: plagiarism. *All Mod Cons* is a veritable jackdaw's nest, littered with familiar licks and appropriated fragments of melody. In this case, another essay on stardom is bolted to the clipped riff of the Beatles' 'Taxman'. Weller's lyric tells of a recording artist who squanders his riches and ends up consoling himself with the thought/refrain/meaningless space-filler, 'But didn't we have a nice time?'

'Mr. Clean' is an incredibly nasty ode to class vengeance. It may even be directed against the not-quite-pitied narrator of 'Tube Station'. Weller informs the subject, 'I don't ever want to catch you looking at me, Mr. Clean' and moreover that he hates him and his wife and, given the chance, will fuck up his life. This is an inordinate degree of malice to direct at someone whose only crimes seem to be that he was born to privilege and is not very rock 'n' roll. It's certainly hardly any more constructive than saying 'destroy.' For all that, though, the track has some power, Weller's vicious hatred being perfectly complemented by a slow, menacing ambience. Coppersmith-Heaven judiciously adds mild echo to Weller's voice at crucial moments to ratchet up the sinister timbre.

Following a new mix of 'David Watts' comes a song that was originally not listed on the album sleeve but which the record label revealed to be 'English Rose'. It's as honeyed as the previous track is spiteful. On the last album, Weller had been groping for a way to express his love for his girlfriend and had achieved results that were not very impressive. On 'English Rose', he nails it. Crooning against only his own acoustic finger-picking and overdubbed wind-and-wave sound effects, Weller sweetly declares that no temptations on earth can keep him from his lover. Some lines are gauche, but one shines clear and true in both its emotional beauty and clever switchback of expectation: 'I've scoured the whole universe, caught the first train home.'

Buckler recalls the absence of the song from the tracklisting as being down to the lateness of its inclusion, but Weller says, 'I probably was a bit embarrassed by it because it was so stark and so naked, just a voice and guitar. I thought maybe it should just be like a hidden track. It was quite a tender moment.' Once again, Coppersmith-Heaven showed more perspicacity than his client: 'It took our producer to get me over that. He was like, "No listen, we've got to go on with this. It's gonna be good."'

The vinyl side one closed with 'In the Crowd', at more than 5½ minutes by far the longest track on the LP. It's the third of Weller's songs to express a terror of conformity. Yet just as 'The Combine' was inferior to 'Away from the Numbers' (whose title refrain this song actually quotes), so this represents another incremental waning. The track does have a pleasantly woozy ambience and boasts some fine bass. However, not only is it riddled with atrocious lines but it's the nadir of *All Mod Cons'* second-hand air. It recycles the riff from the Jam's version of 'David Watts' and lifts part of the melody of the Kinks' 'Johnny Thunder', while arbitrary washes of backwards guitar betray the fact that Weller has been listening to a lot of late-Sixties music.

That 'Billy Hunt' is cockney rhyming slang for 'cunt' may have been a reason for Polydor's reluctance to issue as a single the track that kicked off side two. Around this point in history, Radio 1 – then the country's only national pop radio station – was notoriously censorious. In 1982, for instance, it insisted its DJs refer to Marvin Gaye's hit 'Sexual Healing' only by its second word. In naming the titular protagonist, though, Weller seems to have been thinking of *Billy Liar*, the daydreaming fantasist of Keith Waterhouse's celebrated novel and its subsequent film and TV adaptations. The music is not quite as anthemic as it's trying to be, and Weller is still showing his youth and lack of education in lines that sound good but don't quite make sense, such as the one where he informs an individual that if it's not them crying then it's probably him. However, it's clear from the song's brisk and chant-worthy nature why it was a contender for single status. Moreover, when Weller gets it right lyrically he's bang on the fantasist button: 'I'll spy like James Bond and die like King Kong.'

'It's Too Bad' finds Weller ruminating on the imminent demise of a deteriorating relationship to a backing decorated with arpeggios and a cooing chorus. Judging by the way he rhymes 'break up' and 'make up,' he's still got the lyric of 'So Sad About Us' swimming around his head, but that's less an issue than the fact that the comparison the lyric invokes reminds us that he's not in Pete Townshend's league as a tunesmith. 'Fly' is a love song cut from a more devotional cloth wherein the author wishes for blissful solitude with his partner. Finger-picking acoustic sections sit side-by-side with keening, electric passages. Weller, though, is still too green to make much of a philosopher.

'The Place I Love' finds Weller talking about a favourite rustic beauty spot – possibly inchoate metaphor – to accompaniment that is incongruously electric. '"A" Bomb in Wardour Street' and 'Down in the Tube Station at Midnight' round out the album.

Rather than possessing the heightened musical sophistication attributed to it by many, *All Mod Cons* is a step backwards. The band's obvious power-pop objectives are never quite achieved, the music possessing neither that genre's infectious melodies nor its crunching impact. When remembering the taut, tuneful stylings of highlights of their debut like 'Non-Stop Dancing' and 'I Got By In Time', this is surprising indeed. Nicking other people's stuff is part of the retrograde process. *In the City* lovingly embraced musical

106

archetypes but rarely, if ever, left the listener shouting, 'Stop, thief!'

Also woefully stranded between ambition and achievement are Weller's lyrics. His first problem is that he doesn't quite know what to write about. The opening brace of music industry-oriented songs reveal rarefied concerns. They also seem informed less by personal experience than received wisdom about evil entertainment corporations. Even if we give Weller the benefit of the doubt and assume that 'Mr. Clean' is not an anxious attempt to scrub from public memory his previous pledges of allegiance to conservative ideology, the song remains deeply problematical. In his short and circumscribed life, Weller's direct knowledge of posh office workers was almost certainly nil. His pejorative perceptions of the lifestyle and values of his subject are clearly gleaned from popular prejudice and are no less reprehensible than bourgeois snobs dismissing the working class as uncouth and unwashed. Where Weller is not undermined by his lack of life experience, he is left helpless by his paucity of education. That, unlike Mr. Clean, Weller is no Cambridge graduate is made manifest in a line where he promises to stick Mr. Clean's nose in the 'grind'. Told this doesn't quite make sense, Weller responds, 'It does in my mind.' He does concede, though, that he was confusing 'grind' with 'gravel'. Moreover, not only is he rarely poetic, but often he can't even express himself with any lucidity. 'In the Crowd' finds him referring to an 'equilibrium melting pot' and to catching falling cans of baked beans on toast. 'Fly' contains an almost stream-of-consciousness verse in which he moves from a messy Peter Pan simile to meaningless word association based around 'sand' (which he lazily rhymes with itself) to a non-sequitur rumination on the fate of the human race. His statement to his lover in the same song that they should travel to the 'demi-monde' suggests a principled stand against any instinct to reach for a dictionary.

Most people overlooked both that *All Mod Cons* showed Weller straining for a lyrical ability he didn't yet have and the Jam straining to be as pleasing a proposition as they had been on their debut. The album was easily their most commercially successful so far, climbing to number six and remaining in the UK album chart for seventeen weeks. It was also greeted by some effusive reviews, one of which in particular has stuck in Weller's mind. 'We had a full-page in the *NME* of Charles Shaar Murray reviewing the album and taking it seriously,' he recalls. Parry: 'Charles Shaar Murray was really a big fan of Paul. They were hanging out.' Murray – a veteran critic not known to be overly excitable – gushed of *All Mod Cons*, 'It's not only several light years ahead of anything they've done before but also the album that's going to catapult the Jam right into the front rank of international rock and roll; one of the handful of truly essential rock albums of the last few years.' Murray praised Weller's responsible attitude toward violence ('if these songs mean that one less meaningless street fight gets started then we'll all owe Paul Weller a favour') and the verisimilitude of his romance numbers ('Weller has the almost unique ability to write love songs that convince the listener that the singer is really in love'). Weller notes that Murray's praise for his lyrics 'had the effect that it made me take myself more seriously and think, "Oh okay, people are listening now, so you've got to refine this thing and explore it, the craft of writing." Before that, to be honest, I was just copying other people, as most bands do on their first records, whether it's Dylan doing Woody Guthrie or the Beatles doing the Shirelles.'

Dennis Munday is one of the many people for whom *All Mod Cons* remains the Jam's long-playing masterpiece. 'It's where you can really hear him as a songwriter,' he says of Weller. 'Before that, he was a budding songwriter.'

For Buckler, the reception to the album put into perspective the failure of *This is the Modern World*, which he is now able to view as 'a fantastic learning curve,' adding, 'It was a necessary lesson to learn.' He also says, 'We did get criticised at the time that this band had been signed too early and it shouldn't have been signed until *All Mod Cons*, but that's with hindsight. That's lovely to say, but it means nothing.'

Munday recalls that it was around this time that Polydor finally began to take the Jam seriously, making the effort to attend their shows rather than waiting for punk's death throes. He recalls, 'I went to see them with one of the execs at Birmingham Odeon and he said, "They really are a good band, aren't they?" I said, "Well they've been a good band for at least eighteen months now."' Weller himself publicly pronounced on the difference in the label's attitude: 'The British branch of Polydor are really nice to us now, but as I remember, nobody spoke to us for two years.' He added, 'And I've got a really long memory. I don't forget things like that.'

Precisely one week after the release of *All Mod Cons*, the Clash released *Give 'em Enough Rope*. Even if one accepted the idea that the new Jam album constituted progress, the Clash's second LP put that progress into context. There were justified complaints that its overall effect was bludgeoning, but the record underlined that the compassion and street poetry of Joe Strummer's songwords were still well beyond the fumbling and sometimes mean-spirited lyrical profferings of Weller, while Mick Jones' melodies and arrangements proved that one could write in a classic tradition without resorting to pilfering. 'Tommy Gun' was a far more cogent and musically exciting condemnation of violence than 'Tube Station' or '"A" Bomb in Wardour Street', 'All the Young Punks (New Boots and Contracts)' explored working-class misery more acutely than any Weller creation yet, and 'Stay Free' – an anthem imploring an old rapscallion mate not to get into trouble again – was shot through with a blush-making humanity that made the arbitrarily vicious 'Mr. Clean' feel even grubbier. In this face-off, only 'English Rose' could be said to have trumped the Clash. Many new-wave bands shied away from love songs, viewing them as a symptom of the spiritual softness to which rock had succumbed in the first half of the Seventies. In insisting on including such compositions alongside his songs of social commentary, Weller gave his band's art a dimension that the Clash unwisely denied their own: the latter ensemble would only ever unequivocally visit such territory in the songs '1-2 Crush On You', 'Train In Vain' and 'Should I Stay or Should I Go'. Moreover, Weller's post-*In the City* love songs broke with two disagreeable traditions. Not only did he decline to render them in a pseudo-American accent, but he spurned braggadocio and paternalism. This latter is a remarkable but little remarked-upon fact about a man so often perceived as a 'lad'.

Not that the Clash and the Jam had the territory of People's Band to themselves. A fortnight after *All Mod Cons'* release, the Boomtown Rats' 'Rat Trap' became the first record by a new-wave act to reach the top of the UK singles chart. The Rats – middle-class Dubliners with a line in rough-hewn pop decorated by singer Bob Geldof's morbidly humorous lyrics – were dismissed by some as a bandwagon-jumping joke. However, 'Rat Trap' was not just a superb record, but as acute a dissection of the dreariness of proletarian existence as anything in a similar vein – before or subsequently – by Weller or Joe Strummer (or come to that Bruce Springsteen). That it was no less than the third single the group mined from their June album *A Tonic for the Troops* was another cause for derision, but, avarice aside, it couldn't be denied that the latter was one of the year's best LPs.

There was also a joker in the punk pack that was in danger of turning into a trump card. Sham 69 had three hits in 1978, all infectious plebeian anthems: 'Angels With Dirty Faces', 'If The Kids Are United' and 'Hurry Up Harry'. It tends to be forgotten now, but if punk was a race for the twin prizes of success and authenticity, in '78 Sham 69 were perceived as fast coming up on the outside. Both Caroline Coon (credited by some with giving the

110

punk movement its name) and *Sniffin' Glue*'s Mark Perry have stated that Sham – particularly lead singer Jimmy Pursey – were the real guttersnipe deal in a way previous punk acts (implicitly including the Sex Pistols, the Clash and the Jam) were not.

Buckler told Ian Snowball in *The Dead Straight Guide to the Jam* that the troubled preamble to *All Mod Cons* changed the Jam's songwriting process: 'From here on … Bruce and I … got more vocal when it came to the songs' arrangements and putting forward our ideas. We also became more vocal when it came to … saying that … this or that wasn't working.'

Considering this, it's richly ironic that one thing *All Mod Cons* did establish beyond doubt was that the Jam's songwriting strength lay outside their rhythm section. Excepting 'David Watts', all the album's tracks were Weller-written. Although Foxton – and even Buckler – would receive writing credits in the future, Paul Weller would from here on be perceived as unequivocally the apex of the triangle. There would certainly be no more indulging of the idea that Foxton's songs were as valid candidates for the A-side of singles as Weller's.

Buckler feels that that difficult third-album preamble, and the brutally-articulated assessment of the demerits of Foxton's songs, did the bassist something of an injustice. 'I think he got one or two unfair comments, either from Paul or from other people, 'cos Paul's songwriting is so strong it's a very difficult one to stand up against,' he muses. Referring to a future Foxton composition, he says, 'I love 'Smithers-Jones'. I think it's a great song. There's some things that Bruce did which were really good and it's a shame that he was standing next to Paul, because I think it made him shy a little bit away from writing.'

The fact of one member being a band's chief songwriter inevitably means that that person is perceived by the public and critics as not just the most important of its personnel but even its essence. It also puts said member's colleagues in the slightly humiliating position of being dependent on him. It's a pattern that has been seen over and over in music history, with perhaps its apotheosis being represented by the Rolling Stones. That group's guitarist Brian Jones had incredible sex appeal, breathtaking multi-instrumental abilities and for a long time enjoyed the status of the band's leader. However, when Mick Jagger and Keith Richards grew into the role of the Stones' songwriting axis and hence the band's meal ticket, it made all those facts secondary. It was something that must have been psychologically devastating to what was an already insecure person, and may have played a part in Jones' ultimate destruction. Neither Foxton nor Buckler suffered from Brian Jones' personality disorder, and a trio by definition is more of a democracy than any bigger permutation of musicians because of its instrumental interdependence. However, the Jam rhythm section would have been no less aware of their lower status.

Which leads to the $64,000 question: did dependence on Weller unbalance the band in the sense of causing the rhythm section to defer to him, to be humbled by feeling the necessity to bite their tongues in arguments? 'I never looked at it like that,' says Foxton, adding, 'We didn't have that many fallings-out really.' 'No, not at all,' insists Buckler. 'The press will for obvious reasons single out somebody as a spokesman for the band and obviously the easiest target is the frontman. If you talk to the fans now, they don't regard Paul Weller as the Jam. They certainly don't regard any individual in the band as being the Jam. It is literally the fact that there's three guys, all contributing their part, no matter how great or small, and that is what the Jam is. The Jam is certainly not Paul Weller.' Mentioning a prominent DJ and Weller friend, Buckler says, 'Even Gary Crowley at the time quoted that there was three guys in this band and two of them weren't called Paul Weller.' It should be noted that Weller himself publicly agreed with such sentiments. In

1979, he told Paul Morley of the *New Musical Express*, 'The Jam is a group. I don't like the idea of getting singled out.' He also told *The Hot Press*, 'If a band's only got one writer, it means that a lot of influence is coming from him, but if you took one member away from the Jam, I don't think you'd have the same sound.'

Foxton adds, 'I couldn't write any more than I did for the Jam. I tried, and if the song is just not up to it, it's not up to it.' Despite his frank assessment of his own compositional abilities, the bassist has issues with the fact that Weller's name alone appeared in the parentheses below so many Jam song titles. 'Real Jam fans knew it was a three-way effort in terms of writing, although it generally appeared that it was Paul's song,' Foxton avers. 'We were so young and naive and so pleased to be able to give up your day job, it didn't seem that important. Our verbal agreement was, "Well, whoever comes up with the initial idea, it's their song." Which was very green and naive. Realistically, probably two-thirds of all the Jam songs should have been credited to the three of us because songs stem from a drum pattern, some songs stemmed from a bass line. It's water under the bridge now and it's not sour grapes at all because we've all done pretty well out of the band financially over the years, but, looking back, what would have been fairer would have been a three-way split on a lot of the songs … There are ways of splitting royalties. You don't have to say, "Well, it's all mine" or, "It's a third each." You can have lyrics fifty per cent, whoever wrote the lyrics, and then split the music three ways or whatever. There are ways around it, but you only become aware of this when you start to see record sales and the penny drops that there's a lot of money to be had here, and by that time it's too late. Which would be a very touchy subject once you've actually drawn up the guidelines. It's very difficult to backtrack and say, "Hang on, can we have a look at this?" That would have only thrown another spanner in the works.'

'I'm not very happy with that at all, but I wouldn't be, would I?'

responds Weller. 'To me, if you write the words and you write the chords and you write the melody, you've written the fucking song, really. So whatever the drummer cares to play or the bass player or the keyboard player or whatever it may be, it's entirely up to them, but it doesn't [constitute] writing. Different thing, really.'

Foxton does concede one wrinkle in his argument. 'We did make that verbal agreement initially, and to be honest that was reflected in some of my songs. If Paul hadn't have come up with the middle eight, or coda or whatever, on a song, it wouldn't have been finished, but because I had the initial idea I got the full writing credit.'

BUILDING UP TO SOMETHING

March 9, 1979 brought a new standalone Jam single, 'Strange Town' backed with 'The Butterfly Collector'. The record demonstrated that in the band's six-month absence from the release schedules their sound had undergone significant changes.

Weller – who wrote both tracks – revealed heightened levels of insight. 'Strange Town' is another Jam song about London, but this time the composer's view is unobstructed by youthful naiveté. Instead of perceiving it as a hive of envy-worthy activity whose ambient sounds are worth immortalising on a C-60, Weller is suddenly seeing the capital the way that so many visitors from elsewhere in the UK do: hard and unfriendly. The narrator has been in London (despite the use of the word 'town', it's identifiable as the capital city by the song's reference to Oxford Street) for three weeks. He finds himself unable to acquire not just friends but even travel directions, the indigenous people bustling past him and declining his requests for assistance with an 'I've got to go, mate.' Weller also seems to perceive London as just as restrictive as he'd found Woking, although this conformity is different in being oriented around wearing the latest clothes, buying the trendiest records and adopting the fashionable socio-political causes. (Some journalists, incidentally, got the impression from Weller that the visitor to London was not a provincial but a spaceship passenger.)

The music evinces a similar degree of evolution. The track's marching tempo, pleasantly squalling guitar riff, throbbing bass work and hint of keyboards are all melded with unprecedented slickness. While never being quite whistlable, the melody swells and subsides agreeably. In the guitar solo, Weller rocks out in a way rare on Jam tracks.

The B-side is even better. 'Butterfly Collector' is a more elegant way of describing what the Rolling Stones called a 'starfucker'. The lyric is one of Weller's best yet, full of memorable observations about an individual enveloped in second-rate perfume who is obsessed with sussing out the week's climbers. 'There's tarts and whores but you're much more' the composer sneers of someone who can find validation only in the number of famous faces that end up on her pillow. The causticness is counterpointed by a delicately winding guitar figure and a gentle arrangement, albeit one possessed of a malevolence similar to that of 'Mr. Clean'. As in the latter track, the menace is ramped up by echo on Weller's voice. One feels rather uncomfortable admiring the craft of this merciless denunciation. However, it's interesting how much opprobrium this track has attracted where, in contrast, 'Mr. Clean' – whose malice is far more extreme – is celebrated rather than condemned.

The figure standing below a crossroads signpost on the single's bleak cover is Bill Smith, who went to the Isle of Sheppey to fulfil his vision of depicting 'someone deciding what they wanted to do, not necessarily with life in general but where they were at that particular time.' Smith ensured the picture was out of focus so that, 'You could look at it and make your own interpretation of who that figure is.' The pin-sharp beauty of the back cover – depicting a petrified butterfly against a pink backdrop – is a complete contrast. The rear also featured an open-verse Weller poem.

The record was the second consecutive Jam single to reach number 15. Polydor, far from being happy that the Jam had recovered their chart mojo, were dissatisfied with such positions and once more agitating for a new producer. Although Munday hadn't bothered telling the Jam of the label's suggestion of Martin Rushent, this time he felt compelled to reveal to them the identity of the man Polydor now had in mind: George Martin. He says that the issue was not simply Coppersmith-Heaven: 'What bothered them more than anything, punk came along and they wanted to make the records they wanted to make. They weren't interested in having the latest producers. They saw George Martin as a way of smoothing the Jam out, rather than making a great record.' Foxton and Weller suggested to Ian Birch of *Melody Maker* that Polydor were enthusiastic about Martin 'in order to get the American market.' While the ex-Beatles producer's technical proficiency was doubted by no one, Munday was completely opposed to the idea of his appointment. 'George Martin didn't like punk music,' he reasons. 'I can't see the point in getting someone to produce a type of music that they don't like, no matter how good they are.' There were also practical objections: 'He may have been able to do a single, but he couldn't have done an album – he would have been booked up for at least eighteen months.' The band had other objections. Referring to the big-league producer appointed by CBS to helm the Clash's second long-player, Weller complained to Birch, 'It's just like the Clash getting Sandy Pearlman. They're always suggesting people like that.' Foxton said to the *Melody Maker* scribe, 'It would just become George Martin, or Phil Spector, or whoever it is. It wouldn't be the Jam any more.'

A similar scenario played out when the Jam were recording their next single, 'When You're Young' b/w 'Smithers-Jones'. The record had a troubled gestation before its release on August 17, one involving three different versions and the same number of studios. After the second version had been deemed unsatisfactory by both band and producer, Polydor demanded a meeting with the Wellers and Coppersmith-Heaven. The latter has recalled being told by Polydor MD AJ Morris that he didn't know what he was doing and that an American producer might be taking the helm. Coppersmith-Heaven says, 'There was a fashion at the time by record companies to bring in American producers, probably to try to gain more overseas sales, without really considering whether it would benefit the bands or the music.' Coppersmith-Heaven has reported that Weller stood by him completely and forced the label to back down. The Jam wouldn't always be so loyal to Coppersmith-Heaven, but their resistance to Polydor's entreaties during this period was wise, for the producer would be key to a further massive development of their studio sound and consequent commercial success.

The front cover of the sleeve of 'When You're Young' showed the Jam sitting amidst a typical photographer's studio set-up – white sheets draped over objects to provide a blank backdrop – but with the entire artifice exposed by the fact of an angle that revealed the band posing for a lens. 'Part of my post-modernism period,' explains Bill Smith. The back-cover photograph of commuters at London's Piccadilly Circus underground station seems to be a reference to the record's flip, which is about another character imprisoned in a three-piece cage.

'When You're Young' is the second successive Jam A-side to explore ambiguity. It finds Weller articulating the defiance common to the young mindset – the school-leavers who swear they're never going to stand in line or work nine-to-five – only to dash such illusions on the rocks of a bridge which starts with the deflating line, 'You find out life isn't like that.' Weller told Paul Morley, '…you're not in control of your future. There's a line in 'When You're Young' – "The world is your oyster but the future's a clam" – that's just how I feel about it really.' For one who had exalted – and who, in reality, would continue to exalt – the 'young idea', this is unexpectedly self-aware stuff. It's also nice phraseology which indicates the rapid pace at which Weller's lyrical craft is developing. The music doesn't quite live up to the words, with the melody too frantic and the arrangement a little blurred.

Although B-side 'Smithers-Jones' is another Jam song that follows an upper-middle class office drone through his day, the fact that it's written by Foxton ensures it's more good-natured than 'Mr. Clean'. Its contents are no less received than those of that song, however, with its clichés beginning with the protagonist's generic double-barrelled name and continuing with the assumption that the subject cannot possibly be content in his employment. Smithers-Jones has cause to mourn the loss of his dreary daily routine when he is suddenly made redundant. Weller throws in a last verse (which he also sings) that might have been a favour to the bassist in providing a resolution he couldn't conjure himself, but it's actually inferior to Foxton's parts, incongruously using the words 'groovy' and 'arse'. Despite its flawed and cartoonish nature, though, 'Smithers-Jones' is a sprightly, melodic three minutes. Additionally, its clean lines come as a relief after the indistinct musical margins of the A-side. Mystifyingly, this progression in Foxton's songwriting craft was a dead end: he would never write another song – in the sense of a composition with a lyric - while in the ranks of the Jam.

The record charted two places lower than its predecessor, making number 17. However, if Polydor were as unhappy with that showing as they had been with that of 'Strange Town', their unhappiness was soon to be spectacularly alleviated.

Their standalone singles of 1979 had revealed the Jam to be travelling in a promising direction. With 'The Eton Rifles', released on October 26, 1979, they made a mighty jump to greatness.

B-side 'See-Saw' was emphatically not the great element. A Weller composition on which Weller and Foxton alternate vocal duties, its chugging riff is too similar to that of 'Smithers-Jones' while the fact that its titular metaphor bears no relation to its theme of the aftermath of a love affair indicates Weller is once more lazily deploying phraseology without stopping to think why. Nothing here suggests the brilliance of the record's other face, also written by Weller, or the artistic heyday the group are about to enter.

The sleeve features military-stencil lettering and a picture of Eton army cadets. As might be imagined, then, 'The Eton Riles' is about warfare. However, it's not formal military engagement that is under discussion. Rather the song is about a failed insurrection in which beer-swilling, fag-puffing working-class malcontents leave the security of their local to take on representatives of the ruling class. They come off humiliatingly worse against people who are better educated, better connected, better fed and better equipped.

The composition has a comedic tinge: the narrator, lamenting that his comrade-in-arms turned out to be a poor catalyst for change, observes, 'Loaded the guns then you run off 'ome for yer tea.' 'It's a piss-take on class,' Weller told Paul Morley. '...it's like "The revolution will start after I've finished my pint."' The song, however, sprang from deadly serious events. Weller was motivated to write it after hearing about Eton schoolboys jeering at people participating in a Right to Work match protesting against the rising unemployment caused by Margaret Thatcher's economic policies.

Also deadly serious is the soundscape. Following an urgent, doom-laden introduction, Foxton's bass provides a broiling bottom end as Weller's multi-tracked guitar parts stutter and crash. Slivers of organ are the only glints of light in the all-encompassing gloom. Yet 'The Eton Rifles' is very easy on the ear. In fact, it's the epitome of the way Weller could make a slight melody feel substantial through adroit and dramatic shifts in key. Adding to the infectiousness is a staccato shouted chorus, one which – appropriately for a military-related song – has the flavour of parade-ground call-and-response.

This paradoxical concoction shot the Jam to dizzying heights in the UK singles chart, ultimately climbing to number three. 'Can you imagine that being on the radio or top-three record now?' marvels Weller. 'Wouldn't happen, would it?' Even then, it was a hard-won achievement. Munday: 'We changed promotion managers in between 'When You're Young' and 'Eton Rifles' because everyone was unhappy with the in-house promotion. Maybe that made a difference. The guy that I took on was positive about 'Eton Rifles'. This is one of the problems that I had with the rest of Polydor: their reticence. "Oh it's punk music, [DJs] don't play punk music." People forget in '77, '78, you only heard records at night. It was very rarely that they would play punk records on the breakfast show, for instance.' Weller was also aware of the difficulty of reaching the public without the support of 'the nation's favourite'. 'Radio 1 refused to play us and 'Eton Rifles' was the first tune that they actually played,' he says. 'I don't think they had too much choice. We were too popular. But prior to that, it was a real fucking effort to try and get any radio play. There was less options at that time. There was Radio 1 and that was it. [London's] Capital [Radio], maybe. 'Eton Rifles' was the first time we actually got played on radio and reflected our popularity around the country. So it felt like it was building up to something.'

That growing fanbase was, from what Munday observed, not purely down to the increasing quality of the Jam's music. Before gigs, the Jam would let fans into soundchecks. After gigs, they would stay around to sign autographs for anyone who wanted one. 'I've never known other bands to have that kind of interaction,' he says. 'Most bands used to disappear in the dressing room or back to the hotel and get pissed. So they had a very loyal following.' Munday says the single's success was the proper turning point in Polydor's appreciation of the group: 'What it did is it woke them up ... After 'Eton Rifles', they were a mainstream act.'

The sleeves of 'When You're Young' and 'The Eton Rifles' had declared the records inside to be produced by 'Vic Coppersmith-Heaven & the Jam.' Meanwhile, the back of the previous album had stated it to be 'Produced by Vic Coppersmith-Heaven, arranged by the Jam.' Those who detected from this a shift in the power axis toward the artist might have been surprised that *Setting Sons*, the album that appeared on November 16, 1979, not only stated it to be produced by Coppersmith-Heaven alone but carried an additional credit: 'Arranged by Vic Coppersmith-Heaven & The

Jam.' 'I've no idea,' says Weller when asked the story behind the obviously carefully phrased credit. Asked whether Coppersmith-Heaven helped shape the soundscape, however, he readily concedes, 'Absolutely.' Weller is effusive in his praise for the producer, revealing, 'There's lots of things even going back to 'Down in the Tube Station'. He was very encouraging, 'specially with layering guitars and double-tracking. He was very, very good on that and I learnt an awful lot from him.'

'Quite rightly,' is Foxton's view of Coppersmith-Heaven receiving a co-arranger's credit. He adds, 'He was very valued as far as I was concerned throughout the whole Jam career. He had a good ear. Nine times out of ten the arrangements pretty much we'd sorted, but he really was very valued in terms of hit singles: putting the choruses, repeating a chorus or whatever. He had some great ideas. I would say in the studio he was the fourth person.' Buckler agrees with the latter sentiment, adding, 'He was a very meticulous worker. It did certainly add another element to the band, because it was just like having somebody who could stand back from the whole thing. He did manage to pull some good ideas out of us.'

Not that Weller didn't have interesting ideas of his own. His lyrics on this album – as hinted at by 'The Eton Rifles' – demonstrated that since *All Mod Cons* he had made a quite extraordinary leap in ability. In the space of just one year, he had overcome his linguistic awkwardness and begun reaping the dividends of the self-education he'd embarked on after his early exit from school. During the Jam's lifetime, Weller tackled texts by – amongst others – Geoffrey Ashe, Adrian Henri, Roger McGough, Colin MacInnes, George Orwell, Brian Patten, Erich Maria Remarque, Percy Bysshe Shelley, Alan Sillitoe and Robert Tressell. In light of the consumption of such diverse and intellectually elevated writers, it's little surprise that keen observation and exquisite lyricism began to inform his songwords.

122

Also evident were grand thematic ambitions. Weller had toyed previously with the idea of writing a concept album. In the run-up to *All Mod Cons* he told Chas de Whalley, 'For the next LP, right, by the lyrics I'll have it like a play. With different people singing the lyrics so that everybody will understand.' After *All Mod Cons'* release, he explained to Dave Schulps why he had abandoned the idea: 'You could just take a character like Billy Hunt and centre it around him. The trouble is that there have been so many things like *Quadrophenia* and Sham 69's *That's Life* that I decided that I'd let it hang loosely rather than connect it.'

Running into the fourth album, Weller regained enthusiasm for the idea of LP-as-narrative. Originally, *Setting Sons* was to have been a concept album based on a collaboration with Dave Waller, some of whose poems Weller had already published in the Jam's *In the City* songbook. Sources variously state the collaboration as taking the form of a short story or, putatively, a teleplay or novel. In any event, the idea was to depict three once-idealistic friends who meet up after a civil war to find that their political philosophies have diverged, one of them remaining a leftist, one having turned to the right and one having become ideologically neutral. Those three friends, according to what Weller much later told Paul Lester, were based on himself, Steve Brookes and Dave Waller, even if the splintering of that real-life trio was more about different ambitions and desires than political views: 'Because we had these teenage ideas, with the band – like, "We're gonna make it." Which we did, but it wasn't the same line-up as we started off with.' Although Weller's concept may sound quaint now, it didn't at a time when the country's political opinions were being polarised by the Thatcher government, which was already embarking on an economic strategy that would see the growing prosperity of some counterpointed by the increasing hardships of others.

In the end, though, *Setting Sons* was a concept album only

insofar as *Sgt. Pepper's Lonely Hearts Club Band* and *The Rise and Fall of Ziggy Stardust and the Spiders From Mars* are: mere remnants survived of the original, overall idea. (Another remnant seems to be the title, a confused pun on the decline of Empire.) In the case of the Jam album, conflicting accounts have been given as to why. 'I could have had it mapped out in me head, and there's four or five songs that could have been in the concept,' offers Weller. 'I think after a while I just thought, "Oh fuck this, let's make a record." I just lost interest in it. It got too complicated in my mind.' Asked if there is a part of him that wishes he had fleshed out fully his original vision, Weller shrugs, 'There's a bigger part of me that couldn't care less. I'm not really sure about concept records.' That feeling of being sceptical about the genre was something he discussed with Schulps, whom he told, 'I received letters from a few kids asking if it was true we were doing a concept LP, because, they said, the last thing the world needs is another concept album. I thought about it and realized they were right; concept albums go along with Jethro Tull and bands like that.' Buckler tends to agree. 'It's not a term I'm particularly in love with because it just seems to always conjure [up] pictures of being bloated and pretentious,' the drummer says. 'It's a bit of a hangover from the previous generation.'

Foxton's most vivid memories of the *Setting Sons* sessions are nocturnal hours and a quick turnaround from composition to finished track, both of which he attributes to 'pressure of the label and pressure on Paul.' Recording the album in Townhouse Studios in Shepherd's Bush over August to October '79, the Jam faced the novel situation of extemporising. 'They weren't all completely finished,' says Foxton of Weller's latest batch of songs. 'And it was quite experimental, a lot of it. We were playing cello on certain parts – I don't think you can write for that ... Paul was finishing off songs in the studio. Normally you'd do pre-production before you go into the studio because studios are so expensive ... Normally you kicked the ideas around in the rehearsal room, the three of us, before we go in, but this was kind of writing to order.' He further says, 'Paul was finishing off songs during the day in the studio and Rick and myself would work through the night a lot of the time, working out parts to record the next day or record in the early hours of the morning. It was very hard work. It's amazing that we came out with a great album, actually. It was the first time and last time we ever worked like that.'

In fact, pressure of time has been cited as another reason for the concept-album idea being discarded. Weller, though, denies that the record company were leaning on him unduly. 'Not that I remember, ' he says. 'You're talking about the days when everyone made an album once a year. I don't remember being pressurised.' Yet, in 1998, Weller told Paul Lester of the album's genesis, 'I was constantly stressed, to be honest. I'm a natural writer but though it comes easy, you've still got to work at it. So there was always that deadline: "I've got to make the album by this time" … I was always under pressure, and I really didn't feel like I had much support from the other two, either, when the chips were down.'

Interestingly, Bill Smith started working on the LP's sleeve at a point when the record was still intended to be a concept album. 'I only heard the first two or three tracks before we had to get the cover organised,' he recalls. He found a way to represent the concept, as well as the military leitmotif of a brace of the songs. Although Benjamin Clemens' 1919 sculpture *The St John's Ambulance Bearers* may have nothing to do with Weller's discarded theme, the fact that the people depicted are in militaryesque uniform and the fact of them being a trio is just enough to suggest it does. 'Paul's ideas were a Britain at war and all that sort of thing and I found a picture of that little statuette in the Imperial War Museum,' Smith explains. 'We were just researching various different images and pictures … It's two army Red Cross medics carrying the wounded soldier and I just thought: three people. It summed it up really nicely ... I said to Paul, "This'll be really strong." So we got that photographed.' Military paraphernalia decorates the inner sleeve. Meanwhile, the rear features a Weller-commissioned Andrew Rosen photograph taken at Brighton Beach – famous in mod mythology for Bank Holiday battles between them and rockers – featuring a bulldog and a Union Jack-patterned deckchair. Further evidence of time running out during recording is provided by the fact that the tracklisting on original pressings of the album consisted of a sticker belatedly slapped on the back cover.

Whatever the reason for its abandonment, the five songs that seem to have materialised from the concept idea are mostly superb.

'Thick as Thieves' is a song lamenting the loss of a boyhood allegiance, one in which Weller may be immortalising the other founder Jam member. 'I think that's pretty much about him and Steve Brookes,' Foxton says. Romantic and political song tradition, as well as macho awkwardness, has led to the rock canon containing few songs about male friendship. Those that do get written, perhaps partly because of the fortitude necessary to overcome taboo, tend to be very good. Witness the Beatles' 'Hey Jude', Free's 'Wishing Well', the Moody Blues' 'Lovely to See You', Simon & Garfunkel's 'The Only Living Boy in New York' and the Clash's 'Stay Free'. 'Thick as Thieves' deserves a place in that honourable roll-call. The track features the quintessence of Weller's Jam melody style: big key changes going hand in hand with emotional or chronological shifts to powerful effect. Meanwhile, in an example of the massive advancement this album demonstrates in Weller's grasp of language, the title metaphor not only makes sense but is a conceit carefully sustained throughout: a pair of mates whose solidarity has been forged by their propensity to nick stuff grow so much apart that them being, as the saying goes, thick as thieves becomes just a melancholy memory. Paradoxically, the overall result is both poignant and rousing, particularly an end section where the tempo quickens and Weller and Foxton sing simultaneous but contrasting lines until coming together on the words, 'We're no longer as thick as thieves.' There is also what seems to be an additional play on words when it's stated that the pair are not as thick – i.e., stupid – as they used to be.

Weller's vocal also deserves mention. He has always been an above-average singer without ever being a great one (something that must have caused him some distress during the Style Council days, when his records began indicating soul-man pretensions). On this track, however, his delivery boasts a real power. It also has authority: he now sounds a man, not a callow youth.

To a vaguely oriental, mid-tempo backdrop, 'Burning Sky' tackles the same theme from both a more adult and more conservative perspective. In another excellently-sustained conceit, the narrative is in the form of a letter. The sell-out component of the once solid trio starchily sends his regrets that he can't make it to a proposed reunion. The phraseology is acutely judged, right from an opening lightly weighted with contempt in which the writer asks how things are in your little world. Throughout, Weller uses words and phrases from the business and bourgeois worlds that will have been familiar to him only via the media, yet because he is learning not to show off or descend to poesy, as well as beginning to grasp the art of a good rhyme, nothing jars: his narrator states that the values that he and his friends held once upon a time now seem stupid because the rent must be paid 'and some bonds severed and others made.' Only in a couple of minor instances – the meaningless title metaphor and Weller's insistence on throwing in another incongruous profanity in the shape of 'bastard' – is a wrong note struck.

The protagonist of anti-war anthem 'Little Boy Soldiers' is suspicious of the political machinations that result in him being drafted but – made powerlessness by his caste – goes meekly off to the battlefield. Although Jam biographer Paul Honeyford did not get the impression that 'Little Boy Soldiers' was part of the storyline, there has subsequently been speculation that this song would have actually formed the centrepiece of the abandoned concept album. It certainly has the multiple contrasting act format of an opera. Despite this, and its ambitious sonics (it features timpani, military drumming and the sound of cannon shells), it's a weak track. Melodically it often comes close to being a formless chant, while lyrically it throws in a perplexing reference to the American Revolutionary War, as well as another instance of the cursing Weller seems to think confers shock value and/or coolness but almost always sounds contrived and out-of-place. Yet the slightness is ultimately made forgivable by pleasing production tricks, razor-sharp instrumentation and a stunning kiss off-line where, to the accompaniment of a spiralling piano line, the narrator imagines his mother receiving his coffin with an attached letter reading, 'Find enclosed one son, one medal and a note to say he won.'

'The Eton Rifles' is another element of the concept. It is also effectively made the centrepiece of the record by being represented in an extended form (more than half a minute of additional music compared to the single) that makes it the longest track. It also has a slightly different ending (a single crash instead of a rabbit punch of chords).

Weller told Dave Schulps that the concept 'ends with a meeting on the wasteland, the old playground, after the war.' This would seem to indicate that 'Wasteland' (which closed side one of *Setting Sons*) was originally intended as the concept's finale. One could even put forward the argument that the concept would have been pretty much fulfilled by placing the above five songs in the following order on one side of the album: 'The Eton Rifles', 'Little Boy Soldiers', 'Thick as Thieves', 'Burning Sky' and 'Wasteland'. Displaced, 'Wasteland' instead becomes an examination of the dreariness of proletarian existence. Its florid phraseology is unconvincing ('A brave but useless show of compassion'), but what does strike a chord is the evocation of the aching misery of underprivileged teenagers idly traversing their litter-bedecked concrete jungle and wondering, with the quiet terror of youthful inexperience, if life is ever going to get any better. A flute and a yearning melody accentuate the wretchedness.

While the quality and intriguing vistas of the above quintet indicates that *Setting Sons* could have been an even better album if the initial concept had been pursued, there was still great music amongst the rest of the cuts. As with the concept tracks, it's noticeable that the music and lyrics are rarely less than substantial, but also that, even where they are slight, they don't sound it. The multi-layering and additional instrumentation not only enables proper aural fulfilment of Weller's increasingly ambitious visions, but provide something to enjoy when basic song-related inspiration is lacking.

It's not lacking in 'Private Hell', a brilliantly observed depiction of an empty-nester housewife. Who would have imagined that a conventionally masculine and unusually self-absorbed 21-year-old male would be able to get inside the head of a middle-aged woman enduring quiet, Valium-fuzzed agony over the fact that her looks are fading, her husband's sexual attentions are no longer wanted and her children have lives in which she is an irrelevance? When Weller refers to the subject's son still being at college and then triumphantly finishes the couplet with, 'You send him letters which he doesn't acknowledge,' it's the perfect summation of how in the space of just twelve months he has turned from an embarrassingly inept lyricist into an assured wordsmith.

The instrumentation on this domestic drama is even more broiling and relentless than on that earlier, much more kinetic story 'Down in the Tube Station at Midnight'. As with that song, there is a suggestion of contempt for the ostensible subject of sympathy. Despite this, one's admiration for this artistic, psychological and philosophical achievement is only increased by a couple of things we now know about its birth. Weller was partly prompted to write it by the fact that one of his favourite bands – Sixties freakbeat outfit the Creation – had spoken in interview of planning songs called 'Private Hell' and 'Closer Than Close', but never got around to composing them. (The latter title became the first line of 'Private Hell'.) The other impetus was a simple deadline. Asked if he considered 'Private Hell' a milestone in his writing, Weller responds, 'I didn't, to be quite honest with you. I like that song as well, but the circumstance in which I wrote it [was] we needed some more songs for *Setting Sons* so I was put in a room in our old rehearsal rooms with a typewriter or notepad and acoustic guitar and I bashed it out. Knocked out that, and the same day I did 'Girl on the Phone' as well. It was kind of, "Get in there, son, and get some more tunes together." Both them songs are good. 'Private Hell' I think's exceptional, but even 'Girl on the Phone' I like. They were just songs I had to get done to fulfil a quota, but luckily they come out sounding alright.'

'Saturday's Kids' could conceivably be viewed as a companion piece to 'Wasteland'. However, it feels more like a precursor to 'Town Called Malice'. As with that future Jam hit, it contains specific topographical references to the Woking of Weller's youth, but there is universality in its exploration of the mundanity, predictability and cruelty of the lives of the unskilled. In an existence where work is seldom fulfilment and surroundings are rarely inspiring, the chief pleasures to be obtained are sex and its flirtatious build-up, holidays at British seaside resorts, and ostentatious hedonism, much of it revolving around the cigarettes whose long-term effects – Weller points out – often make the closing act of unhappy lives even more miserable.

A song like this is obviously not joyous, yet it still manages to be anthemic. Weller lurches back and forth between lazy (he finishes a line with an antediluvian comment that girls in the Light A Bite 'dig' being chatted up) and inspired: the Saturday Kids who live in council houses 'wear V-necked shirts and baggy trousers.' As with 'Tube Station' and 'Burning Hell', the accusation can be levelled that it is not compassion in play here but contempt. However, the context feels different: chroniclers of the working class often ridicule the very people they posit as oppressed simply as a paradoxical but inevitable function of their superior intelligence serving to distance them from their own kind.

Like 'The Eton Rifles', 'Smithers-Jones' makes a retooled reappearance. This recalibration is wholesale. Emblematic of the LP's rich production, the song is a re-recording to the backing of a twenty-piece orchestra. It's not necessarily better than the rock arrangement but – in this current age of marginally differentiated CD bonus tracks – is an alternate version worthy of the name.

The album could be said to begin and end weakly. Some of the standalone self-written singles and B-sides of the period would certainly have been more logical inclusions than the opener 'Girl on the Phone' and the closing Motown cover 'Heat Wave'. That's not the same, though, as saying either are displeasing to the ear. While 'Girl on the Phone' is a glorified jingle with no sociological import, it's also perfectly enjoyable. Addressing in heightened form Weller's real-life experience of being stalked, it purveys bright, poppy tones and a disciplined rhyming scheme. The inclusion of 'Heat Wave' is on the surface bordering on the absurd. Whereas 'Girl on the Phone' is at least a slice cut from contemporary life (albeit a rarefied sector of it), the Holland-Dozier-Holland classic made famous by Martha and the Vandellas has absolutely nothing to do musically or thematically with what precedes it. However, such is the Jam's ever-increasing prowess that it – unlike the soul cover closing the second album – doesn't seem dispensable. It's a powerful, driving rendition decorated by sweet sax work by Steve 'Rudi' Thompson of X-Ray Spex and a pumping piano part from 'Merton Mick' Talbot of mod-revival band the Merton Parkas. It also constitutes an exit whose joyousness cleanses the palate after all the preceding grimness.

'We were running a little bit short,' says Weller. 'That's why we put on 'Heat Wave'.' Buckler's recollection is different: 'It was one of them songs we used to do in the clubs that we were probably itching to record ... It was pretty much live in the studio. It was great fun to do. I think it just adds another dimension. Maybe even reminds people where we came from.' Would it not be more appropriate for a B-side? 'I don't know,' says the drummer. 'We always tried to stay away from hiding tracks away on B sides. If we felt that we wanted to do it, we just did it.' Munday, though, is unequivocal when he says, 'I know that 'Heat Wave' went on 'cos they didn't have another song, and they couldn't put the album back because they'd booked the *Setting Sons* tour.'

Certainly, the fact that 'Heat Wave' seemed filler and/or a non sequitur was a motif in the album's reviews. So, however, was the record's extraordinarily high quality. Asked if *Setting Sons* is the Jam's masterpiece, Foxton initially deflects the question by suggesting that it's for people outside the band to judge. However, he then allows, 'I would be tempted to agree. *All Mod Cons* [was] the big turning point, and *Setting Sons* was probably the one. But that varies. I'm put on the spot. It's like when someone asks can you give me your top ten all-time favourite singles and you could list them off now, but then five minutes later you say, "Well actually, I'd rather that one was in."' Buckler also sways toward the idea of *Setting Sons* as the band's magnum opus, but also does so with caveats: 'I think it's a great album. There again, I tend to change my mind. I think, "*Sounds Affects* wasn't that bad either."' While Weller has never cited *Setting Sons* as a high-point, he says, 'There were some great songs to come out of the record: 'Thick as Thieves', 'Burning Sky', 'Eton Rifles'. There's some great tunes on that record: 'Little Boy Soldiers', 'Saturday's Kids'.'

132

Against a background of critical hosannas, *Setting Sons* climbed to number four. Both the position and the record's nineteen-week occupancy of the album chart were Jam milestones. *Setting Sons* even secured the first-time Jam feat of cracking the US LP top 200, reaching number 137.

Vic Coppersmith-Heaven's album royalties, though, were not as healthy as those sales might suggest. An indication of how squeezed were the schedules is the fact that Polydor insisted that *Setting Sons'* vinyl master be cut the day after the album was finished. Coppersmith-Heaven booked a session at Townhouse, where he spent a day with head cutting engineer Ian Cooper deciding the levels, the dynamics and the equalisation. However, in 2007, the producer told Richard Buskin of *Sound on Sound*, 'My ears were pretty shot by that time, having worked for several weeks on the recording and mixing, and when the pressing came back from the factory it sounded absolutely terrible ... I then had to give Polydor the bad news that I had to reject it.' Coppersmith-Heaven was permitted to re-cut the record, but revealed, 'The record company people made it clear they were not happy with me, and when my next royalty statement arrived they'd deducted the cost, which came to about £2,000 in studio charges. That really upset me, because it wasn't something that I was personally responsible for.'

For Chris Parry, the album's commercial success was partly the result of Polydor finally putting the promotional muscle behind the group that they had neglected to when he was on the scene. 'Everyone was struggling with hits in '77 into '78 because radio wasn't playing them,' he says. 'I got a little bit disillusioned by that. The Jam were still being looked after by Polydor internally.' He gives fond credit to Polydor's Roger Holt for early promotional assistance: 'He had a specific promotions budget that did stuff. He came up to my office and said, "I'm going to help you with the Jam. I don't believe these fuckers about the punk thing and the Sex

Pistols stuff – we should have had them.'" However, he also says of the label, 'There was a lot of people that didn't particularly like the band ... *All Mod Cons* was the last album I was involved in and we were still struggling. Number one was a way, way, way away.' Parry attributes the sea-change to a decision to contract PR man Nigel Sweeny. 'Polydor started to get more serious with the band and brought in outside agencies to deal with Radio 1 and suchlike and reposition them. They started to get a lot more play on the radio ... Polydor Records, who were a bit sluggish and lazy, they galvanised around the band. All of a sudden, they had a good team around them corporately and the Jam just rammed home. Nigel Sweeny and his team were close to the BBC and they just picked the Jam up. And they had good records to break.'

Parry made a return visit to Stratford Place where a playback of *Setting Sons* happened to be occurring in the very demo room where he had recorded the Jam approaching three years before. 'All the people that didn't like them, didn't like punk, didn't like any of it, they were all packed into that room,' he recalls. 'All the people that gave me shit, they had a different view. They were all packed in there like sardines listening to this record and they were going, "Wow, that's good."'

It wasn't only their improving art which brought the Jam a whole new slew of fans that year. 'Seventy-nine marked the full flowering of the mod revival, whose steady, organic growth since the previous year was given a sudden outside boost by the November 1979 release of the movie adaptation of the Who's *Quadrophenia* album. While the whole new mod cult might have been nebulous (a patchwork, never quite convincing avowal of adherence to Sixties mods' musical and fashion interests) and contradictory (nostalgia for the values of 'modernism'), it nonetheless existed. This mini Parka-clad army naturally gravitated toward a band considered to have a long association with mod.

'I thought it was quite good really,' says Dennis Munday of the new breed of the tribe he once ran with. 'They took it a lot more serious, whereas when I was a mod it was something you just became. Certainly, for me the music was more important than anything, including the dress sense or haircuts ... My generation of mods, we listened to a lot more different kinds of music. I found that that generation of mod was a little narrow-minded. We were listening to rhythm & blues, blues. I went to see Jimi Hendrix and there was loads of mods there. The Rolling Stones had a big mod following.'

Although Weller assisted the revival by offering Jam support slots to mod bands the Chords and the Purple Hearts, he was also publicly sceptical of the movement. In 1980, he told Dutch paper *Musical Express*, 'I'm not really interested in the whole revival thing. It's a bit pathetic.' Funnily enough, that is pretty much what the residents of Woking are reported to have felt about Weller when he instigated a one-man mod revival a half-decade before. One would have thought he might have felt some sort of validation about the fact that the world had finally caught up with him.

The year had been an extraordinarily febrile one for music, and most of its significant artists were young and British. 1976 and 1977 might have been the juncture at which punk exploded, but it was '79 when it all came to fruition. New-wave acts effected their full maturation, while there appeared an intriguing new genre, an angular, slightly dispassionate field that, despite not being punk, was so inconceivable without it that it was given the term 'post-punk'. That Britpop would give 1995 the reputation as a great year for British music seems laughable when looking at a list of some of the albums released in 1979: *Armed Forces* by Elvis Costello & the Attractions, *Look Sharp!* and *I'm the Man* by Joe Jackson, *Inflammable Material* by Stiff Little Fingers, *Scared to Dance* and *Days in Europa* by the Skids, *Secondhand Daylight* by Magazine, *Squeezing Out Sparks* by Graham Parker and the Rumour, *Cool for Cats* by

Squeeze, *Y* by the Pop Group, *Replicas* and *The Pleasure Principle* by Tubeway Army/Gary Numan, *Unknown Pleasures* by Joy Division, *Ghostown* by the Radiators, *Drums and Wires* by XTC, *Join Hands* by Siouxsie and the Banshees, *Entertainment!* by Gang of Four, *154* by Wire, *Cut* by the Slits, *A Different Kind of Tension* by Buzzcocks, *Reggatta de Blanc* by the Police, *One Step Beyond...* by Madness, *Metal Box* by Public Image Ltd., *Machine Gun Etiquette* by the Damned, *Quiet Life* by Japan, and the eponymous debuts of the Specials and the Undertones. Not all can be said to be great records (although many are), but each contains much that is musically and/or sociologically fascinating.

The two most impressive artists amidst this ferocious creativity and innovation were the Jam and the Clash. It was clear by now that it was this pair alone who were tussling not just for artistic supremacy but the crown of leaders of new wave. The Damned might have released the very first UK punk record in the form of 'New Rose' but they had never really possessed sufficient gravitas to be seriously considered as contenders for the role of pack leaders, even without their split (albeit one made hazy by reunions under the original name or subtle variants). The Boomtown Rats had had another good year singles-wise with 'I Don't Like Mondays', 'Diamond Smiles' and 'Someone's Looking At You', but the quality of those singles wasn't matched by that of the parent album, *The Fine Art of Surfacing*. Said LP concluded with 'When the Night Comes', an acute, epic dissection of the quiet desperation behind conventional lives, but elsewhere on the disc the group were losing their common touch and descending into the quirkiness and whimsy that would blight the rest of their career. Meanwhile, Sham 69 were losing their lustre as a consequence of acquiring a distasteful and disruptive far-right fanbase. While this may not have been their fault, it was also becoming increasingly obvious that despite their likeable, raucous hits – of which 'Hersham Boys' had been another example this year – they didn't have the capacity to ever make a top-quality long player.

In its review, *Record Mirror* adjudged *Setting Sons* 'the last great album of the Seventies.' Not quite. It being so close to year's and decade's end, the music weekly's precipitousness was understandable, but December 14 brought *London Calling* by the Clash. It was a joyous, barnstorming double-set that saw the band, like the Jam, exploding beyond the musical parameters of punk while determinedly retaining the genre's social conscience. Even Jam fanatics would have to concede that, in all honesty, it left the Clash the head of the field. It was undeniable, though, that the Jam were catching up fast.

VOICE OF A GENERATION?

The Jam's first proffering of the new decade made the band superstars in their homeland.

Double-A sided single 'Going Underground'/'Dreams of Children appeared on March 14, 1980 housed in an ostensibly prosaic sleeve featuring what looked like stills from the record's promotional film. However, Bill Smith reveals, 'Funnily enough, they did the video after I'd done the picture bag. I wanted to make it look like they were stills from a promo and then they made a promo round that.'

The Jam intended 'Dreams of Children' to be the side of the record that received airplay. That the 500 copies of the DJ demo disc pressed by Polydor turned out to designate 'Going Underground' as the A-side was down to the machinations of Dennis Munday. He bluntly opines of the tradition of double-A sided singles, 'I've never seen the point, because you're not going to get both sides played ...You can't split airplay.' Munday instructed the pressing plant to clearly mark 'Dreams of Children' as a B-side. He then needed to devise an explanation for the Jam about why their wishes hadn't been observed. 'I made up a story that it was a pressing error,' he shrugs. 'It was the right thing to do.'

Musically, the mid-tempo 'Dreams of Children' is vaguely psychedelic in the strain of *Revolver*-era Beatles. Lyrically, it proposes that such are the complexities and problems caused by adult awareness that sometimes the lack of knowledge of children seems preferable. Overall, it's an agreeably gothic affair, although the haunting effect aimed for by the bridge is undermined by Weller seeming to confuse the word 'choke' with 'crack', and even then using it inconsistently.

The narrator of 'Going Underground' starts out with a relaxed attitude to life but is soon reduced to a sickened state as he contemplates what such self-satisfaction results in: complicity in

The Jam's debut release was adorned with an instantly iconic logo designed by Bill Smith.

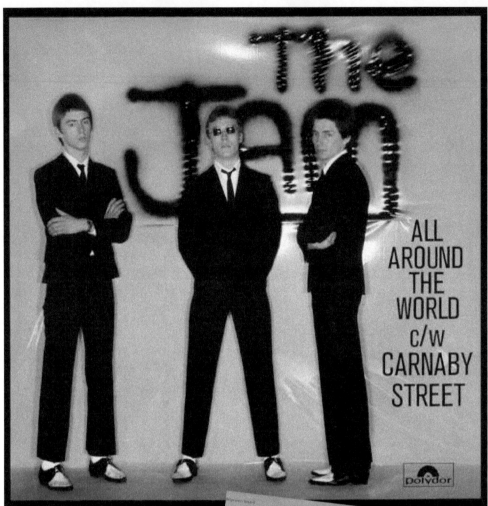

The Jam's mid-1977 single 'All Around the World' featured (l-r) Weller, Buckler and Foxton in their famous mohair-and-spats uniform. The look would be abandoned by the following year.

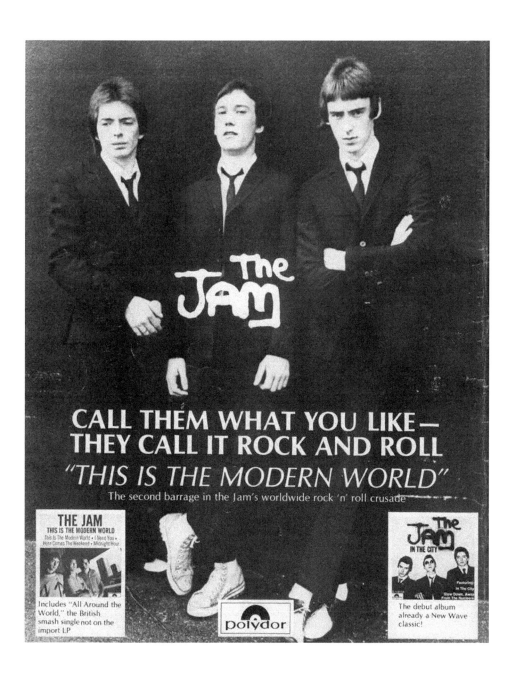

This advertisement sought to sell the Jam's second album to the American market, but the group and the USA never gelled.

Connie Wong's illustrations for the inner sleeve of This is the Modern World *were bizarrely incongruous for a band like the Jam.*

The Jam on TV. Host Mr Bolan is seen playing with Jam badges prior to their appearance on Marc *(1977, above); the band perform 'Billy Hunt' on* The Old Grey Whistle Test *(1978, below).*

The front of the sleeve of the Jam's 1978 single 'Down in the Tube Station at Midnight' saw the use of the fonts from both their iconic logos, while the rear paid tribute to the recently passed Keith Moon.

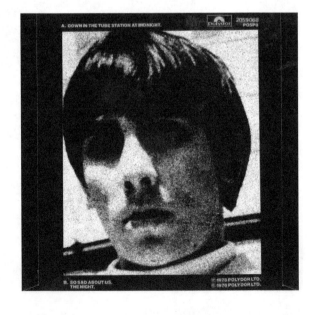

Third album All Mod Cons *(1978) was a sumptuous package.*

THE JAM   SETTING SONS

Military themes dominated the sleeves of Setting Sons *(1979) and its precursor single 'The Eton Rifles'.*

Contrary to appearances, the sleeve of 'Going Underground' (1980) inspired its video, rather than vice versa; the single also inspired a 2000 AD comic strip, 'Comic Rock: Terror Tube'.

*As the Jam grew ever more successful, they
became regular magazine cover stars in the UK.*

The Jam's 1980 album Sound Affects *took its title and cover design from a series of BBC LPs, while its preamble saw Weller extol in print the virtues of rawness and minimalism.*

THE JAM ★ THE GIFT

In 1982, the last Jam album featured a puzzling stagnation cover message, but the sleeve of their final single proffered a more comprehensible literal image.

THE JAM
BEAT SURRENDER

BEAT SURRENDER
SHOPPING

the crimes of politicians. He concludes he wants to opt out of life: going underground, which could be interpreted literally or as a description of an escapist mentality – 'internal exile'.

The music commences with a joint bass-and-drum attack and proceeds with stabbed, reverberating guitar and brutal bass runs. This vice-tight, harsh soundscape, though, is alleviated by pretty touches, including organ swells and tom-toms. Foxton's breathy, almost delicate, echoing of the title phrase is contrasted by parade-ground barks alluding to the Boys' Brigade to which Weller sarcastically likens military sabre-rattling.

That Weller's vocal lines frequently overlap adds to the impression of a spluttering state of fury. The lyric he seethingly enunciates is frequently stunning. True, it's speckled with the not-quite-right phraseology and confused reasoning of a man whose youth and meagre educational hinterland doesn't serve well his natural intelligence and social concern (e.g., deciding to go underground is identical in effect to the insulated complacency which the narrator denounces). However, by this point the same natural intelligence and social concern gives rise to phrases, lines and couplets that positively dazzle. One example involves the narrator being upset about his taxes being spent on nuclear textbooks for atomic crimes. The truly resplendent section, though, is a verse in which – possibly with Margaret Thatcher's victory of ten months previously in mind – he castigates the electorate, stating that having chosen their leaders and placed their trust, '...their lies wash you down and their promises rust.' Kidney machines, he avers, will be replaced by rockets and guns.

'From the moment that we struck that one up we knew we had something that sounded really good,' recalls Buckler. 'Still stands up very, very well.' Bill Smith offers, 'It's like the Jam live rather than anything else ... The Jam live were more ferocious than they were on record.'

Weller would over the next few years become increasingly

involved with the Campaign for Nuclear Disarmament. His Jam colleagues were sometimes brought along for the ride, whether it be by playing a benefit for said pressure group or 'Little Boy Soldiers' being included on a 1982 anti-nuclear fund-raising album, *Life in the European Theatre*. Buckler reflects, 'Unfortunately, with the nuclear bombs there's no un-inventing them.' Nonetheless, 'Going Underground' was a form of social commentary he could get behind. 'For people to constantly throw up warnings about these things is quite healthy, the same as people are constantly questioning why we have to have nuclear power. There's no way we're ever going to get rid of it, not realistically, but it shouldn't be accepted glibly.'

That the Jam were moving into the mainstream was demonstrated by the fact that the Radio 1 DJ accorded the privilege of being the first to play 'Going Underground' was not John Peel, as was the custom, but Mike Read. Peel presented a late-night show listened to by young, hardcore music lovers, while Read was the host of the evening slot just before his that was listened to by a slightly wider demographic. This may be one of the reasons that on March 22, 1980 'Going Underground' debuted at the top of the UK singles chart, the first time a single had entered at number one since Slade achieved that feat in 1973 with 'Merry Xmas Everybody'. Of all the records that might be imagined going to the top, such a ferocious concoction as 'Going Underground' was not it. 'I was surprised by it being number one,' Weller admits. He adds, however, 'It did feel like we were boiling up to something. It was getting pretty big in a fairly short space of time.' Despite his conviction of the record's special quality, Buckler says, 'I don't think we ever thought it would do as well as it did.' Foxton's mind boggles at the numbers involved. 'It amazed me,' he marvels. 'I still remember the publisher saying, "Well, you're selling 40-60 thousand singles a day." I can't visualise that amount of people going out and buying a record each day for a week.'

There arose a controversy about Polydor's sales methods. It was said that the label engineered a clustering of sales by delaying the release date. If true, the machinations wouldn't have been a first. Parry says, 'We held 'In the City' back a week just to give us an extra bite.' However, Munday denies any dirty tricks, averring that the release date was only put back because the Jam were late finishing the tracks. He asserts of the record company, 'We were one step ahead. They did a good job. They authorised [them] to go in Saturday and Sunday. So come Monday, everything went out. Normally, you start packing the orders on the Monday and you're aiming to get everything out by Friday and Saturday for the charts. Also, our singles sales force took double the amount of stock that they would normally carry.' Weller says of the alleged chart-rigging, 'I don't know whether that happened or not. All I know is that we had quarter of a million advance sales, so I was pretty sure it was gonna be near the number one spot. Those days, we shifted out a quarter of a million records in a week. You'd be number one for, like, six months now.'

Moreover, from Munday's point of view it was at this point that the intensity of the Jam's fanbase really reaped dividends. 'They toured constantly and they'd just built up this ferocious following,' he says.' I think that that probably sold seventy per cent of the total sales in the first week ... Before 'Eton Rifles', they could sell about 150,000 records. So you follow that, you knew you were going to sell 300,000 records. And they sold in a very short space of time. It was just the buying power of the fans. They all went out and bought it. Literally, their records lasted three weeks, and then there's a sudden huge drop in sale, whereas if you take most bands, it takes five, six weeks to get to number one and they can generally sell half a million or more.'

The Jam weren't the first new wavers to hit the UK top spot. Not only had The Boomtown Rats racked up that milestone back in '78 with 'Rat Trap', they had since scored another with 'I Don't Like

Mondays'. Acts like Ian Dury and the Blockheads, the Police, Tubeway Army/Gary Numan, Blondie, the Pretenders and the Specials had also topped the charts. Some might dispute the punk credentials of any or all of the aforementioned, but all had gone to number one with records infused with values and techniques uncommon, and in some cases unthinkable, before punk. Moreover, the first punk number one had probably actually happened as far back as June 5, 1977, when all the evidence suggests that the Sex Pistols' 'God Save the Queen' was denied by political imperatives rather than sales statistics the formal status of the nation's top-selling single in the week which inconveniently happened to coincide with the monarch's Silver Jubilee. It could now be stated that the Jam were in that gainsaid-but-exalted company. 'Going Underground' hitting number one was therefore a generational triumph. Although there had seemed a certain element of deliberate self-parody in Tony Blackburn's complaint about punks not singing about flowers and trees, his allegation that they were 'disgusting' wasn't too far off the opinion of the majority of music lovers of the time, especially those who paid less attention to the evidence of their ears than to the gag reflex provoked by tabloid headlines. Essentially, the Jam were helping to prove that the records of new-wave artists were music too.

The Jam's ascension to the top spot was also, of course, a personal triumph. Not just in the sense of the validation that comes with being endorsed by the record-buying public in the ultimate way, but in the fact of them having overtaken and outstripped all the London punks who had once laughed at them. Some people were now beginning to think the previously unthinkable: could it be that, of all the groups that had emerged from the punk revolution, it was the Jam who had turned out to be the most important?

Ammunition for Munday's denial of chart-rigging is provided by the fact that the success of the record seemed to take the Jam by surprise. When the disc scaled the summit the band – having assumed that there would be the usual incremental climb up the chart after release date – weren't even in the country. Instead, engaged on their fourth US jaunt, they were in Los Angeles when they received the news that 'Going Underground' was the UK number one. Weller later reported that the news left him close to tears. This surprises Munday, who says, 'Paul has always kept his emotions under check. He wasn't the sort of guy who's going to leap up and down.' Nonetheless, Weller and his bandmates were sufficiently moved to take the decision to abandon their American dates and fly back to perform the track on that week's *Top of the Pops*. An appearance on said show was always followed by a huge sales boost (Munday estimates one of 20 to 30 per cent), proof of the fact that the BBC's hegemony could work for artists as much as it could penalise them (such as failure to gain airplay on Radio 1). Moreover, the Jam were perennially haunted by the suspicion that trying to effect a breakthrough in the States was futile. However, while a desire for more sales and a resentful what-the-hell-are-we-doing-here? feeling may have partly motivated the decision to return home, it also seems to have been made because of a humbled affection for the band's native fanbase. 'We were always very faithful to the UK audience,' says Buckler. 'We finished the American tour early because we felt we had more allegiance to come back to the UK than trying to play to some guys in Texas. We always felt that we had a duty to playing in the UK. That was a good strength and a good bond.'

'Going Underground' remained at the top for three weeks. It has been claimed that the extended stay was also contrived. Polydor were said to have staggered sales by releasing stock to distributors in dribs and drabs. Additionally, releasing a limited-edition double-pack edition of the single can only be viewed as having one purpose. (The extra disc in this edition contained live versions of a trio of Jam songs.) However, the fact that the Jam would have more chart-toppers, and the fact that they would never score lower than number four for the remainder of their existence, proved that the group's popularity was not manufactured.

Then there is the fact of the plethora of Jam records that soon filled the UK singles chart. Polydor wasted no time in cashing in on the Jam's new high profile by reissuing all their previous 45s. Although only one of them made the top 40 – 'In the City', replicating its original placing of number 40 – all except 'Tube Station', 'When You're Young' and 'The Eton Rifles' made the top fifty. Moreover, if a definition of stardom is the fact of cropping up in the public arena in wholly unexpected ways, the Jam now indubitably fit that bill. In July 1980, the science-fiction oriented boys' comic *2000 AD* published a phantasmagorical six-page strip called 'Comic Rock: The Terror Tube', the first panel of which proclaimed, 'Story suggested by the Jam's Going Underground.'

Says Buckler, 'It became more and more difficult to appreciate our position. We're so close to the woods you just don't see the trees. I remember we drove up to Deeside to do a gig there. There was this huge queue and we quite honestly thought, "Well, what the hell's going on here? Somebody must be selling something or they must be giving free money away around the corner," and then when we did turn the corner we realised that they were queuing to see us. It was incidents like that that struck you about how much the band had grown.'

During 'Going Underground''s tenure at number one, Bruce Foxton in particular had cause to feel pleased. 'Turning Japanese', a record which reached number three at this precise juncture, was the work of the Vapors, a band in which he had a financial stake. After spotting them playing at a venue in Guildford, Surrey, Foxton began to manage them in partnership with John Weller. Although the Vapors were the archetypal one-hit wonders, 'Turning Japanese' cracked the US top 40, a feat never managed by the Jam.

Following up 'Going Underground' – more a phenomenon than a record – was, of course, somewhat difficult. Almost five months elapsed before the Jam's next release.

Of the new songs Weller had ready for the task, Polydor favoured 'Pretty Green' while he inclined toward 'Start!' Weller agonised about the choice. Munday: 'We did two sleeves: one 'Start!', one 'Pretty Green'. I had to say to Paul, "You gotta make your mind up."' Munday was pleased when Weller opted for 'Start!' 'I always thought that 'Start!' had legs whereas 'Pretty Green' was a very, very good Jam number, end of,' he says. 'It didn't stick out like other singles they'd made.'

Recalls Bill Smith, 'Because no one was sure what to do I [designed] basically the same thing but different colours. That's why it's such a simple bag.' The front of the sleeve featured just band name and title. The shot of a record-player deck on the reverse seems designed to fit in with the A-side's theme of music as a form of communication, but Smith is vague about this. The developing cracks in the relationship between him and the Jam are evident in his comment, 'It might well have been, and now we're getting into the area where Paul's voice, musically and visually, is starting to be wanting to be heard. Basically, everybody was telling him that everything he did was brilliant. By that time a lot of artists get surrounded by sycophants. Record companies – 'cos they're making money out of them – they tell them how brilliant they are.'

'Pretty Green' has a bass line that – at a pinch – could be said to be a variation on the riff of Homer Banks' 'A Lot of Love' (and thereby the Spencer Davis Group's 'Gimme Some Lovin''). However, there was no ambiguity about the plagiarism involved in the bassline of 'Start!' It was the Jam's second nod to the Beatles' 'Taxman'. It was so blatant that it caused Munday some concern. 'I remember going in the studio with a multi-track and trying to sing 'Taxman' to it,' he said. He was relieved to find that he couldn't. 'I just wanted to see. People borrow. And the Beatles were one of the worst bands for that and people never say anything about it. My view is that, as long as the melody and the lyrics are new, then it's not a problem.'

Neither this nor any of the other examples of appropriation littering the Jam's catalogue made Rick Buckler fearful that the group could find itself embroiled in legal action. He reasons, 'It's like '[Town Called] Malice': taking that sort of Motown feel. All we done with 'Start!' was just plagiarised a particular feel, that's probably the best way of looking at it. Because they don't actually sound the same. When you listen to them side by side, they are very much different, but there's a certain vibe that those particular songs have.'

'Bruce wrote the bassline to 'Start!' Buckler recalls. Weller doesn't pin the blame on Foxton for the 'Start!' lift, but in any case has always publicly defended his and the Jam's jackdaw tendencies. Now that he has been around long enough for young musical devotees to rip him off, has he changed his position on pinching? 'No. If I ever hear someone who I think might have lifted a bit from one of my tunes, I'm more than flattered. I take it as a compliment. I don't ever get offended by it or want to get on the case with my lawyers. Music just goes round. There's only so many notes and so many chords.' He explains of the origins of the jackdaw habits, 'I did it more when I was a kid. You're still looking for what you want to sound like. I've always been a fan and often it's just 'cos I get enthusiastic and I'd want to do something similar to what I've just been listening [to] and digging. I don't think there's any ill intent behind it. Sometimes it's just a cheeky nod to something, a little wink to something you love.' He also insists, 'There's hundreds of other tunes I've written that don't sound like anything else. So, give a fuck.'

It has to be said that the above arguments cut no ice at the time of the release of 'Start!', not least because its guitar solo also seemed to owe something to the Beatles' template. The controversy about plagiarism, in fact, was part of the reason for the subdued critical reaction to 'Start!' when it appeared on August 15, 1980. Another factor was that, on the first few hearings, the track sounded a bit odd: it was scant of melody, bare-boned arrangement-wise, slightly soulless in its echoing mix and possessed of a lyric devoid of a rhyming scheme. Even the record's minimalist sleeve design fitted into this ersatz feel.

'Start!' turned out to be a record in the vein of the Rolling Stones' album *Exile on Main St.*: disappointing on first (even second, third, fourth) hearing, but ultimately yielding extreme rewards. The riff is infectious, which was sort of the point of considering it worth nicking. Moreover, the bass-playing throughout – purloined and original – is excellent. The tune may be more chant than melody, but still lodges itself in the brain. The words may be that most lazy of forms, open verse, but are interesting in the way they examine the Jam's relationship with their fans.

A motif in Weller interviews was a very un-Clash like assertion that music doesn't change society (e.g., 'I don't think the group have got any power at all, even if a million people buy our records and listen to each word it's not going to do anything' – *NME*, November 1979). However, one thing in which he did believe was a band's ability to have an effect on *individuals*. In 'Start!' Weller addresses an abstract version of one of the Jam's legions of followers. He tells the fan that it doesn't matter if they never meet again because the bond they have forged is a start. Weller is rejoicing in the fact that other people feel as fervently as him about social issues – or, as he oddly puts it, 'Knowing that someone in this life loves with a passion called hate.' Interestingly, another of the song's key lines was foreshadowed by Weller at a New York gig in 1979 when he told the audience, 'I have to say in all honesty this place ain't really us and I'm sure it ain't you either. What we give is what we get.'

Some prefer 'Liza Radley', the record's B-side, to 'Start!' and even feel it would have done better commercially. Against his own acoustic strumming, Weller croons a paean to a mystical female who feels a deep compassion for the residents of her small town even though they hold her in nothing but contempt. Percussion is inaudible but embellishment is provided by Weller's overdubbed picked acoustic work and Foxton on – of all things – accordion. The rustic sonics are utterly lovely, and mixed to a mountain-stream purity. (The Jam and Coppersmith-Heaven share production credit.) The sonics are, however, rather damaged by the lyric, which starts as it means to limply continue with the banal observation that the subject has long hair. Lines like 'See her creeping across summer lawns at midnight' grope desperately for profundity and have the air of something heard elsewhere. His profundity objective might have been helped if the composer could only make the effort to find rhymes. Incidentally, although the song is attributed to Weller alone, Buckler claims to have written some of the lyric after the singer, short on inspiration, turned to him.

The process whereby 'Start!' pulled into focus as a very good record would possibly not have happened without the success of its predecessor. Having had a chart topper, the Jam were automatically on Radio 1's playlists, which meant that the public were able to acquire a taste for 'Start!' by the osmosis resulting from forced exposure. Despite its slow-burning attractions, though, the fact that 'Start!' was never going to be as intoxicating as 'Going Underground' is illustrated by its chart trajectory. The record debuted at number three, and although it impressed enough people from that point to jump in successive weeks to number two and number one, it remained in pole position for just a week.

*

With the exception of the complicated situation surrounding *All Mod Cons*, a Jam LP had always succeeded a precursor single within weeks. *Sound Affects*, though, only made its appearance on November 28, a gap of 3½ months after 'Start!' In fact, if Weller had had his way, there would have been no 1980 Jam album at all.

After some sessions at Townhouse in June and July, Weller told Dennis Munday that he didn't foresee a Jam long-player in the immediate future. Munday recalls, 'He came to me and he said, "I can't finish it. I want to put it off." So I said, "Fine." I couldn't see the point in arguing with him. You can't force someone to make a record.'

However, for Munday's bosses it wasn't as simple as that. With two consecutive number one singles to their name, the Jam were looking like they could rival the value to Polydor of cash-cows like the Who, the Bee Gees, Eric Clapton and James Last. They were certainly now mainstream enough to feature on kids' Christmas-present wish-lists and to be on the radar of the important post-Christmas record-token-gifted demographic. When Munday went in to tell AJ Morris Weller's news, the Polydor MD transpired to be so desperate for a year-end Jam album that he made a suggestion to Munday that was utterly bizarre. Godley & Creme had recently signed to the label and were one of the other acts for whom Munday had responsibility. Like 10cc, the band of which they had until recently constituted fifty per cent, Kevin Godley and Lol Creme purveyed arty, whimsical and decidedly non-political fare (an example of such, 'Under Your Thumb', would be a hit for them the following year). Morris, though, seemed to feel that they would be a good match for the Jam. Munday: 'He said, "Well Godley & Creme could write the album for them." I said, "I know they could, but I don't think the Jam fans would appreciate it." He was quite serious. I was trying not to laugh.'

If Morris' attitude was bizarre, that of others at Polydor was decidedly nasty. Munday claims that some superiors refused to speak to him, and that those who did deign to do so claimed that his failure to persuade Weller to come up with the goods meant that people at the company might have to be laid off. With feelings running so high, it's perhaps understandable that Weller was eventually persuaded to get his muse into gear. The remainder of the album was recorded from August to October at RAK (Upper London) and Eden Studios.

Then again, Munday feels the creative drought hadn't been as severe as Weller had suggested. 'At the time, I was far too busy to analyse what was going on, because they weren't the only group I worked on,' he says. However, as a consequence of later compiling several Jam compilations, Munday would become *au fait* with the details of Jam recording sessions. 'Most of the songs were demoed before they went in the studio,' he says of what he found out about *Sound Affects*. 'Why it took so long, who knows? They certainly were fucking about, there's no doubt about that. It cost 120,000, *Sound Affects*. That's probably as much as all the previous albums put together ... I was getting the bills through. The girl who did the studio bookings would come in to see me and say, "It's going up Den, it's going up." And I just said, "Look, we got to get it done – fuck it."'

Whatever the circumstances, for the second year in a row the album the Jam delivered to their label was of a very high quality. Moreover, at a shade over 35 minutes it was this time even of a respectable length, which extent, furthermore, was reached without recourse to throwing on an incongruous cover version.

Weller would often take his cue from contemporary sounds. The records he was consuming at the point of recording *Sound Affects* were sonically skeletal. Munday recollects in particular a penchant for Gang of Four. As well as that Leeds quartet's brutal and bare political funk, Weller was listening to – according to a list he supplied *Smash Hits* in late '79 – Wire, the Slits and Joy Division. It was inevitable, then, that *Sound Affects* ended up both muscular and unadorned.

Some interpreted that timbre as a deliberate turning away from the ornate sweep of the Jam's last long-playing offering. Demurs Weller, 'It was trying to do something a bit different every time, as much as you possibly can with a three-piece. I don't think it was a reaction to the sound of *Setting Sons*. We just didn't want to make the same record again. The template for me is growing up with the Beatles, always that anticipation of what they're gonna do next and where we're going next on this trip. I guess I always thought that's what bands should do.'

Buckler doesn't see a contradiction between the two issues. Asked if *Sound Affects* was a self-conscious stripping back of the multi-layering of the previous album, the drummer flatly says, 'Yes.' However, he adds, 'We just simply tried to do different approaches on different albums. It was just really another path on the experimentation of what we could do with a core three-piece.' Foxton responds similarly to the was-it-a-reaction-against-*Setting-Sons* question: 'Yeah. That's the short answer.' In the long answer, he says, 'It goes full circle. You start off and you're a novice. Hopefully over the years your musicianship improves and you get to know your instruments more and you start to branch out and you want to bring in other sounds, like we did on *This is the Modern World*, and start doing a lot of overdubs and almost like Thin Lizzy harmony guitars on a lot of stuff, 'Strange Town' and that. And then you think, "Hang on a bit, it's getting a bit carried away here and we won't be able to recreate half of this live" and it comes full circle. You strip it back down to the bare bones again.'

Sound Affects was the third Jam album in a row to feature a punning title, although this one made more sense than those of its predecessors. Weller was playing with the name of the BBC's famous, if rather specialist, series of sound-effect LPs, his purpose being to make another point about the influence music can have on individual lives. It even lent itself to a cover conceit mimicking the

BBC LP sleeves' distinctive image-grid designs, the pictures chosen for which were linked to the litany of scenarios featured in one of the album's songs, 'That's Entertainment'. After the aerosoled logo, the cover became the most iconic of Bill Smith's Jam designs, something which he finds somewhat bemusing. 'It's the one that was really more or less Paul's idea right from the get-go,' he says. 'They were in a recording studio and I had a meeting with them and he pulled a few BBC sound effects records down from the shelves. I thought they were awful in terms of the actual design and layout. It's not my favourite album cover of the Jam by quite a long way, but it does seem to stick in quite a lot of people's memories in terms of being one of their better ones.' With regard to the images used, Smith says, 'Martyn Goddard and I took the photos between us. The dog is my wife's family pet. The telephone box is in Gravesend, where I used to live. Martin took the funeral directors just because he knew them. It was just convenience of where those images were.' He confirms that the image of rooftops on the top right are from the opening titles of gritty working-class soap opera *Coronation Street*, a favourite of both Weller and Buckler.

The white-dominated back cover features, alongside the tracklisting, a segment of 'The Mask of Anarchy', a revolution call by Percy Bysshe Shelley. Says Smith, 'I thought it was nice that it was a poem rather than one of the lyrics of the songs, because it would have pulled that out, whereas that Shelley poem I think for Paul said as much about the album as his own lyrics.' Smith chose the picture on the back, in which the Jam are seen in the recording studio. Although Buckler (temporarily bearded) is to the fore, Smith says, 'Paul was quite happy with it.'

The inner bag featured contrasting sides: one utilitarian, containing the album's lyrics and a scattering of monochrome in-the-studio photographs; the other lustrous, featuring an outdoors colour shot of the group members that shimmers with early-morning tranquillity. It was taken by Andrew Douglas, the *Setting Sons* cover photographer.

Album opener 'Pretty Green' finds Weller observing that, 'Power is measured by the pound or the fist.' 'Pretty Green,' of course is a phrase meaning naiveté. Weller, however, heard it in the United States, where a game-show host made a reference to a 'big barrel of pretty green.' With British pound notes being the same colour as the alluded-to American dollars, he pressed it into service to question the profit principle and the peculiar societal process of handing over valueless scraps of paper for goods and services. The lyrical conceit made sense for British listeners of the time, but has little or no resonance for anyone born into a UK where a quid is a coin. That unforeseeable issue aside, there is no serious flaw in the clipped lyric, although one could be petty and make the point that the theme of the song is trite to anyone past their twenties. In any case, the attractiveness of the music makes the listener inclined to be charitable and view the song as a valid snapshot of the thought processes of a stage in life. It is, though, a peculiar kind of attractiveness. The track's hard-edged bass and reverbed drumbeat sum up the album's coldness. Weller's playing, meanwhile, sums up its frequent abrasiveness: nobody who values their fingers would want to put them near his guitar parts.

'Monday' demonstrates that the album's cold musical tone doesn't rule out warm sentiment. It's another Weller creation that confirms a then-new principle: that a romantic song doesn't have to sound ridiculous because of it being sung in estuary English. Weller touchingly thanks his 'sunshine girl' for both telling him he's not special and for curing his embarrassment about love. Discrete piano work bobs about in the gently lapping instrumentation. Although covering similar territory, 'But I'm Different Now' is sonically a world removed, boasting a blazing guitar riff (one of Weller's best ever) and a hell-for-leather pace. Less than two minutes long, it makes its simple but sweet point

('I'm glad that you're my girl'), then departs the stage in a Rickenbacker howl.

Conversely, 'Set the House Ablaze' is a veritable epic. An impressionistic piece, across the course of five minutes it constructs a sense of dread via a nagging guitar riff, a militaristic whistling motif, relentless drum work and an urgent spoken-word verse unsettlingly mixed just below audibility. Buckler in particular builds a menace that brilliantly evokes the sick feeling in the pit of many a Briton's stomach at this point in history. Although Weller never actually enunciates the names of the National Front or British Movement, it is clearly this type of then increasingly visible – if rarely electorally successful – far-right organisation to which he is alluding in a lyric that laments the increasingly closed and bitter mind of a friend. Although the mate looks good in his black boots and belt, and comes out with rhetoric so superficially rousing as to gain loud plaudits (or set the house ablaze), Weller insists to him, 'Hatred has never won for long.' The track, though, is no didactic treatise. This is partly because it is one of several on *Sound Affects* influenced by *Camelot and the Vision of Albion* by Geoffrey Ashe, a book whose thesis is that humanity has lost sight of spiritual goals. It seems safe to say that such lofty literary inspiration didn't underpin the Dead Kennedys' similarly themed 'Nazi Punks Fuck Off'.

Following a slightly remixed 'Start!', side one closed with 'That's Entertainment'. The song was inspired by 'Entertainment', a poem by one Paul Drew that appeared in an anthology issued by Weller's new publishing house, Riot Stories. Drew's free verse sarcastically counterpointed the cheesy showbiz phrase 'That's entertainment' with a list of social maladies, including crime and disease. Weller told *Mojo* in 2015, 'I wrote to him saying, Look is it all right if I nick a bit of your idea, man? And he said, It's fine, yeah.' Although Weller doesn't here pilfer lines the way he did from Adrian Henri in 'Tonight at Noon', he co-opts the phrase and the juxtaposition conceit. The fact that the two works are drawing from the same well is underlined by the fact that neither rhyme. For all that, it has to be said that the lyric is not that impressive. Like Drew's original, it's rather confused. Weller doesn't seem able to make up his mind about whether he's complaining about life's everyday mundanities (glumly feeding ducks in the park) or its unrepresentative traumas (a kick in the balls).

Musically, 'That's Entertainment' was one of what Buckler has described as 'the very rare occasions' when Weller presented the rhythm section with a finished song. Weller re-uses the chords from 'When You're Young'. However, he has now mastered the trick of not sounding like he's repeating himself. He scrubs an acoustic guitar in a bare arrangement a world removed from that single's busy, electric ambience. Foxton adds a nimble-fingered bass bottom, while Buckler keeps the percussion between subtle and undetectable. With his sublime mixing job, Coppersmith-Heaven truly stakes a claim for position of honorary fourth member: the subtle muffling of Weller's guitar and the slightly distant and helpless quality given to his vocals work to perfectly convey the notion of there being no love in the heart of the city.

Despite its bleakness, there is something poppy in the chant-like nature and atmosphericness of 'That's Entertainment'. It wasn't too much of a surprise, then, to in early 1981 see it in the charts. However, a convoluted story lay behind its hit-parade presence. Although the Jam, as was now standard, declined to pull a second 45 off their new LP, a West German single featuring it as an A-side was imported into the country. Its B-side was a live version of 'Tube Station' already available on the 'Going Underground' double-pack. The sleeve was a section of the *Sound Affects* cover, with the album's full cover artlessly occupying the back. Despite it constituting such an unprepossessing package, and despite the fact that Jam fans knew that second singles from albums were frowned upon by the group, the record sold sufficient quantities in Britain to be a minor hit. It may even have become a major hit were it not for Dennis Munday. 'I was in America and it was done behind my back and they actually misled [Paul],' says Munday. 'They said it was demand. It wasn't demand; they saw it as a way of re-promoting the album and selling more records.' When he discovered Polydor's ruse, Munday was so angry he ordered that the importing cease, thus causing the disc's chart progress to halt at number 21.

The four-minute 'Dream Time' opened side two of *Sound Affects*. Like 'Set the House Ablaze', it's a relative epic whose grim mood is assisted by pitiless yet excellent instrumentation. Its lyric recounts a nightmare in real time. The narrator finds himself wanting to run away from a town he knows too well, but finds himself unable to move his feet. He can't speak when he hears his name called. Perceiving an overwhelming emptiness beneath the surface gaiety he sees around him, he concludes that the world is a tough place and that this leaves him no option but to adopt a similar callousness. He is scared because people's hate and love 'comes in frozen packs.' This latter invoking of life options taken as casually and enjoyed as cursorily as shopping purchases doesn't ring true, coming across as Weller lazily using an easy but unconvincing target for social critique (rather like the Clash's equally unconvincing 'Lost in the Supermarket'). However, the track does hit the bullseye in its evocation of the surreal, fractured sense of unease created by a harrowing dream.

'Man in the Corner Shop' is another abrupt change in tone. Although in some senses as glum as the preceding track, it boasts a radiant melody, sweetly chiming guitar and a resplendent 'la-la-la-la-la' vocal refrain. The lyric is cleverly constructed. Each verse is a shift in focus: the first follows the thoughts of a self-employed shopkeeper who reflects that, despite his job being hard, he is glad to be his own boss; the second verse follows the thoughts of the last customer he served before closing, a man who, sick of factory work, is jealous of the shopkeeper; the third verse switches back to the shopkeeper and reveals he is jealous of the freedom enjoyed by the factory owner to whom he sells cigars. In the final verse, the district's residents congregate in church, where convention has it that they all enjoy equal footing. It's a lyric that ingeniously feels like both a relay and a loop. The track's aural sweetness, meanwhile, comes pretty close to exquisite.

'Music for the Last Couple' has a rare three-way Jam composing credit, one of only two in the group's corpus. This is a result of it being a glorified instrumental. It has four lines of verse, sung twice, about how thoughts of boats and trains make the narrator want to get away. The music is about as inconsequential, boasting a nicely keening guitar riff but little else of note. The fact that the first minute is taken up with ambient noises, including the buzzing of a fly, suggests a scrabbling for ways to finish a product so as to placate Dennis Munday's superiors. While it's admirable that the Jam spurned any temptation to include 'Going Underground' on the album – it could conceivably have added a nought to its sales figures – most Jam fans would probably have preferred its inclusion to this non-track.

In a way, 'Boy About Town' is the album's biggest triumph. Most would have assumed that, whatever his advancing songwriting skills, a life-affirming anthem was beyond a self-confessed miserable bastard like Weller. However, 'Boy About Town' perfectly evokes the elation it intends to. The narrator is as free and untroubled as a piece of paper fluttering in the wind. When Weller enunciates the line, 'There's more than you can hope for in this world,' it's genuinely heart-stirring, not least because it's suffused with a humility rare for him. The music is perfectly suited to the lyric's exuberant sentiment, with the icing on the cake a trumpet solo which raises the mood to new euphoric heights.

The album closes with the final tranche of the album's trio of doom-laden marathons in the shape of the four-minute 'Scrape

Away'. Despite technically being a different song, its length, second-person narration and indignant timbre give it the feel of 'Set the House Ablaze Part Two'. This time, Weller is telling his friend, 'Your twisted cynicism makes me feel sick.' He avers that his mate is jaded, ill and scraping away, and – in order to be cured – needs to effect a change of pace and place. Scrabbly guitar work, an unyielding bass line and bullet-shot drumming all collude to create yet more menace, which this time is intensified by disconcerting echo on Weller's spat vocals.

As with *Setting Sons*, the Jam were so late delivering the album that it caused problems with both mastering and the printing of the sleeve. 'There wasn't enough time to mix it,' says Munday. 'I remember cutting the lacquers for pressing. The guy was pulling his teeth out. We did thirteen or fourteen cuts. You can't ask a cutting engineer to do something that needs to be done in the studio … I thought several of the tracks needed a re-mix. But I had to get the thing out. But I'm talking about perfection. It's unlikely that other people would hear it.' Munday adds, 'I had to get it pressed in France because they were so late on delivering it that our factory had no capacity and the guy whose job it was to get the albums processed said, "Oh, I'm too busy. I don't want to know. Do it yourself." I went to the factory in Paris and the printers in Saint-Denis. I flew over and spent three or four days organising it.'

No deficiency in the sound quality could be inferred from the critical reaction, which was very good, or the public response, which was enough to send the LP to number two, making it the band's highest-charting album yet. Once again, the LP remained in the chart for 19 weeks. A quarter of a century later, Weller told Phil Sutcliffe that *Sound Affects* was the Jam's masterpiece. 'We had the sound together, the energy and there was a darker side to it, we were pushing ourselves.'

That the album was more than all this, though, was confirmed by the end-of-year *New Musical Express* readers' awards. As the

NME was the hippest of the four weekly UK music papers, appearing in its 'Pop Poll' was considered by recording artistes a genuine accolade. The Jam were not strangers to the upper reaches of said poll, having won the best group award the previous year and the best album award the last two years. Yet *Setting Sons* had probably benefitted from the fact that *London Calling* had been released so late in 1979 and thus been heard by commensurately fewer people. Although 1980 was another year with a November Jam LP and a December Clash album, this time it probably made no difference: *Sound Affects* was up against *Sandinista!*, a bloated triple-set viewed by most at the time as the Clash's grand folly. Moreover, the Jam swept the board, taking the prizes of best group, best bassist, best drummer, best guitarist, best male singer, best songwriter, best single, best album and best-dressed LP. Weller even picked up an unlikely additional prize. When a self-acknowledged miserable bastard is awarded the title Most Wonderful Human Being, he is unequivocally on a roll.

There was another award the following February. Although not possessed of the hip cachet of the *NME* poll, the *Daily Mirror* British Rock & Pop Awards was an important date in the music calendar. That it was broadcast at prime-time on both BBC television and BBC radio ensured that stars as big as David Bowie and Paul McCartney could be persuaded to turn up to accept its baubles. In its awards ceremony for records issued in 1980, 'Going Underground' took the prize for best single.

It was a significant achievement, perhaps even the final confirmation that the spirit of punk had conquered the mainstream. Yet Weller didn't want to know. While Buckler and Foxton trooped onto the stage to collect the award, Weller refused to get out of his seat. Munday: 'I was sitting next to them and he just said, "Can you go?" I thought, 'No, I'm not gonna do that.' I don't think it was pre-planned. He doesn't like that sort of thing, and I don't blame him. It was a bit cheesy.'

While the anti-showbiz gesture might have been valid – especially as the awards were presented by Smashie & Nicey-type DJ Dave Lee Travis and the matronly Sue Lawley – it was a little insulting to Jam fans who would have been proud of their heroes' achievement. It also raised the question of why Weller had attended the ceremony in the first place. 'It's just Paul,' says Munday. Referring to a future Weller composition, he elaborates, 'He just is, "My ever changing moods." That's how you sum him up.' What about Buckler and Foxton? 'They were different. Rick was probably the best out of the three, because he was never a problem. Bruce could get a bit up and down. There were times that he was unhappy, like when Paul would do something like that – it kind of leaves him and Rick in it.'

As Munday intimates, Weller's gesture could be viewed as a rebellious act in the long rock 'n' roll tradition of uncooperativeness with showbusiness corn. Additionally, Weller may well have been increasingly tempted to make such gestures because of the weight and glamour of a new status upon his shoulders. It was increasingly being suggested by media commentators that he was the Spokesman for a Generation, implicitly equating him with the early-to-mid-Sixties Bob Dylan and the mid-to-late-Sixties Mick Jagger. 'I don't think it sat well with him,' says Munday. 'I don't think he quite saw it. I think that he was pushed into that. That was more the press than him, because he always had a lot to say. He didn't speak for a generation, but he spoke for those people that followed him.'

'I never thought of myself as a spokesman for a generation,' says Weller. 'I was just writing songs that other people related to, kids my age. I wouldn't have been articulate enough or intelligent enough to be a spokesman for fucking anything apart from what I think myself. But I think I was in touch with what people similar to me were thinking and feeling. A lot of the best music does exactly that – it reflects the mood of the time and people's feelings.' Weller seems to be revising history a little, and not just because of the leadership role he envisaged for himself that he revealed to Chris Parry at their early meeting. The youth-leader status may have been projected on him by media and fans, but at the time he was visibly enjoying it – if in his own dour way. He frequently acquiesced to media gigs that clearly worked on the assumption that he was a figurehead of youth. Witness, for instance, his involvement in an October 1981 edition of BBC TV programme *Something Else* in which an upper-class schoolboy and a young, working-class factory worker described their wildly different lifestyles before meeting on camera. He also got involved in pop-magazine readers' discussions about current affairs, and, when he did so, adopted an air – painfully unnatural – of diplomacy and sagacity. However, it's no crime that his ego was as susceptible as any young man's would be to being placed on a pedestal higher even than that granted a standard rock idol. The incident at the *Daily Mirror* British Rock & Pop Awards, though, typified a strain within his mindset of nothing more elevated than scattershot petulance.

A YEAR OFF

The back cover of *Sound Affects* bore a joint Jam/Vic Coppersmith-Heaven production credit. This could have been interpreted as a slight shifting back in the power axis in the Jam's favour. However, it hardly seemed to auger that Coppersmith-Heaven's name – which had so far appeared on every single one of their discs – would never feature on a Jam record again. It was primarily replaced by that of Peter Wilson.

'That was more Paul,' says Foxton of the change. 'You're getting more experienced yourself, obviously. Paul had been demoing a lot of stuff with Pete and was getting on well with Pete Wilson anyway and we felt may be a time for a change. I wasn't so sure about it, but went with it.' Buckler offers, 'It was a matter of not really wanting to get stuck in any particular rut, wanting to move on and explore other things. I think that [Coppersmith-Heaven] brought some great things to the table. We probably had the view that to go to Pete Wilson would also do the same thing. It would give us a change and put a different perspective on it. I think for no more reason than that really.' Recalls Weller, 'Pete Wilson was this funny old hippie bloke who was the house engineer at Polydor Studios up in Stratford Place. I would do demos there on me own and I just liked the sound he was getting and I suppose I talked us all round to using him. I don't know if it was a diss on Vic. I thought I wanted to try something different.'

The averagely sensitive antennae will detect in the banalities above both lack of concrete answers and the whiff of a party line. Certainly, Dennis Munday tells a very different story about Coppersmith-Heaven. 'He was fired after *Sound Affects* because of the cost,' he says. By Polydor or the Jam? 'It was a combination of both. My boss particularly didn't like Vic at all. He found him to be obnoxious. And the album cost 120,000, which in those days was a phenomenal amount of money. It cost them 20,000 each personally. That's the way it was put to John [Weller]. I was called up very late to the meeting. If I could have stopped it, I would've. So it cost 120k – there were mitigating circumstances. You could blame me, you could Vic, but at the end of the day you could also blame the group because they *were* fucking about it in the studio. It's their money so you can't say anything. I think a lot of groups don't understand that when they do this sort of thing, it's their money. Polydor pay for it, but it comes back out of their sales ... It sold a phenomenal amount of records. I think 350, 400 thousand copies, so it wasn't a problem ... It just gave the company an opportunity to lever Vic out.'

Coppersmith-Heaven says he 'was very unaware of budgets at the time' and admits he 'probably did' spend an inordinately long time on mixes. However, he also says, 'In hindsight, if I hadn't spent the time creating the mixes I did, we probably wouldn't still be talking about the Jam forty years later. The mix is the final stage of the art, and if the mix isn't completed to the highest standard, the art is not complete.'

If the motivation for the Jam and their manager to go along with the coup had something to do with resentment about reduced profit margins, the logic can be questioned. Not only does Munday allege that *Sound Affects* was costly due to the Jam as much as their producer, but Buckler himself told author Ian Snowball, 'It would be Vic who'd remind us that time is money and that we only had a certain amount of time and money to play with.' Leaving that aside, *Setting Sons'* commercial success, for instance, was surely not unrelated to its splendid soundscapes, which Coppersmith-Heaven played such a large part in constructing.

However, finances may not actually have been as much of an impetus for the producer's dismissal as Munday suspects. Although the Jam members have made favourable remarks about Coppersmith-Heaven down the years – including in this text – they have not always been so complimentary. In 1981, Weller told journalist Chris Salewicz, 'I thought *Setting Sons* was a bit too slick, a bit too polished. I don't think it's a really true sound.' Foxton noted to Paolo Hewitt of *Sound Affects*, 'We were well disappointed, and that's when we parted with Vic ... It sounded flat. A lot of tracks were really quiet and we knew it was on the tape, it was all down.' It's not uncommon for recording artists to be mystifyingly unaware of the merits of their art, even when it has charmed critics and delighted the public. The Small Faces scoffed at praise for their power-pop classic 'Sha La La La Lee'. John Lennon was routinely dismissive of some of the Beatles' finest works. Robert Plant once said of 'Stairway to Heaven', universally recognised as Led Zeppelin's magnum opus, that it was not a song he particularly cared for. Musicians – indeed any creative person – can simply get too close to their work, and too embittered by frustrations relating to its creation, to see what others see in it. In failing to view *Setting Sons* and *Sound Affects* as artistic triumphs, the Jam slotted right into this tradition.

Coppersmith-Heaven must have been bewildered. He must also have been a little hurt, for he had been as loyal to the Jam as – previously – they had been to him. In 1980 – the very year he was ousted – he told Phil Sutcliffe, 'The opportunity to grow with the material is really important. That's why I've turned down dozens of other offers over the last two years and kept my involvement down to three acts ... That means I have time to go to Jam gigs in the US or Europe often. Getting the real picture of the band. I want to be as familiar with a song as the writer himself – or almost.' The Jam's treatment of Coppersmith-Heaven seems to betray an extraordinary lack of gratitude for, or even understanding of, his role in their rise from second-tier punks to pop gods.

If he is bitter, Coppersmith-Heaven doesn't betray it. 'I got a phone call from Paul, who said he wanted to make a change, and they wanted to do the next album with someone else or on their own,' he blandly says. 'It was a bit sad to leave the project at that stage, but now was a time to make plans and move in other directions. I'd had a fantastic five years working with them.'

Munday had, at least, no issue with the man who replaced Coppersmith-Heaven. 'Pete was one of our house studio engineers and he did an awful lot of the demos,' he says of Wilson. 'When Paul came in to demo his stuff, he always had Pete, and Pete played on a lot of the demos. It was a good move.'

'I suppose it was from the time of *Sound Affects* or perhaps even earlier,' says Peter Wilson of his engineering Weller's demonstration tapes. 'You'd do whatever came in. They'd come in and do demos and routine stuff, and Paul would come in on his own sometimes to knock down a rough demo version for the other members to hear, or just to work it out in his head. Sometimes he'd book two or three days and he'd run out of songs, so we'd just do covers for fun. Beatles covers and so on, or Kinks songs. I'd play drum kit often, or organ, or something like that, maybe even do some backing vocals. His mum often said that she preferred the demos. And I thought Paul did, actually. There was an argument that the demo of 'That's Entertainment' was in some ways superior, had a feel about it.'

Wilson hadn't heard any rumours in the Polydor corridors that the Jam were unhappy with Coppersmith-Heaven. 'I wasn't quite sure what was going on, 'cos they seemed to have a winning formula,' he says. 'They'd had big hits. Brilliant records. What did they want to change? But I wasn't going to question that … They wanted a change, I seemed like a safe pair of hands, Paul thought he could get on with me, I had something to contribute, I could do a good job.'

Wilson admits that, although of an older generation, he was a little intimidated at being offered the formal role of the Jam's producer. 'They were at the time absolutely massive,' he notes. 'I wouldn't say I was in awe of them, but I was very conscious that this was big shit. I wasn't going to mess up. I'd had some top-ten singles with Sham 69 and so on, but I couldn't have been called an

A-list producer.'

As he began working with them, Wilson didn't find the Jam offering him much in the way of enlightenment as to what they wanted from him that they hadn't obtained from his predecessor. 'Paul would say things that weren't very clear. He would sometimes say things like, "I want it to sound more real and less produced." He often said that. I didn't want to produce a record that didn't sound produced, because *my* name was on it. It wasn't just about pursuing the artist's intention. It's also about – with due respect to the artist – doing my job. So I wasn't quite sure what he meant by that. But, anyway, I think he was happy with what we did. I thought that the records that he'd done with Vic were great, but I suppose they were a bit guitar-heavy. There was a sort of progression, which you might say came to bigger fruition when he went on to do the Style Council.'

How did Wilson find Weller as a person? 'Quiet. I suppose shy in a way. He didn't dominate, as some people like Jimmy Pursey would dominate. I did four albums with Sham 69. I saw Pursey as an example of somebody who's very different and they dominate in not always a helpful way. Whereas Paul wouldn't dominate, but he had the respect because he was writing nearly all the songs, lead vocalist and so on.' Wilson reports Buckler and Foxton as 'easy to get on with' and that the Jam was a democracy. 'People put opinions forward and they were respected. Bruce did contribute a lot of harmonies and bass lines and things.'

'Funeral Pyre' b/w 'Disguises' was the first result of Wilson's work with the Jam to reach the public's ears. Released on May 29, 1981, it was the first of two singles in a row to feature the credit 'Produced by Peter Wilson and the Jam.'

Bill Smith's sleeve design was printed on thick black card. The front featured the 1897 monochrome painting *Funeral March* by Edvard Munch, best known for *The Scream*. 'That was what Paul wanted,' says Smith. 'It's a great picture and I think it worked really, really well with the single.' The sleeve revived the Immediate-style band logo because its 'spikiness' was adjudged to work well with the image. On the sleeve's other side was a confusing circular photograph of trees, whose rationale Smith vaguely recalls was that it worked well with the front cover. Alongside the trees was the A-side's lyric, which revealed Weller to have got away with smuggling the word 'pissing' onto daytime radio, perhaps a development of some sort considering his previous airplay-oriented self-censorship.

'Funeral Pyre' was the Jam's first single for 9½ months, and their first record of any kind for six months. What with their fanatical fanbase, its release was attended by considerable anticipation. That anticipation swiftly turned to disappointment.

The first warning sign about the record's quality was that 'Funeral Pyre' was another Jam composition attributed to all three members (the formal credit was 'Words: Paul Weller, Music: The Jam'). 'I don't recall him ever demoing it with me and I think they'd worked it out before I was in the studio with them, so I can't really comment on the writing process,' says Wilson of 'Funeral Pyre'. One thing the producer does feel able to comment on is the song's quality: 'It's a bit of a mess. Let's call it torrid. It's not an obvious candidate for a single.'

Indeed, one listen to the track raised the suspicion that the writing credit was not an honest or generous acknowledgment by Weller of his colleagues' inordinate contribution to an unusually instrument-heavy recording, but rather probably merely reflected the fact that Weller's inspiration at this point did not extend to being able to devise a song on his own. Moreover, 'Funeral Pyre' engendered a feeling of déjà vu: in its circular structure, atmosphere of foreboding and allusive condemnation of the weakness of the fascist character, it sounded for all the world like the third instalment of a song cycle started on *Sound Affects*. Weller,

Foxton and Buckler had already more than made their case on this subject and style in 'Set the House Ablaze' and 'Scrape Away', and that's not to mention the new track's resemblance in its epic feel and menacing timbre to the same LP's 'Dream Time'. The Jam sounded like they were treading water. The record also ignored a music-industry cardinal rule, which can be broadly stated as: an LP track can be a newspaper report, but a single should be a newspaper headline. To put it another way, 'Funeral Pyre' lacked punch, focus, brevity and immediacy.

This is not to say that it's bad, or even mediocre. It would have made a very good album track (if still one that involved the Jam repeating themselves). Weller's lyric states that those attracted to the cause – one not defined, but which can be guessed at in that it involves contempt for love and the strong getting stronger and the weak weaker – are throwing responsibility on a fire and thereby ultimately running the risk of fatally immolating themselves. This use of non-didactic metaphor is as valid as – and arguably preferable to – the likes of the Special AKA's 'Racist Friend', which bluntly urges listeners to shun anyone without a simpatico viewpoint on race, not to mention the Dead Kennedys' aforementioned self-explanatory 'Nazi Punks Fuck Off'. The music not only has a dark power, but contains the finest drumming ever heard on a Jam record – which, given the abilities of this particular drummer, is saying something. The final thirty seconds are effectively given over to Buckler, and he rises to the occasion with furious patterns that are utterly mesmerising.

The B-side was a cover. 'Paul wanted to record it,' says Wilson of 'Disguises'. Bunging a Who song on the flip didn't this time have the justification of a memorial. Wilson: 'It was a homage, if you like. I didn't get the impression it was because he hadn't got a song to put on the B-side.' However, if 'Funeral Pyre' was the best original song the band could muster for the A-side, it hardly suggested that they had much in the way of original material worth putting on the obverse. Although 'Disguises' was the lead track on the same 1966 *Ready Steady Who* EP that featured 'Batman Theme', Weller seems to have come across an alternate version on bootleg. 'It was referencing a Pete Townshend demo, which is slightly different to the Who's version,' says Wilson. That the Jam's interpretation features a lot of tape delay seems an instant contradiction of Weller's wish to make records that didn't sound 'produced'.

Underwhelming though 'Funeral Pyre' may have been, the same could not be said for its video (as promotional films were increasingly being called). That Bill Smith had the gumption to petition the band to let him write and direct it was the result of the reverse-process surrounding the 'Going Underground' promo. Recalls Smith, 'It was after that that I said, "Well hang on, you've just done a video promo that's based on my sleeve, so I think you should let me come up with some ideas for maybe your next video."' Smith's experience in this area amounted to, 'none whatsoever.' In a then heavily unionised country, this meant double-manning. 'The lighting and the cameramen and all that sort of thing couldn't apparently do anything unless there was someone there who had a director's card,' recalls Smith, who also states that the unionised director 'just sat in a caravan all day.'

The video was shot on a winter's day on Horsell Common, near Woking. Smith: 'I said to Paul and his manager, "We need to get quite a lot of people. Can we get people from locally?" Of course, everybody came and all of Paul's friends and acquaintances. We started shooting mid-afternoon and went right the way on into very late evening.' Despite the inevitable jollity of an occasion that took on the air of a triumphant homecoming, Smith was successful in his intent to make a finished article that was quite unsettling. The video opens with a dramatic sped-up zoom on Buckler's bass drum, which is followed by the sight of processions of people wielding flaming torches while the band play before an ever-rising bonfire. The Jam were far too unglamorous and modest to be much interested in the increasingly cinematic genre of the video, but this was a very impressive example of the developing artform. Unfortunately, the video was shown just once on British television. This was partly the consequence of the smallness of the UK media in 1981 (there was really no outlet for it other than *Top of the Pops*), but it was also partly down to the fact that the record climbed only as high as number four in the charts before its quick descent.

'It's not a surprise,' says Wilson. 'I think a lot of the chart position was to do with what you might call the fanbase rather than any new people hearing it on the radio saying, "Oh, I've got to have that."' It's a measure of how far the Jam had come in such a short space of time that number four qualified as a disappointment: it was only since late '79 – a matter of eighteen months – that they had even been able to crack the top ten. 'Funeral Pyre' was later remixed for its appearance on posthumous Jam compilation *Snap!* 'The vocals really needed to come up,' explains Wilson. 'It needed to be a bit clearer.' No amount of work, though, was going to make the track seem a classic. 'To me, 'Funeral Pyre' could have been written two years before,' says Munday. 'He'd always gone forward with his songwriting and he hadn't gone forward there.' However, Foxton says he never viewed 'Funeral Pyre' as an artistic dip. 'I just thought it was a slightly different, moody vibe,' he reasons.

Buckler, asked how he got such a starring role, says, 'That was something that, as a backing track, myself and Bruce were playing with. Then Paul came in with some lyrics one day and we put that together.' Buckler also demurs from the idea that 'Funeral Pyre' was substandard, and does so quite strongly. 'We just really felt that it had something. It was just one of those songs you think, "Well this is the one."' He does concede, 'It was a bit of an unusual one,' but adds, 'We were never known necessarily to go for the bleeding obvious. That would have been boring.' For Foxton, the track's publishing split underlines his regret about the set-in-stone verbal agreement regarding other Jam songwriting attributions. 'We all got a credit on that one and there was not that much difference between writing that and writing 'Tube Station' or any of them,' he notes.

In retrospect, 'Funeral Pyre' was the beginning of the Jam's artistic decline. This was hardly obvious at the time: only the most precipitous would posit artists to be on an unstoppable slide on the basis of a very good album being followed up with a quite-good single. However, we now know that the Jam would never again quite scale the artistic heights of *Setting Sons*, 'Going Underground' and *Sound Affects*.

Nineteen eighty-one was the only year of their existence as a recording outfit in which the Jam failed to release an album.

Since the very start of their contract, Polydor had hustled the band for product, whether by rushing them into the studio to record their first single as though afraid the punk bubble would burst, persuading them for similar reasons to put out a second album with unseemly haste, or holding their feet to the fire in order to facilitate Yuletide releases for *Setting Sons* and *Sound Affects*. Only during the troubled gestation period of *All Mod Cons* had the label shown any particular patience with regard to delivery of material, and even then it managed to ensure that that album came out a hardly unreasonable twelve months after its predecessor.

Things were initially no different with what would become the Jam's next album, *The Gift*. 'There was a lot of pressure,' recalls Wilson of its recording. 'The record company wanted the album out for Christmas.' The producer remembers the pressure also coming from Weller's father, who he says was 'in and out all the time.' Wilson notes, 'John wanted to line up a tour to promote the album, so it's, "Paul, when is the album gonna be finished?"' However, it eventually became clear that the now traditional

November release of a Jam album simply wasn't possible. 'That would have meant delivering it to the record company by September,' says Wilson. 'Well, that wasn't going to happen. We were recording almost up to Christmas, and we never finished in '81 – we had to come back in '82.'

The year of 1981, in fact, would see the release of only three self-written Jam songs. Munday says Weller's lack of productivity was 'fairly deliberate,' adding, 'I don't think he wanted to do an album that year.' However, he suggests an additional reason for the slowdown: 'It was after *Sound Affects* that he started to perhaps give thought to maybe the Jam wasn't going to continue ... He was listening to other stuff. He was listening to soul music. He was listening to all sorts of stuff. He was changing direction as a songwriter.' While the change of direction part is palpably true, Munday's additional comment, 'I don't think he dried up,' seems just as categorically untrue. Weller himself later admitted to Paolo Hewitt of this period, 'I, as a songwriter, had exhausted all my supplies and ideas.'

Buckler observes, 'At that particular period, what I really can remember was planning what we were going to do. That sort of thinking had kicked in. We knew roughly what our album commitments were going to be, so therefore what our touring was going to be and all that sort of stuff. The whole thing started to turn into very much a planned campaign. We could look six months in advance and know exactly what we were going to be doing.' Of the sudden lack of productivity, he says, 'I think that could have been one of the contributing things. Paul obviously knew what the pressures were going to be in advance, that he was going to have to come up with particular products by a particular time and there did seem probably to be no end to this treadmill, simply because of the way that the contracts were. If they said, "You've got to do five albums," then you're contracted to do those and that's that. We hadn't really thought too much in the early days of saying,

"Well look, maybe we'll only sign for one album because then we can think about it a bit more, we can plan things." I think that just got to Paul in the end where he decided that he didn't want to be on this treadmill.'

Once again, though, Weller disavows pressure, even if this time ambiguously. Asked if an annual requirement for a full album plus a clutch of standalone A- and B-sides was too much in terms of his natural level of productivity, he says, 'Not really, because pretty much most of the time I fulfilled it – apart from the year you're talking about. I just needed a break from it really. It was a big workload. But we had a break from it and we came back with an album like *The Gift*, which is another one of my favourites, another great record ... I think I was just creatively tired by that time. I just needed a little break from it to come up with another twelve songs.' Was it a writer's block? 'I don't know. I just didn't really want to do it. I wanted a little time away.'

Not that the group were idle. In only four months of 1981 did they fail to play gigs. Weller as an individual, meanwhile, was rather busy. During this period, he became a publisher and a record-label head. 'Giving something back, but also to have a channel for communication for people,' is Weller's rationale for these activities. He and Dave Waller were company directors of Riot Stories, set up in January 1980 to publish streetwise poetry and prose. Although essentially a mail-order outfit, Riot Stories was actually both prolific and aesthetically impressive. Probably its most notable offering was *Jambo* by Dave Ward. Jambo was a character quite visible at the time, also turning up in prose form in the likes of *Transatlantic Review* and teenage magazine *Kicks*. Essentially a cypher, he enabled Ward to note the sort of minutiae of proletarian and unemployed life not usually given much exposure in the media. As it branched out into other areas, Riot Stories was even responsible for the first-ever Small Faces biography, if a slim one, in the shape of Terry Rawlings' *All Our*

Yesterdays. Had it not been for tragedy, the company may even have blossomed into something bigger and more mainstream.

Weller's Respond Records was initially funded by Polydor. Weller had grand plans for the label, publicly expressing a hope that its name would become a byword for quality the way Motown's had once been. Munday was sceptical. 'I just couldn't see how him and his father could put the time in to run their own careers and a label,' he says. 'If you look at the most successful labels, they're not [run by] artists. [Motown's] Berry Gordy, Chris Blackwell at Island – they're music men rather than musicians ... The Jam were at their peak then and they had to record songs, they had to go on tour. John was managing the Jam. I've been a label manager. I know what it's like. As a product manager, I would handle perhaps a dozen different groups. But I had 52 weeks of the year to do that. I wasn't going to go on tour for three months, or go in the studio.' Meanwhile, Weller seems to have been sceptical with regards to Polydor's attitude toward Respond. Before long, he had transferred the label to A&M Records.

Weller's Motown-level quality ambitions were eyebrow-raising at the time, but they become close to laughable when examining Respond's ultimate roster, which consists of a litany of unfamiliar or unimpressive names: A Craze, the Big Sound Authority, Dolly Mixture, the Main T Possee, M.E.F.F., ND Moffatt, the Questions, Vaughn Toulouse, the Rimshots, Urban Shakedown and Tracie Young. 'I didn't rate the artists he signed,' says Peter Wilson. 'And he never asked me to work on any of them, which was fine. He did put quite a lot of work into Respond early on, but I didn't think the records were very good. I don't know quite what was in his mind. It was sort of teenage pop music.' Of all Respond's artists, only Tracie Young – whose records were released under her first name – made serious waves, and those were restricted to having one top-ten hit and being voted Most Fanciable Human Being (Female) by the readers of *Smash Hits*.

174

Ironically, Respond was outperformed by Jamming, a record label Weller set up separately to be run by Tony Fletcher, Jam fan and publisher of the music magazine *Jamming*, originally a humble fanzine titled *In the City*. Apocalypse, Rudi and Zeitgeist may no more be names to conjure with than Respond's artist list, but the six records they recorded between them all made the UK independent chart. This was quite an achievement considering a label budget so meagre that it could be thrown off course by Fletcher drawing his £17 weekly wages, itself only the equivalent of what he had previously claimed on the dole.

Whatever the failings of his three ventures, Weller could assert that – as he put it in 'Sounds from the Street' – at least he was doing something. 'No one else was doing it,' he says. 'The Clash, bless their hearts, for all their fucking chat and all the rest of it, I didn't see them doing that.'

One day in 1981, Weller came into Dennis Munday's office to play him a cassette tape containing a demo of a new song. 'I listened to it and before I could say anything, he threw it in the bin and said, "That's a fucking load of shit" and walked out the office,' recalls Munday. 'When I spoke to him, I said, "Well, it's a demo. You don't sit there and say, "Oh that's great." It's work in progress. You gotta produce it."' Some might suggest that Weller's first adjudgment on 'Absolute Beginners' – released as a single coupled with 'Tales from the Riverbank' on October 16, 1981 – was in fact correct.

The front of the single's sleeve featured a moody photograph of rows of rooftops, with an industrial chimney stack in the foreground. It was so evocatively in the style of kitchen-sink cinema dramas and early *Coronation Street* title credits that one would be forgiven for immediately assuming it to be the work of a professional snapper, but in fact the picture was taken by none other than Rick Buckler, who filled the longueurs of touring life with his shutterbug hobby. Its relation to the A-side's lyric, though, remains mysterious. The spindly font superimposed on the picture spurned both previous Jam logos. The record's back cover, as well as its inlay lyric sheet, featured colour Jam images taken by a young Surrey photographer called Derek D'Souza. Weller had been impressed by the amateur gig pictures D'Souza habitually sent in to the fan club, run by Weller's mother and sister. Accordingly, he instructed his mum to give D'Souza a call. It was a Cinderella-goes-to-the-ball scenario that as much as anything sums up the Jam's genuine common touch. As D'Souza told Guy Martin of *GetSurrey* in 2014, 'That would never happen now, a band would normally choose a big-name photographer. And even then it was unusual, having the family running a fan club.'

The A-side's title phrase was already familiar to those who had had heard of Colin MacInnes' celebrated 1959 youth-culture novel of the same name. It would become familiar to many more people five years hence upon the release of Julien Temple's motion-picture adaptation of the same book, which itself bequeathed another single called 'Absolute Beginners', this one written and recorded by David Bowie. Bizarrely, although Weller would read it later and be impressed enough to in 2007 choose it as his castaway book on *Desert Island Discs*, he hadn't read MacInnes' tome when he wrote the Jam song named after it.

While the cold, skeletal likes of Wire and Gang of Four had been evident as an influence on *Sound Affects*, Weller was less successful in decanting into it an album he has said he was inspired by at the time: Michael Jackson's 1979 offering *Off the Wall*. 'Absolute Beginners', however, made clear the new black direction in which Weller wished to take the Jam. The track starts dramatically with an explosion of brass. The stylistic intentions are further demonstrated by the fact of a funky rhythm track. Weller was inspired these days not just by the Jackson disc but 'Chant No. 1 (I Don't Need This Pressure On)', a hit earlier in '81 by Spandau

Ballet.

Unfortunately, whereas the Ballet boys created an impressive concoction whose flaring brass runs were a fully integrated and delightful component of their song, the horn charts on 'Absolute Beginners' just do not mesh with the Jam's instrumentation. Moreover, while splinters of guitar on Spandau's record perfectly complement the brass, here Weller's alternately chugging and growling axework clashes with it. Consequently, despite tilting for passion and drama, 'Absolute Beginners' is stiff and unconvincing.

Another clash comes in the fact that the uptempo soul on offer here is associated with a euphoria or assertiveness strangely absent in this song's expressions of uncertainty. Weller is unhappy about something which he doesn't define beyond 'I saw no warmth in life – no love was in my eyes.' The words sometimes approach poetry, such as when he states that a feeling he had of emptiness quietly turned and walked away, but ultimately are as under-developed and without impact as the music.

Wilson recalls Weller's announcement of the new direction for the band amounting to, '"Here's the song, I'd like some horns on it." Not a lot of discussion, really.' Of the trumpets played by Martin Drover, Michael Laird and Luke Tunney, Wilson says, 'We should have maybe got in an arranger. I did the arrangement in as much as I wrote the notes out ... but Paul produced most of the tune in his head and he had a view about the instrumentation, so I went with it.' Weller's inexperience of orchestrating a brass section shows in an over-trebly arrangement. 'If I did that arrangement again I would put in perhaps some tenor sax,' says Wilson. 'Paul was always averse to tenor saxes and trombones and things. In a horn section, you might want something down the bottom just to give it weight.'

Both Buckler and Foxton say they were neither surprised nor unhappy about brass appearing on a Jam single, trilling the familiar refrain about the group's innate and admirable itch to expand its boundaries. However, the bassist also reveals, "Absolute Beginners' was one of my least favourite singles. I wasn't quite sure about the song being released.' "Absolute Beginners' was a step forward, but it was a bit messy,' says Munday. 'It probably needed Martin Rushent to produce that, or Trevor Horn. It doesn't gel. It doesn't quite work. Perhaps it needed to be played in. I think it would have been better to go with 'Tales [from] the Riverbank'.' Wilson offers, 'There was discussion at the time about whether 'Tales from the Riverbank' should be the A-side, though whether that was by the band or the record company I don't know. I think 'Tales from the Riverbank''s a great song, but perhaps not as snappy and radio-friendly.'

While 'Tales from the Riverbank' may have been too slow and vague to have made for an A-side, its experimentation is more successful than that of 'Absolute Beginners'. A thin, serpentine guitar part and intriguingly-mixed percussive effects decorate a Weller peroration on a 'dream mixed with nostalgia,' a harking back to the rustic, waterside bliss of a part of his life when innocence trumped cynicism. Only a few instances of Weller not bothering to find a proper rhyme and of inappropriately heavy drumming mar an unusual and absorbing creation.

The public were as unsure about the record as Foxton. Once more the Jam proved to have enough core aficionados to send their new single to number four, but once more the wider populace – unencumbered by a fan's sense of duty or loyalty – declined to improve that position.

Although the sleeve for 'Absolute Beginners' was officially designed by Bill Smith, the record's inlay sheet featured the following wording: 'Rick - front photo; Bruce – sleeve layout; Paul – art direction. Cheers Bill!' Smith laughingly comments, 'That might say it all.' A pointed 'Fuck you'? 'It probably is. By that time, it was very much, "We'll come up with everything, we'll do everything, can you just put it together for us?" As a designer, you might as well forget it, basically.' However, Smith's dismissal as the Jam's art director after four years in the role might perhaps have been less blunt were it not for the group's reaction to his video for 'Absolute Beginners'.

Smith wrote the video's script with famous rock photographer Gered Mankowitz, who had provided the dynamic photography for the back cover of *This is the Modern World*. Smith: 'Paul really liked Gered and liked his photography so I said, "Well, we could do the video together." I came up with the concept and the script for it. Everybody approved it, the record company and the band. We shot it over a day or a day-and-a-half. Paul saw the rushes through the day and liked a lot of the images. We had a meeting scheduled to show them the first cut, which I took through to them. They didn't throw their hands up in despair and go, "This is awful." They just said, "We'd like to change this" or, "We'd like to change that." I made my notes, I went away and then the next day I got a phone call, probably from Dennis, saying, "The Jam no longer want to use you or that video. They're shooting another video, so please put a stop on anything you're doing." That was it.'

Of his film, Smith says, 'It was a performance video with some acting bits and pieces in it as well, and some extras that had relevance to the lyrical content. It was a fairly harmless video, so I don't know quite why they got so upset about it and why they thought they had to go and do another one. By that time, Paul and I had reached a point where he probably thought he knew better than I did about what was a good design and what was a bad design and I suppose he thought he had a better video in his head than the one I'd produced ... I've never understood what it was they disliked so much. I just think it was more that maybe this was a good way of putting a full stop on our collaboration.' Smith says there had been no particular needle between him and the band, but adds, 'We became further and further removed. It was less my input and more what they wanted. It didn't begin and end with *Sound Affects*, but that was the first real point where [they said], "This is what we want." Completely different from *In the City*, where it was, "This is my idea of the band and what you're about and what I think you're representing" and they were quite happy with it ... Where I met the band to show them the video was the last time I spoke to anyone in the band until probably 2005 or six.'

Although he says he is impressed by the artwork of Weller's solo albums, Smith says he felt that the design on the remainder of the Jam's releases after his departure – one album and three singles – was not up to the standard he had set. Should he be so inclined, Smith could further brood on what fate did to his Jam legacy. At the time of his dismissal, for all he knew the band still had another five or ten years of life. As it happened, they would be defunct within little over a year. This left him in the excruciating position of being almost, but not quite, responsible for the design of their entire oeuvre.

TRIUMPHANT REVITALISATION

As 1981 progressed, Weller once more found his songwriting touch returning to him.

Undeterred by the artistic and (relative) commercial failure of 'Absolute Beginners', he continued to turn away from white rock, and even the black R&B of the Jam's early days, and to venture further into the territory of modern soul and funk. To this end, he brought in more musicians and different instruments to populate the Jam's soundscapes. His Jam colleagues had, of course, little option but to come along for the ride. Whether they did so with enthusiasm, or even armed with the requisite musical abilities, has been a matter of debate ever since.

In furtherance of Weller's new visions, *The Gift* would be graced by the work of trumpeter/trombonist Steve Nichol and saxophonist Keith Thomas. The pair's contributions would fit into the Jam's sound far better than had those of the trumpet trio on 'Absolute Beginners'. The two were quite short in the tooth. Explains Wilson, 'Paul had this policy of using young people if at all possible, rather than seasoned veterans. That was something he believed in quite strongly.' In devising the more complicated horn riffs, Weller took advantage of Wilson's ability to write musical notation. 'If they needed to be written out, he'd sing them to me,' says the producer. 'If they were very simple, he'd just sing them to the [musicians].'

Weller's expanding horizons were interpreted by some as a sign of him becoming bored by the limitations of a rock trio, with all the ramifications that had for the Jam's future. For his part, Buckler seems to have perceived in them nothing more portentous than a thirst for fresh musical waters. 'It certainly started to pull his guitar playing back,' Buckler recalls. 'We all noticed that, especially with things like 'Town Called Malice'. It led onto Paul's evolvement, but all I can really say is, at the time, it was just another way of experimenting.' Foxton says he wasn't worried that the changing

Jam sound might alienate their audience. 'We did what we felt was right,' the bassist reasons. 'I know it sounds big-headed. We just wanted to [do] what we would term pushing forward and trying different things, not just write for a particular market. We hoped that what we were doing appealed to our audience, but we weren't going to just find a formula and stick to it. That just wasn't us. We'd go out on a limb and, nine times out of ten, it worked.'

The Gift was recorded in AIR London, Oxford Street. Sessions took place in the second half of '81 and, after a break, concluded early the following year. Wilson says that 'hardly any' of the album's songs were demoed beforehand, adding, 'They were put together in the studio, really. That is a luxury that successful bands often go to. Budget is much less of an issue.' More of an issue was paucity of songs. The end-of-year hiatus was necessary so that Weller could compose the remaining half of the album. Wilson says of Weller, 'He was, I wouldn't say struggling, [but] there's not a magic tap you can turn on. You just have to work round it.' However, Wilson notes of 'Circus', an instrumental whose composition was credited to Foxton, 'It's not a strong track, but we might have been short of tracks.' Wilson recalls that Buckler was also given an opportunity to contribute an instrumental. 'We spent a day getting really nowhere, which was a waste of a day in retrospect. That didn't go down too well with Paul.'

An anecdote has emerged from the *Gift* sessions involving Buckler observing to Weller that his latest creations were 'not drummer's songs.' Wilson can see what Buckler means in that he was being required to play in a 'slightly different way; they weren't guitar-rock things.' However, he also says that he detected no lack of whole-heartedness from either Buckler or his partner in the rhythm section as they helped Weller tread his new musical path, including on 'Precious', which Buckler has stated is the only Jam song he doesn't like, and 'The Planner's Dream Goes Wrong', unanimously considered the album's stinker.

While the rhythm section may have exhibited a game attitude, Weller was in a peculiar mood during the making of the LP. Observes Buckler, 'Paul's always been a very tense guy, especially when you're under pressure to record stuff. We were all fairly tense at that time. But Paul was becoming more and more so during the year.' Citing the fact of Weller being domiciled in London once more (this time in Pimlico), Buckler says, 'He'd detached himself from the band.' Foxton also felt Weller was restless, saying, 'He certainly didn't appear totally happy.' Munday observes, 'It was a difficult album all round. It was very difficult to produce. It was very tense in the studios.'

'I'd put it down to pressure of the music business, the demands on Paul as a songwriter, the touring,' Foxton expands. 'It's not all glamour and at the time, particularly when we were abroad, Paul was miserable. You think, "Well, fucking hell, we're in Japan, what's up with you?" Wouldn't tell him because didn't want another argument or whatever. You think, "Well, if he's in a bit of a mood I'll leave him, he'll get over it, or it'll blow over." You get to know each other so well, you know when to mention something and when not to.' Foxton never found Weller inclined to bare his soul to his colleagues: 'He had quite a long-term girlfriend at the time. He would have maybe discussed his concerns to her. But he didn't really say, "Guys, I've got a bit of a problem here."' Like Foxton, Buckler appears to have attributed a change in Weller's mood to pressures related to his elevated profile. 'He hated the idea of having to have bars on his windows when he lived in London, because he obviously felt under threat," he says. 'There were pressures that he was beginning to feel that myself and Bruce escaped from.' Munday, though, has a different theory. 'I think that Paul had an inkling at the time that things weren't gelling ... If you listen to that [album], that's half the Jam, half the Style Council.'

Weller later wrote in a Jam fan-club newsletter that he had been considering his decision to leave the Jam 'for almost a year.' It's also the case that in the final year or so of the Jam's existence, Weller's public persona was as belligerent as his Jam colleagues found it in private. His print interviews in particular exhibited a grating generalised animus, leading to accusations of him being 'snotty.' In retrospect, it all makes sense if there was something on his mind that carried the potential to have a profound, even devastating, impact on his career, family and workmates.

Whatever the tenseness of *The Gift*'s recording process, and whatever the bleak long-term prospects Weller's increasing gloominess may have implied for the Jam, none of this was visible come January 29, 1982 and the release of the group's third double-A-sided single, 'Town Called Malice'/'Precious'. Certainly, no one could possibly have extrapolated from this record's artistic and commercial triumph that, come the end of the year, the Jam would be no more. Hailed as both a return to form and a successful conclusion to the Jam's quest to incorporate soul-based sounds into their music, it entered the charts at number one.

That 'Malice' was the side favoured by DJs was once again the consequence of Munday engaging in what he viewed as noble-cause corruption. 'I just said it was another pressing fuck-up,' he says. 'My view on that is it's a white lie.' The fact that the Jam were not long for this world was fortunate in at least this respect. How many more times could they have been expected to buy the same excuse?

It was the second successive Jam single to take its title (albeit this time punningly) from a novel Weller had not read, this one being *A Town Like Alice*, Nevil Shute's 1950 tale of the adventures of an English émigré in Australia. The title may have entered Weller's brain via an Australian-produced TV mini-series based on the book from the previous year, or else by the osmosis involved in the occasional appearance in TV schedules of the novel's 1956 movie adaptation.

The song had even less to do with its ostensible inspiration than had the 'Absolute Beginners' single. The subject of 'Town Called Malice' is Woking and the economic and spiritual poverty of its inhabitants. Weller's lyric, like that of 'Saturday's Kids', contains references to local landmarks, him talking of the place's train track and its recently closed dairy yard. This time, though, his observations about lifestyles and mentalities are not dripping with scorn. Moreover, his (brilliant) observation that a big decision in this town involves choosing between beer or new gear for the kids is not an accompaniment to resignation. The traditional contempt of the cultured product of an uncultured hinterland is present in Weller's depiction of lonely housewives 'hanging out their old love letters on the line to dry' – and eminently forgivable because the latter may well be the best line he's ever written. Otherwise, however, his lyric is suffused with compassion and hope, even if the latter is something he effectively concedes has to be forced. He kicks off proceedings with the narrator observing to (implicitly) his spouse that they should stop dreaming of a quiet life because it's hardly a likely prospect. This, though, is not a putdown: although the narrator implores his partner to cease daydreaming, he also admonishes her to stop apologising for their lack of achievement, on the grounds that life is short and they should make the best of their surroundings, and even – where they can – change them. The narrator concludes his peroration by observing that, although he could go on for hours about the lack of fulfilment and lack of happiness which drapes the area, he'd rather spend the time trying to inject some joy into it.

The lyric, littered with eminently quotable lines and couplets, and with imagery as grainy as an Alan Sillitoe novel or a Ken Loach film, ranks as one of Weller's masterpieces. So much so that it pretty much makes irrelevant the ordinariness of the music it's set in. There's little wrong with the melody, which is appropriately sad and replete with the key shifts a songsmith as expert as Weller knows are necessary to maintain interest. The instrumentation, though, is functional where it's not derivative. Unlike, say, 'I Got By In Time', 'Town Called Malice' doesn't assimilate black music but simply appropriates it. The track's pumping bass riff (echoed on organ) is almost a straight lift from that of 'You Can't Hurry Love' by the Supremes. Buckler's cymbal-heavy drum beat is a simple imitation of a hundred and one Motown rhythm tracks. The refrain of "Ooh-ooh-ooh, ye-eah" is also Motown-generic. On a first, shallow hearing, the track sounds not Motownesque but like a Motown cover. That on subsequent hearings it doesn't come across as uninspired is only because the listener appreciates that its accompanying words are leagues beyond those of – for all their estimable popcraft – any Motown composer.

The other side of the single also confused being influenced by someone with mugging them. 'Papa's Got A Brand New Pigbag' by Pigbag was a joyous, brass dominated instrumental that had been a permanent fixture in the UK indie chart over much of 1981 but had not yet been a mainstream hit. It was most notable for its horn riff, but its bassline was also memorable. The Jam used something extremely similar to the latter in 'Precious'. That 'Precious' also features wah-wah guitar work that veers toward generic also helps give it a second-hand feel. The difference with 'Malice', though, is that the music is overall a fine concoction and the fulcrum of the track's aesthetic accomplishment.

'The way it was done was completely different,' recalls Wilson of the development of 'Precious'. 'We did a demo of it at Polygram Studios. It may have been just me and Paul. I got a bass drum off a multi-track, put it on a quarter-inch tape, made a tape loop of the bass drum and ran that round and round and round, recorded it onto a multi-track and then just put everything else one thing at a time. So when Rick came in, he wouldn't be playing bass drum, he'd just be playing snare drum and hi-hat and so on. The loop's what's on the record.'

Weller's lyric was reasonably good – there's always room for love songs rooted in the vulnerability in which Weller specialised at this point in time – but sentiments like 'Your precious love that means so much' hardly have the gravitas of a statement like 'Town Called Malice'. The music, though, positively cooks. Buckler's clattering drums are tricked up to dramatic effect, Weller's vocal shows utter commitment to his estuary soul-man role, the wah-wah guitar is infectious enough to make one understand why it became a cliché in the first place, but most pleasing of all are the horns. With their lung-busting contributions, Nichol and Thomas exhilaratingly take Jam music places it's never been before, including the field of jazz.

'Town Called Malice' was the second successive Jam single to feature a surprisingly evocative aerial poverty tableau provided by Buckler. (The back featured more of those Mod-associated arrows, perhaps because Sixties mods had liked Motown.) The record itself was the second Jam number one to be accused of grabbing the top spot by unfair marketing methods. The early Eighties was the era of the twelve-inch single. For a brief period – before the vinyl market was decimated by the arrival of the compact disc – the format seemed ultra-modern. It was an advancement in the sense that it granted greater aural clarity to tracks previously restricted in fidelity by the squashed-up grooves of seven-inch singles. However, it also led to the dubious phenomenon of the extended version, whereby – in either an attempt to provide value for money or else to induce people to buy the more expensive twelve-inch version of a single (or even both seven-inch and twelve-inch versions) – a song was made longer than the 'standard' iteration, often by contrived methods. 'Town Called Malice'/'Precious' was the first UK Jam single to receive a twelve-inch release. The latter featured, instead of the studio version of 'Malice', a live version recorded at Hammersmith Palais the previous December, plus a version of 'Precious' that was 2½ minutes longer than the not-included standard version. It being the case that sales of the two versions of the Jam release were aggregated by the chart compilers, the Stranglers – whose 'Golden Brown' was prevented by the Jam disc(s) from becoming their only official UK number one – had some cause for grievance. Not according to Munday, though. 'Well, everyone did it, so if it was fair for every band it was fair for the Jam,' he shrugs. It was also the second Jam number one to remain at the summit for three weeks, once again a sufficiently long spell to at least suggest that marketing methods were less important to its success than the fact that it was genuinely liked beyond Jam completists.

It wasn't liked so much, apparently, by its composer and producer. 'He wasn't that impressed with it,' says Peter Wilson of Weller regarding 'Town Called Malice'. 'I wasn't sure at the time either. His dad insisted it was brilliant, and in retrospect his dad was absolutely right. I don't know why I couldn't quite see it. Sometimes you're too close to things.' Wilson was 'very moved' to see the track used in *Billy Elliott*, the 2000 movie about an aspiring ballet dancer set against the backdrop of the 1984/85 miner's strike. 'It was used so appropriately. It complemented the film and it complemented the record.'

'I never, ever thought he lost form,' says Munday of Weller. 'Like all songwriters, he's going to go through the period where he can't write as much, and you can't write great songs all the time. I was personally never worried.' However, there's no denying that the single was a triumphant revitalisation for the Jam. That triumphant revitalisation was completed on February 18, 1982 when the band – at number one for the second week – were granted by *Top of the Pops* the symbolic accolade of being allowed to 'perform' both sides of their record back-to-back. They were the first act to do so since 1966, when the Beatles had mimed to their double-A 'Day Tripper'/'We Can Work It Out'. 'I loved it because

I loved the historical thing that before us it had been the Beatles,' Weller says. 'I thought we were in very esteemed company.' If any moment truly constituted the anointing of the Jam as the most important artists to have emerged from the punk revolution it was this. Says Munday, 'I think it *was* symbolic in a way, what the Jam meant.'

They certainly currently meant more than the other candidate for keeper of the punk flame. The public perception of the Jam and the Clash as bookends and rivals was given formal voice in 1981 by the works of Tony Marchant. A 21-year-old clerk from London's East End, he was actually one of the writers given a break by Weller's Riot Stories, who published a selection of his poems when he was eighteen. Marchant's first play was produced in 1980. In 1981, he wrote *London Calling*, a play inspired by the Clash, and another called *Dealt With*. The two were combined in a double bill with the umbrella title *Thick as Thieves*, produced regionally in '81 before moving to London's West End.

Until recently, deciding whether it was the Clash or the Jam who were the best was both as difficult and pointless as the similar Sixties debate about the Beatles and the Rolling Stones. Each of those latter groups had possessed a profound socio-political significance, if one not as ideologically explicit as those of the groups which emerged from punk. They had also each made wonderful music. Choosing one over the other was nothing more than a parlour game: most people loved them both, and were made proud to be British by the fact that such a dilemma even notionally existed. The Clash-Jam debate, however, had over the last year taken a turn that the Beatles-Stones discussion never really did. The Clash had undermined their own appeal, both aesthetically and sociologically. Weller had been disgusted by *London Calling*'s glossy production, internationalist subject matter and occasionally smooth arrangements. He fulminated to Dave Schulps, '*London Calling*'s a cop-out. It is for British people anyway. It's alright for

Americans ... I used to be a fan of theirs, but ever since they started getting it together in America every picture of them you see is this quasi-American gangster sort of stuff and there are all the Americanisms in their music.' To Chris Salewicz, he complained that the record's closing track, and minor US hit, 'Train In Vain' 'sounds like something by Nils Lofgren.'

Although that point of view now seems wrong-headed – it's long been the consensus that *London Calling*'s aesthetic brilliance made irrelevant its supposed compromises – before long few were doubting that the Clash had become a self-parody. *Sandinista!* did contain some great music amongst a welter of garbage, but the cover showed the group draped in a ridiculous jumble of military and rebel clothing. As well as purveying guerrilla chic that seemed absurd next to the Jam's down-to-earth smart-casual look, the Clash were neglecting their home country. While there's nothing wrong with broadening horizons, it creates problems if a group have nailed their colours to the mast of propagating their own culture and analysing their native society's faults. Especially so when that group are frequently working and sometimes living in a particular foreign country with which they have ostentatiously professed to be bored. The Clash were caught in a quandary which wasn't less real for it being slightly unfair: when they wrote songs about foreign topics they were criticised for being out of touch, but when they wrote songs about issues in Britain, they were met with a what-would-you-know-about-it-these-days? response. Album-wise, the Clash had sat out 1981, their sole new record being 'This is Radio Clash', a mediocre, badly produced funk single. Its self-aggrandizing lyric was not unusual. However, while few had minded the band mythologizing themselves in anthems when they genuinely did seem to be the Greatest Rock 'n' Roll Band in the World, in the context of their decreasing songcraft and increasing irrelevance (it had been a year since they were a top-40 singles act in the UK), it now served to make them seem pitifully deluded.

190

The buzz surrounding their reverence-soaked *Top of the Pops* appearance seemed to confirm that the Jam were fairly effortlessly offering things – excellence, relevance, authenticity, humility – now completely beyond the Clash. The punk runts were now the pick of the litter.

The Gift was released on March 12, 1982. The Jam's sixth album came housed in a thematically-appropriate candy-striped paper bag resembling a present's wrapping. It was the archetypal marketing gimmick turned instant collector's item: as it was quickly discarded by most purchasers, few remain in existence. (Weller, who designed it, seems to have gotten his inspiration from an unlikely source: the candy striping was first seen on Jam product on the back of the perfunctory sleeve of the 'That's Entertainment' import single.)

The proper sleeve within featured a design wherein the three Jam members were depicted running on the spot, each of them bathed in a different hue from the traffic-light colour system. The same image featured on the record's labels. The back cover contained a black-and-white stage shot which pointedly included the Jam's two auxiliary brass players, who also appeared on the inner sleeve. On one side of the inner sleeve, a monochrome photograph of a typically energetic Northern-Soul dancer provided the backdrop to the album's lyrics, with the exception of '"Trans-Global Express"', whose songwords were hived off to the other side.

Production was credited to Wilson alone, as would be the case with all subsequent Jam records helmed by him. He makes himself heard immediately: opening track 'Happy Together' begins with the sort of production trick with which the album is agreeably littered, in this case a backing chant by Foxton of 'Bay-beee!' isolated and given so much delay that it flares out like a fan. 'I like me delays and me reverbs,' admits Wilson. It has to be said that it's about the only attribute Wilson brings to the party. It soon becomes clear that his production sound is unattractively dense and bulky.

'Happy Together' is a pounding number with an incongruously thin guitar riff. It's another song in which Weller expresses gratitude to his partner for the peace of mind she has given him. While that sentiment is, as ever, touching, and while the music is above-average, Weller's puffing, guttural vocal seeks to claim a gravitas for the composition that it doesn't really possess.

'Ghosts' has a gossamer beauty. Weller picks a quiet electric guitar part, Foxton unobtrusively plucks his bass strings and Buckler taps rimshots. The most vigour in evidence amongst such delicacy comes from the trumpet work of Steve Nichol. Weller's lyric implores someone to show his real feelings and take up the cause of love. Peculiarly, it's difficult to get away from the suspicion that he's talking to himself.

The version of 'Precious' that follows runs to 4¼ minutes. Although this fine song is naturally a welcome presence, many will be forgiven for thinking – considering its relentless, unventilated nature – that it's best heard in the seven-inch single version's 3½-minute edit (its smallest dispensed dose). However, this version will probably strike the right balance for those who felt the seven-inch version departed the stage too quickly but that the nigh seven-minute twelve-inch iteration was something of an endurance test.

'Just Who Is the 5 O'clock Hero?' is a song about the working man's economic and spiritual difficulties, written like 'Town Called Malice' as a conversation with the working man's wife. 'He was very clear that it was about his dad and his huge respect for his father,' recalls Wilson. That the working man's economic and spiritual difficulties are things Paul Weller has never really known first-hand doesn't mean he doesn't have the right to write about them, not least because his childhood was blighted by their effects. However, while 'Scrimping and saving and crossing off lists' rings true as a summation of that life's difficulties, the line with which it constitutes a couplet – a complaint that it seems a constant struggle just to exist – is platitude. Moreover, this has all been said by Weller much better in 'Saturday's Kids' and 'Town Called Malice'. The music has a flat and unresolved air, despite the presence of a bouncy bridge whose songwords cleverly explore the cycle of life and death that attends even uneventful existences, and notwithstanding a sweet sprinkling of brass. Not for the last time on the album, the drumming threatens to make the temples throb. As Buckler's playing has been so welcome an element of so many previous Jam recordings, the assumption must be that it's the way the drums are mixed, not the way they're played, that's maladroit.

Side-closer '"Trans-Global Express"' (the additional quote marks are Weller's own) is clearly intended as the album's grand statement, yet the spotlight Weller gives its lyric by isolating it on the inner sleeve is made a nonsense of by the fact that the listener can barely hear those words. The lyric sheet reveals it to be a piece of open verse that exhorts the listener to get on the titular express, a metaphor for a global strike by ordinary people. ('Not just British Leyland but the whole world,' the composer emphasises, a genuinely funny reference to the car company then notorious for its stoppages and walk-outs.) Weller claims that governments keep the common folk divided by threatening them with recession and war, and distracted by the struggle to put food on their plates. It's student-union politics, but that doesn't mean it couldn't have been stirring if executed properly.

'I think the lyrics were written after the backing,' says Wilson. 'I recall seeing them doing this live after they'd worked on the song and played it in and it was better. The vocal's not very strong. It's not just about the mix. It's about the delivery of the singing. He knew what he wanted to say, he knew what he wanted the lyric to be about, but he hadn't really fashioned them into a singing thing. So they're more like a rap narration. He said, "Don't mix them up. Just put them in there, not too loud."'

'I was probably self-conscious of my vocal on it,' offers Weller. 'I didn't have the balls to have it up front because I didn't like the way me voice sounded.' Would he have the final say on a mix? 'Yeah, absolutely,' Weller says, adding, 'Not just me. The band.' On this issue, Wilson says, 'The three of them wouldn't sit through a whole mix session. It would be more often, "Well I'm going to the pub but I'll listen to it tomorrow and I'll tell you if I like it." Which was fine by me.' Did Buckler and Foxton have a veto? 'It wasn't as formal as that. They'd express an opinion and if there was a consensus that something needed fixing, we'd do that. But it wasn't contentious or tricky. And it wasn't like Paul would be sitting at my side during the whole mix session. There was plenty of scope given to me to do something I thought fit and they'd review it as and when.'

Munday observes, 'Paul did have a habit sometimes of wanting the vocals down in the mix, or he never sang them clearly. I don't think that that's Pete's fault.' One wonders whether Coppersmith-Heaven would have acquiesced to Weller's insistence on burying the vocal of '"Trans-Global Express"'. Asked if he should have argued with Weller, Wilson says, 'Yes, maybe,' but points out that it was one of the last mixes completed. 'I think we all were tired by the end and just wanted to get it finished.' Wilson does go partway to making up for the track's deficiencies with an ingenious speaker-panning climax in which vibrating lips transmogrify into a loop of 'Get off!'

'I was hoping we'd make real progress,' despairs Weller in the first line of 'Running on the Spot', as though he thinks that, five years after his songs started pointing out the faults of society, the revolution would already have arrived. Of course, the politically-committed young are often unrealistically impatient for change, but that hardly seems to justify a number in which Weller complains that, no matter how high the building blocks are piled, the structure never gets any taller because he and his generation keep kicking away the foundations. Said generation is dismissed as emotionally crippled and prone to violence when things don't go well (possibly a reference to some recent unpleasant Jam gigs, perhaps also to the youth riots that swept Britain in the summer of 1981). That this message contradicts the album's would-be life-affirming title track is not too perplexing – people can hold contrasting views or be torn about something – but what is a puzzle is that the running-on-the-spot motif is highlighted by the album's cover. It's almost as though Weller is asserting that it is the Jam who are in stasis. As to the music, Weller seems – as in several places on the album – to be groping for an attractive melody. The accompaniment is tiresome, with Buckler's drums once again unnecessarily prominent.

'Circus', Bruce Foxton's writing contribution, is an instrumental. If this signifies the bassist exhaustedly throwing in the towel in his quest to devise a lyric in Weller's league it would be ironic, because his track ends up saying more than do some of Weller's lyrics on this outing. An upbeat affair with an Eastern-sounding guitar riff and some galvanising brass, it's amongst the album's most enjoyable cuts.

Unlike Mick Jones of the Clash, Weller had never done time in a tower block, so writing 'The Planner's Dream Goes Wrong' can be put down either to an expression of compassion or a scrabbling around for things about which to protest. In it, Weller makes the point that while those consigned to high-rises are condemned to a life of piss-stinking hallways, broken lifts, stolen washing, isolation and unbearable ambient noise, the middle-class planners who designed their homes suffer only the fate of embarrassment. This might all be true, but the treatise has no bite. The song has a whimsical air completely inconsistent with the lyric's scorn courtesy of the arbitrary decision to give it a calypso arrangement. Wilson recalls the steel drums being the work of, 'some young players, Afro-Caribbean, who did it all by ear, no notation.' Erasing these 'pans', however, would not have redeemed an atrocious verse in which Weller says that, if people were meant to live in boxes, God would have given them string to tie around themselves at night to 'stop their dreams falling through the ceiling.' 'It's a bit weird really,' says Wilson of the track. 'It's out of their style. Semi-humorous, I suppose you might say. There have been commentators who said it perhaps wasn't worthy of being put on the album.'

'Carnation' is another blast of pessimism, but one with far greater class and coherency than 'Running on the Spot'. Weller's narrator states that if he was given a fresh carnation he would crush its tender petals. There's something mystical in his boasting of trampling all life in his wake and averting his eyes from other people's pain. 'Touch my heart and feel winter' is one of several impressively gothic lines before a final verse provides a clever twist in which it is explained that, to solve the mystery of who the narrator is, the listener should look in the mirror – the narrator is the greed, fear and hate in every human being. Neither the indistinct tune or the unsubtle instrumentation boast the elegant touch of the lyric, apart from a respite in which, one after another, acoustic guitar and piano play the topline and for the first time make it sound impressive.

That 'Town Called Malice' follows is a little fortunate, because without the hope-in-the-face-of-hardship message of that track, album closer 'The Gift' would sound like an over-compensating repudiation of much of this album's glumness. On the latter, Weller declares that he's got the gift of life, a euphoric realisation that means he just has to keep moving. Unlike 'Boy About Town', the joy just doesn't convince. The whoops he emits and the whistles blowing around him are painfully contrived ways to make this stance sound convincing, but worse is a line that a self-confessed grump like Weller should have known better than to include: 'Can't you see it in the twinkle of my eye?' What makes this doubly embarrassing is the way the track invokes the Small Faces via the debt it clearly owes to their 'Don't Burst My Bubble': Small Faces music was routinely and effortlessly life-affirming. The track is another of several on the record where Weller chants a *doo-doo-doo-doo* rendition of the melody, something which cumulatively is groan-makingly repetitive. It also involves a degree of self-regard, as though he's patting himself on the back for his tunesmithery. Maybe the track would have benefitted from a better production: once again the sonics are dull for reasons other than musicianship.

Reviews of *The Gift* were mixed. Some critics seemed pre-inclined to be ecstatic, displaying a Pavlovian pleasure at familiar Jam lyrical and sonic trademarks. Others were more sober, and came to the speedy conclusion that they didn't admire the Jam's latest album as much as they admired the Jam, a sentiment best expressed in the final lines of the review by Graham Lock in the *NME*: 'The Jam have tried too hard to do too much without really having any stronger foundations than their own desperate desire to "keep movin'". It's not enough, but I guess it shows they still care and for that, at least, I'm grateful.'

Despite the ambivalent feelings we now know him to have been nursing about the Jam at this point, Weller told Chris Salewicz in *The Face* two months after the album's release, 'I think it's the best thing we've done … I really felt it at the time we were making it. There were no precious decisions about what we were doing. It was just a case of putting everything we'd got into it. And to me that comes across, especially when you hear it on the radio, next to all the other records. It just leaps out.' Although in the years since he has decided that *Sound Affects* is his favourite Jam LP, Weller continues to hold *The Gift* in high regard. When it's pointed out to him that the critical consensus is that the album marked a falling away in quality, he responds, 'Nah, bollocks man, rubbish. Fucking wicked album. What about 'Precious', 'Who is the Five

197

O'Clock Hero?', 'Town Called Malice', 'Carnation'? Fucking top tunes. There's a few turkeys on it, but generally it's fucking great quality.'

Yet Munday can't shake a memory of Weller from directly after the album's completion. 'We had a playback and we listened to it and I could see he wasn't happy,' he says. Munday cites public comments made by Weller prior to the album's release in which he spoke of trying to hit an artistic peak with the LP. He feels that they were related to his knowledge that it would be the final Jam album: 'He wanted it to be the best Jam album ever, and I always thought that was a mistake to say, because you go in and you do your best. You can't go in to make a great album or a great single. It doesn't work.' Going back to his half-Jam, half-Style Council observation, Munday says of *The Gift*, 'It's neither fish nor fowl. I could see that he wasn't happy with it. I could understand that, because things like 'Planner's Dream' didn't work at all. If he'd have done that with the Style Council, it would have worked ... Some of the things worked. For me, it's worth the money just for 'Carnation'. I think that is one of the best songs he's ever written.' Wilson says he didn't get the impression that Weller was unhappy with the album, but agrees with Munday on the latter point. 'It was a great song,' says the producer. 'Beautiful. Masterly.'

What is indisputable is that *The Gift* sent the Jam to new commercial heights. It was their first long-playing number one in their home country, entering at the summit on March 14. Although its stay at the top was seven days, its 24-week residency in the album chart was five weeks longer than that of previous personal bests *Setting Sons* and *Sound Affects*.

The Gift gave rise to another hit.

Supposedly, 'Just Who Is the 5 O'Clock Hero?' was an unofficial single, a Dutch (some sources say West German) import released on June 11 which happened to soar to number eight based on popular demand. As such, no dent was left in the Jam's reputation for disdaining the practice of milking albums to death. In fact, it was an instance – maybe the only one of their lifetime – of the band engaging in the sort of music-industry fraudulence they had always condemned, 'or 'selling out' to use the prevailing term.

Dennis Munday was ensnared in the subterfuge. Where he had angrily short-circuited the chart ascent of the 'That's Entertainment' import single, now he had to meekly go along with the Jam and Polydor's shady machinations. 'I didn't particularly think that 'Five O'Clock Hero' was a good idea but everyone else did,' he says. 'I didn't have any choice. I can't say to the company and the band, "You're not gonna do it." It would have happened anyway.' Summarising the Jam's two-faced attitude toward the record, Munday says, 'They were happy about it,' then adds, 'They didn't promote it.' Evidence of the fact that the Jam were aware of what was going on was provided by the fact that, unlike with 'That's Entertainment', the single came housed in a sleeve with a fully-fleshed design: a silhouette of an old-fashioned overhead studio microphone against a blue backdrop on the front, a band photo on the back, and phraseology that indicated the involvement of the word-playful Weller (the record had not sides but 'faces'). Moreover, its B-side somehow proffered previously unreleased material, 'The Great Depression' and (on the twelve-inch) 'War'.

The B-side tracks were co-produced by the Jam and Tony Taverner, studio manager of Maison Rouge in Fulham. Taverner recalls working with the group over 'a period of a couple of weeks or so.' He says, 'We did 'War' and 'Move on Up' at Maison Rouge and 'The Great Depression' or a large chunk of it at Red Bus in [the] Edgeware Road area. … He'd just written that and Maison Rouge wasn't available. We went back to Maison Rouge to mix them all … I remember working on some other bits and pieces on some other tracks as well, but those tracks somebody else had recorded the basic stuff. 'Stoned Out of My Mind' might have been one of them. I think we did a few overdubs on that. While we were recording 'War' and 'Move on Up', 'Town Called Malice' was actually number one, or it had just been number one a couple of weeks before.'

Of his recruitment in place of Pete Wilson, Taverner says, 'The thing that I got is they just wanted to try something different and maybe with somebody different.' This suggests that the Jam were not completely convinced by Pete Wilson's production abilities. Taverner, who hadn't met the band before, reveals, 'We got on really well. Certainly enjoyed working with them. I liked their attitude about it. When we were recording, it wasn't too anal. It was like, "Let's get it done, let's get a good feel, and let's see where it goes." It was quite relaxed and open, no tension, no restrictions on anything ... Getting the tracks down was no problem. It wasn't like hours and hours of redoing it and redoing it.'

As a studio engineer for teen sensations Wham!, Taverner was used to witnessing idolatry. However, he found that the Jam's celebrity had a different quality. He says the band were 'quite relaxed sort of stars,' something illustrated by an incident when he and Buckler left Red Bus after a day's work and the drummer offered him a lift home: 'He had some big old American car. It was one, two o'clock in morning and there was still quite a lot of fans outside. We got in this car and the bloody thing wouldn't start and the fans were pushing us down the road.'

A Hammond organist (identity unknown, but Taverner says not Mick Talbot) and a brass section (also unidentified) complemented the trio at overdub stage. Weller sang to the horn players the notes he desired, although Taverner says, 'Not total dictation. It was collaborative, but he certainly knew what he wanted to get out of them.'

Weller's singing on the covers 'War' and 'Move on Up' comfortably navigated the path between soul-man passion and estuary English. Taverner: 'I can remember he was very quick at doing the vocals, at ease doing them.' Taverner felt that the rhythm section were also at ease, contrary to some who have subsequently accused them of not being able to handle black time signatures. 'I suppose you could say they've not got that real slick soul groove in them, but they gelled as a band so I wouldn't say it sounded awkward,' he reasons. 'It worked. There was no sign of any unrest or frustration at getting what [he] wanted to get out of them at all.'

Soul was clearly very much at the forefront of Weller's mind. Taverner recollects that a record-dealer friend of the guitarist's visited the studio several times, product in hand. 'Paul was buying lots of old soul singles from him, collectors' stuff.' However, the soul covers worked on at these sessions were hardly candidates for the A-sides of a self-reliant band like the Jam. Taverner does feel, though, that mid-tempo Weller original 'The Great Depression' – on which he estimates they worked for two to three days – was considered by the group to be single material.

'Move on Up' and 'Stoned Out of My Mind' were held over for later use. On 'The Great Depression' horns shadow Weller's vocal and phasing is applied to the drums. As with several recent Jam tracks, the ornamentation is unable to disguise the fact that the number doesn't seem to go anywhere. The song does at least throw light of some sort on chunks of *The Gift*. The lyric seems to lambast the British public for having voted in Margaret Thatcher's administration and thereby unleashing the depression of the title (technically a recession). 'I think we must have all gone mad,' Weller declares before launching into a condemnation of the public's obsessions with violence and keeping up with the Joneses. Had this track been ready for inclusion on *The Gift* (and it's no worse than some of that record's contents), it might have provided a context to some of the pessimism that confusingly sat cheek-by-jowl with its messages of optimism.

The Jam turn in a creditable performance of 'War', the Whitfield & Strong peacenik anthem made famous by Edwin Starr, even if it does rather underline the fact that, scattered tracks excepted, the Jam had always failed in their quest to create self-composed authentic-sounding black music. It's interesting that this was one area where the Clash had the Jam licked: *London Calling* featured plenty of well-integrated brass, and if the black grooves of that album were more reggae than soul, its final number 'Train in Vain' was (although ironically sans brass) something that sounded like it could have come from one of the Stax writing crew instead of Strummer/Jones.

Perhaps it was the Jam's need to veil their complicity in the release of the 'Just Who Is the 5 O'Clock Hero?' single that prevented them from amending the word 'shit' that appeared in the A-side's second line. If it reduced airplay, it doesn't seem to have had an adverse effect on the record's commercial impact: a top-ten placing was impressive for something so nondescript and which the Jam promoted only via the recording of a video.

Taverner was subsequently invited to a couple of Jam gigs, but didn't get to work for them again. However, the fact that Weller later asked him to helm sessions for Respond act the Questions seems to confirm his impression that the band were pleased with what he'd done.

It was with Peter Wilson that the Jam would later in the year record and release another version of 'War', something that surprised Taverner. However, he was far more surprised when, shortly before that second version was released, the news was announced that the Jam were to split. 'There was no sign of that whatsoever,' he says. 'I can remember socialising with them after the gigs and I can only remember it as all being relaxed and just good fun. No over-the-top star stuff, no wobblers at all, not during the sessions or any other time. They just seemed like three normal blokes who were at ease and enjoying what they were doing.'

A BITTER PILL

There were two finished masters of the next Jam single.

Wilson recalls the first version being recorded at Odyssey Studios, Marble Arch. Munday's memories are more focused on the fact that its string section was recorded on a Sunday, 'which pissed me off because we had to pay them double-bubble.' Not likely to have improved his mood was the news Weller delivered at Polydor's offices the following day: 'He came in Monday and he said, "I want to redo it." I said, "What, you want to re-do the strings?" He said, "No I want to re-do the whole record."' 'I'm glad he did,' Wilson says of the new version, laid down at AIR. Munday concedes, 'It worked better the second time around, for sure.'

This, though, doesn't mean 'The Bitterest Pill (I Ever Had to Swallow)' is any kind of classic. Released on September 6, 1982 along with B-side tracks 'Pity Poor Alfie' and 'Fever', it's a quite bizarre creation. Its theme is the same as that of Gladys Knight & The Pips' 'It Should Have Been Me', but it's no smouldering soul number. Instead, it's a string-drenched ballad not too far removed from what we now term 'cheesy listening'.

On his vocal track, Weller swoons and croons in ways never before heard on Jam product, but in a way that would become very familiar to Style Council fans. The chorus brings another Jam first: female singing, namely that of Jenny McKeown of the Belle Stars. At the start of the track, the narrator is staring at an ex-lover as she stands in her beautiful wedding gown. The sight is such a bitter pill that he wishes himself dead. The mood of the composer, as opposed to narrator, is both poetic and careless. Weller is in search of profundity, but won't take the trouble to come up with lines that are anything more than quasi-embarrassing ('When the wheel of fortune broke, you fell to me'). Similar laziness attends the music. Despite the sonic ambition indicated by the classical overtones, the opening guitar line is a lift from the Small Faces' 'Tin Soldier'. Unlike in 'Smithers-Jones', the strings are not an asset. Formally credited to Wilson and Weller, the arrangement occasionally impresses for its keening sweetness and grand sweep, and there are a few spots involving an impressive syncopation with the vocals, but the overall timbre is tacky. Nor does the production serve it well. The track admittedly sounded a lot better on home stereos than it did on radio and the pre-stereo televisions of the time, but in any setting it remains cluttered. It also sounds as dank as the grim room (jail cell?) featured on the sleeve's front. (This confusing design is accompanied by equally confused ideas on typeface: the title is rendered in an elegant font appropriate to the musical stylings, but the Immediate lettering – previously considered to have jagged qualities that made it appropriate to hard-hitting fare like 'Funeral Pyre' – is brought out again for the artist credit.)

The marching beat and sunny brass work of 'Pity Poor Alfie' are incongruously jaunty considering the song's subject matter. Lines about blood-stained letters and having nothing but memories of Alfie suggest that the narrator's friend is dead. 'We escaped the test and the marathon run,' evokes schoolday skiving, suggesting a long-standing friendship. The fact that Weller's old buddy, ex-Jam member and Riot Stories co-director Dave Waller had died the month before the record's release suggests that the song is an eulogy for him. At approaching the three-minute mark the track segues into a version of the old slinky Peggy Lee hit 'Fever' which is perfectly agreeable but serves no apparent purpose, unless Weller is telling us it was Waller's favourite tune.

'I'm not ashamed of it,' says Wilson of the A-side. 'It's a kind of a piss-take, as Paul has said.' The producer admits, though, that he didn't necessarily get the impression of intentional parody during the recording. He adds, 'I think some people were perplexed, but I wasn't going to stand in Paul's way ... No reason why it shouldn't be different.'

Says Munday, 'I thought it was just experimentation. I didn't think it would be number one, that's for sure. It almost worked, a bit like 'Absolute Beginners' – it's kind of there or thereabouts.' Buckler was also not overly impressed by 'The Bitterest Pill'. 'I don't think it had quite so much life in it as some of the other things that we'd done,' he offers. 'We liked the song, we liked doing it – obviously that's why we did do it. But it didn't seem to have the same energy.' Despite the lack of overwhelming enthusiasm for it in the Jam camp, the record did well. The strings and the non-political subject matter appear to have combined to enable the Jam to reach out to purchasers beyond their core audience, the record making number two.

Perhaps Buckler's perspective on the song has been permanently soured by a bitter pill fed him and Foxton during the recording sessions for its B-sides: it was at this point that Weller told his colleagues that he was leaving the Jam.

In July, Weller had holidayed with his girlfriend in Italy. It was an unusually extended break, and unusually exotic – as recently as 1979, he was vacationing in a caravan in Selsey, West Sussex. That the setting was relaxingly sun-dappled didn't stop Weller engaging in his wont for brooding, him taking time to reflect on his career. The upshot of his ruminations was a momentous decision: he resolved to leave the group he had founded. The Jam members later said that they had an unspoken understanding that, should any one of them leave, the group would dissolve. Even without that non-verbal concordance, however, it was inconceivable that the Jam would be able to continue without their chief songwriter, frontman and public face. Weller's decision was one that could only bring the curtain down on the career of a band who were at the very top.

One of Weller's reasons for his decision was that he wanted to explore different types of music. He insists that he didn't consider that the music he wanted to explore was beyond his Jam colleagues' capabilities. Rather, he felt it was outside their interests and inclination. 'I don't think that's in any way a reflection of their musicianship,' he says. 'I just thought, "I really want to go somewhere different, I want to try all these different things." I don't think we would do that, not because of musicianship. I just didn't think we would do that as a collective spirit. All the kind of things that – some successfully, some very unsuccessfully – I try and did on *Café Bleu*, the first [Style] Council album, it just wouldn't have got past the board. Trying to do a rap track, or something. Which is fair enough as well, and I can totally appreciate and understand that. I just didn't think they would wanna do that, really.'

Munday, though, asserts, 'If you listen to 'Long Hot Summer' or some of the stuff he did in the Council, the Jam couldn't do that. They did a cover of a Chi-Lites record ['Stoned Out of My Mind'] on the 'Beat Surrender' double pack. It doesn't gel. It's like the band are playing one thing and Paul's playing another.' Munday does echo Weller, though, when he comments, 'That's not because they're bad musicians.' He elucidates, 'Very few drummers can play every kind of music. Rick is a great drummer, there's no questioning that, but some of the stuff that Paul wanted to do needed a different kind of drumming. Even some of the greatest drummers can't necessarily go in and play on a jazz track, 'cos it required a different feel.' While emphasising that he considers Foxton, 'a great bass player,' he states, 'Pino Paladino's one of the great bass players 'cos he can play on anything.'

Weller cites a couple of other reasons for his decision: straightjackets relating to both workload and personal relations. 'Don't forget, I'd been in that band since I was fourteen,' he reasons. 'Ten years. A long time in a young man's life and, more than anything else, I really wanted to go off and see who else I could be and who else I was. We'd either tour or be writing or recording, so it was a little bit of a treadmill. I wanted to go off and find who else I could be as a person. You grow up and you all move in different directions.' In the Jam fan-club newsletter in which he explained his decision, Weller mentioned that the constant pressure to write the next album meant he had never been able to enjoy the band's success.

Weller has also claimed that *Absolute Beginners* – which he took on holiday with him to amend for his having failed to familiarise himself with a book he'd written a song about – also played a part in his decision. He told Simon Goddard, 'Reading that totally turned my head ... It just kickstarted me on to the whole mod purism thing. That righteous path. I remember reading *Absolute Beginners* and, that same holiday, thinking I could maybe continue the band for another five or 10 years, and that scared me. I realised I didn't want to.'

There is one reason Weller has not proffered for being unwilling to continue in the Jam, but which seems to be a real possibility, even if subconsciously: his grief over Dave Waller. Waller's recent fatal heroin overdose in a Woking hotel room may well have clouded his friend and business partner's emotions. People in their early twenties are usually directly familiar with death only through the hardly unexpected passing of grandparents. They can consequently be disproportionately, even irrationally, devastated by unforeseen loss. As Waller was a onetime Jam member, the tragedy could easily have led Weller's mind into melancholy meditation on the history of the band. It's not inconceivable that he came to the conclusion that Waller's demise marked the end of an era. It might not have been the impetus for his decision to leave the group, but may have in some way justified it or underlined it. Peter Wilson would later produce 'Man of Great Promise', a Style Council track whose subject unequivocally was Dave Waller. Although he doesn't know whether it was a reason for Weller's decision to leave the Jam, Wilson says, 'It did affect him quite a lot, that death.'

Munday says of Weller's resolve to leave, 'It was a tremendous, brave decision because it wasn't a shoo-in that he was going to be successful.' Weller, though, says there was little agonising involved. 'I knew that's what I had to do,' he says. 'The agonising came with the fact that I had to tell John – me dad – and Bruce and Rick. That was pretty fucking tough, because like any relationship it's not an easy thing to say, "I've got to move on." And obviously it wasn't going to be a popular decision. And with the fans as well. I felt for them. I can remember when the Beatles split. I thought the world had fucking ended. [I was] twelve, thirteen. I can remember me mum working in a newsagent and seeing that headline: "Paul: I Quit" – it was devastating.'

The first person Weller told upon his return from Italy was his father. He might have been his dad, but John Weller responded to the bombshell in his other capacity in Paul's life. 'His first reaction was, "Are you fucking mad? Are you taking the piss?" or whatever,' recalls the junior Weller. 'Which is a pretty natural reaction with any manager.' The Wellers then informed Polydor's senior management, who in turn told Munday. 'I wasn't that surprised,' says Munday, 'because in the Summer of '80 we were in Polydor Studios just talking and he just said out of the blue, "I don't want the Jam to end up going round just playing their hits. I want them to be remembered for being something." I remember thinking at the time, "Strange thing to say. You're at the top now."' Weller's attitude wasn't even new then. In 1978, he gave an interview to Ian Birch of *Melody Maker* about his love of pre-*Tommy* Who music. Lamenting what he considered the Who's lack of recent inspiration, he said, 'I suppose after 14 years that does happen. I'll make sure the Jam aren't around in 14 years' time. If you're not totally creative all the time there's just no point in going on.' Of course, such bravado is common amongst young musicians. Once ensconced in the easy life, few follow it through.

One thing about which Munday was surprised – to say the least

– was the revelation that it had been decided by the two Wellers that Rick Buckler and Bruce Foxton were to be kept in the dark about the momentous decision. The plan was to inform them only in December and the occasion of the last gig of the Jam's next, already-booked tour. It was explained to Munday that this was felt necessary because it was suspected that Weller's colleagues would be so upset about their imminent unemployment that they would refuse to participate in the gigs, thus jeopardising a considerable amount of money. Munday thought the plan preposterous. With several people in the company by necessity already in the loop, human nature would do the rest and the secret would at some point be leaked, with all sorts of ramifications, some of them – depending on the circumstances and chronology – potentially catastrophic.

That was the practical objection. There was also a moral dimension, one that also impacted on the commercial sector. The Jam's image and status were predicated as much on elevated integrity as on great music. When it inevitably became public knowledge that he had deceived his bandmates – whether that public knowledge came before or after the split – it would make Paul Weller look very bad, even to the point of seeming to make a mockery of what he and his songs stood for. That in turn might provoke such disgust as to undermine his subsequent musical career at the outset. A horrified Munday demanded a meeting with AJ Morris. He recalls, 'I told the old man, "Look, for Christ's sake, it's his credibility you're talking about, and that's his ace." I told the old man to talk to John. I said, "It's going to be better coming from you than me."' One thing Munday says he never tried to talk Weller out of doing, though, was leaving the Jam. 'I couldn't see the point ... They were going in two different directions musically. He could, if he'd wanted to, have carried on with the Jam and had a solo career. He didn't have to split the Jam up. The company would have loved it if he'd kept the Jam and done a solo thing. But he didn't want to. Why would he change his mind?'

AJ Morris took Munday's advice and managed to persuade the Wellers of the folly of attempting to deceive Buckler and Foxton. Paul Weller was therefore ultimately able to portray the Jam's dissolution as an act of integrity. However, that still left him the grisly task of telling Buckler and Foxton that the band's time was up.

When the Jam were recording the 'Bitterest Pill' B-sides at Marcus Studios, Kensington Gardens, John Weller informed the rhythm section that he and his son wanted a band meeting. It was immediately obvious that something serious was in the air: the Jam had never had formal meetings. At the gathering in the studio's reception area, Weller told Buckler and Foxton that he wanted to leave the Jam because he wanted to get off the treadmill that the band's career had become for him. Naturally, they took this at face value and responded – after a few seconds of stunned silence – accordingly. Buckler: 'We did try and persuade him that maybe we should take a year out and he could do his other projects or whatever he wanted to do and see how it went, but he was adamant that he wanted to make a very clean cut of it and that was that.'

That Weller wasn't amenable to this solution is because he wasn't being completely straight with his colleagues. As Foxton notes, 'He – as we've all heard and learnt since – did want a change of direction and musicians to work with, etc.' What the rhythm section have heard and learnt since – in interviews wherein Weller no longer felt encumbered by the need to be polite to ex-colleagues he didn't have to see anymore – doesn't give Buckler any greater conviction that the decision was a wise one. 'I still don't really understand,' he says. 'I thought it was a bit rash at the time and I still think it is.'

It does bear mentioning that Weller's reasoning seems to have been a veritable onion, involving multiple layers, some of which have only become visible in the years since. For instance, in 2004 Weller observed of the split to *Mojo*'s Phil Sutcliffe, 'I knew it was right. There was a lot of tension and animosity in that band which was great for us live, because it had this snarl to it. But offstage it was a fuckin' pain in the arse ... Imagine us being the Jam in our 40s.' It's a comment which is effectively backed up by Peter Wilson, who says that he wasn't shocked when he was told the news of the Jam's forthcoming dissolution. 'There were intimations during the recording of *The Gift*,' he notes. 'There were one or two exasperated comments from Paul to me, or to himself in my hearing. Things weren't very happy. It was partly personal, I think, as much as musical.'

'I wouldn't say that we *weren't* friends, because we obviously got on quite well,' says Buckler. 'We had a fantastic time. There was a few fights, but not too many.' Offers Foxton, 'We were good mates in the early days, but then, as the machine takes over, you kind of keep yourselves to yourselves on the road and maybe your friendship dwindles a bit, which is very sad. If we'd been closer at the end, maybe he wouldn't have split the band up. Or spoken to us a bit, explained a bit more why he wanted to call it a day.' On that point, Weller says, 'Maybe, but if you're that close you probably would all be travelling on the same journey. If you're that close, then you kind of all instinctively change and turn. I don't care about what-ifs. What's the point? You can't go back and change anything.'

Buckler states, 'The long and the short of it is that, if any one of us had left the band, that would have been pretty much the end of the Jam anyway, and it was just that Paul said, "That's it."' This is something with which Munday agrees: 'People forget that the rhythm section, especially in a three-piece, is very important and quite irreplaceable. If Rick would have left, I can't imagine they could have got a drummer to fit the bill.'

Particularly difficult to take for Buckler was the fact that the split had come just as the Jam's seeds had started to properly flower. In 2012, he told Barry Rutter of *Working News and Mail*, '…everything that we worked for had come true and we thought we've finally got to the point where we don't have to worry about winning audiences over. We've done all the graft, the sound of the band was really what we wanted, touring had become relatively comfortable because we had decent hotels and decent transport.' In his autobiography, Buckler also pointed out, 'The Jam was only just starting to earn some real money … Up until that time, most of the money that we earned went straight back into the band.' Of course, this was not an acute issue for all of the Jam. Although Weller richly deserved the royalties he had accrued by virtue of his songwriting talent, those royalties cushioned him from any long-term financial impact that might result from the Jam ceasing to operate.

Time and tide have made Buckler and Foxton philosophical about the news that so devastated them that day, and for some time afterwards. Says Foxton, 'Paul never owed us a living. We did what we did for six years or whatever, and it was a great buzz and, financially, we've all done pretty good out of it.' 'Nothing lasts for ever,' Buckler reasons. 'It didn't seem to last hardly any time at all, but that was his decision and so all three of us simply had to just get on with it. There's certainly no regrets over that, because the Jam were so successful. We had a great time. We actually set out to play music live and to become professional musicians and that's exactly what we did, and we were very lucky to become very successful. Paul wanted to move on. Okay, fair enough. We couldn't stop him.' Buckler is less forgiving about one aspect of the split, although manages to express his grievance temperately: 'This idea that Paul and John weren't going to tell me and Bruce until after the end of the tour that the band was going to split up I think would have been wrong. Dennis Munday persuaded them that we should be told as soon as. As soon as you make a decision like that, we should be told.'

'I went to the studio,' says Munday of the day the news was delivered to Buckler and Foxton. 'I knew what was going to go down.' Although Munday absented himself from the actual fateful meeting, he made sure to speak to the rhythm section afterwards. Of Foxton, he says, 'I took him over the pub just to drown his sorrows. I said, "I just found out." I couldn't tell him that I knew. Bruce took it the hardest ... Bruce did quit the band, he was so upset about it.'

'My initial reaction was, "No, I didn't want to do the tour" because I am very sensitive and I knew it would be a real hardship,' confirms Foxton. 'It would be very hard for me to go out and play those songs.' The bassist's phone call to the Jam's office to announce he was leaving the group effective immediately was an act that lived up to the Wellers' fear that honesty would only jeopardise the tour. It's rumoured that Foxton was informed that ex-Sex Pistol Glen Matlock would be recruited to replace him if he remained a tour refusenik. If true, Foxton doesn't mention it as a reason for changing his mind. 'After a week or so you think about it: the fans deserve it and I guess I do,' is what he says. 'So try to get on top of your emotions so that you could go out there and play. It was a very sad time.'

The stage was now set for the Jam's well-organised and dignified exit from the public stage involving a farewell record and final UK tour. Moreover, announcing all this activity as the band's goodbye would actually accrue them a lot more money than if the Jam's final releases and live dates had proceeded, as Weller and his father had intended, without special fanfare.

The announcement of the split had originally been planned for November 5, when the Jam were due to perform on Channel 4 pop television programme *The Tube*, a new sort-of rival to *Top of the Pops*. Proving the folly of the Wellers' original intention to keep the Jam's dissolution a secret throughout the last quarter of the year,

213

the news leaked even before Bonfire Night. On October 30, the Jam's office released a group statement which transformed into fact the speculative gossip that had started to appear in various print outlets. Buckler and Foxton found themselves surprised by Weller's part of the statement, because in it he gave a different reason than he had to his colleagues for why he was walking out: 'I feel we have achieved all we can together as a group. I mean this both musically and commercially.' Weller was, of course, grounded in punk, a movement that was partly born out of contempt for the way that bands like the Rolling Stones, the Who and the Kinks had sullied their legends with a protracted public deterioration of their art. This fact was evident in a passage in which he said that many groups 'carry on until they become meaningless. I've never wanted the Jam to get to this stage. What we (and you) have built up ... stands for honesty, passion and energy and youth. I want it to stay that way...' These reasons, of course, weren't quite the full truth, but if he hadn't been able to tell Buckler and Foxton to their faces that he thought they would be reluctant to explore the musical directions that he wished to, it was inevitable that Weller wasn't going to put it in a communiqué to the wider public. As for the suspicion on the part of Munday and others that, in reality, Weller didn't think the rhythm section was capable of exploring those musical directions, if Weller can't even bring himself to publicly state this decades later it's again not a mystery that he couldn't at the time. The reference to youth, however, may have had a grain or more of truth. Weller had brought the curtain down on the Jam just before he personally reached that crucial credibility cut-off of 25 that he had invoked on the group's very first record.

Sentiment proceeded to sweep the nation upon the release of the shock news. Jam concert tickets were snapped up. Such was the demand to take the last opportunity to see the group in the flesh that not only were extra dates added to the tour, but five of them were at London's 10,000-seat Wembley Arena. Although they'd performed before 23,000 punters when supporting Blue Öyster Cult, this was larger than any venue the Jam had ever headlined. Despite this, demand still hadn't been met when the Jam stopped acquiescing to promoter requests to add more shows there.

Although the Jam's dissolution could be argued to be the date of their last gig – which turned out to be December 11 – the band statement set December 31 as the point at which the Jam would officially cease to exist. Whichever was the fateful calendar date, as time ticked down to it Buckler and Foxton found themselves in the surreal situation of having to build their own tombstone. In October, they trooped into Phonogram Studios, Bayswater to join Weller in laying down the Jam's last studio recordings so as to provide the material for their farewell single. Asked about the atmosphere in which this recording took place, Buckler says, 'It was one of those realities where you think, "Well it's not really going to happen," but you know it is. It was really business as usual in every respect, probably grasping at the hope that maybe he would change his mind.' 'It was a bit awkward after that announcement doing recording sessions,' says Wilson, who acted as producer on them. 'It was difficult. We just got on with it. It was like a professional relationship. The band played, turned up, there were no histrionics, there were no mind games, there were no nasty recriminations that I saw. It was fine.' But not exactly a jamboree? 'Well, it never was.'

The Jam's final single was released on November 22, 1982. It appeared in three formats. The seven-inch edition consisted of 'Beat Surrender' b/w 'Shopping'. A double pack added a disc containing a trio of soul covers, which tracks also made up the B-side of the twelve-inch single. The sleeve designs by Pete Barrett featured photographs of a dark-haired young woman – in fact Gill Price, Weller's partner and muse for so many of the best Jam love songs – holding aloft a white flag of surrender. For the first time on a Jam single, there were sleevenotes additional to simple credit listings, attributed to 'The Boy Wonder'. Style Council fans would get used to the peculiar style of these notes: platitudes expressed in exclamatory vocabulary and eccentric lettering.

'Shopping' is a delightful track, and certainly disproves the suggestion never made by Weller but levelled by plenty of others that Buckler and Foxton did not have the ability to tackle, let alone execute well, music beyond their knowledge or interest. A whimsical, circular, jazzy concoction, it finds Buckler brushing his drums and Foxton tickling his bass to sublime effect. Weller throws in an understated, cascading guitar break, and the auxiliary members contribute pleasing flute and cornet. The non-rhyming lyric that Weller breathily enunciates condemns the one-upmanship of consumerism. It could be said that this is not just rather banal stuff but the height of hypocrisy coming from a perennially sharply-dressed man who clearly did indeed have 'clothes at the top of my list.' The track is such well-crafted, good-natured bliss, however, that one is not inclined to make an issue of it. For once, Wilson's production touch is light and crystal clear.

Foxton and Buckler are no less adroit on the soul covers. Said tracks could all be posited as filler proffered in the absence of a willingness by Weller to give any new songs to a band he had reduced to a lame duck. Yet they're also all classics of the genre being tackled by a band possessed of vast skills, and therefore supremely listenable. 'Move on Up' is a propulsive rendition of the 1971 Curtis Mayfield expression of solidarity with a young person whose parents don't understand their values. The Chi-Lites' 1973 single 'Stoned Out of My Mind' – the complaint of a betrayed lover – is given a more experimental treatment which slightly downplays the prominence of the original's brass (although not its falsetto) for a fuzzy ambience. Buckler shuffles an impressive beat and Foxton plays his funkiest bass yet. The new recording of 'War' is differentiated from the version on 'Just Who is the Five O'Clock Hero?' not just by the fact that at 2:40 it's more than a minute shorter, but also because it features female vocal group Afrodiziac and quasi-psychedelic effects. It's just as good.

The Jam recorded a version of new Weller song 'A Solid Bond in Your Heart' but – even though a Jam tour had already been named after it and the Boy Wonder's sleevenotes carried the heading 'A Solid Bond' – they issued only part of that number. Explains Munday, 'Originally they were going to do 'Solid Bond' as the last single. Paul decided he wanted to keep that for the Style Council. The original version of 'Solid Bond' had a bridge. They took the bridge and put it in 'Beat Surrender'. It did improve, having that bridge in there. It gave the song a dimension, whereas 'Solid Bond' is just verse, verse, verse.'

'Beat Surrender' is an anthem which celebrates both the power of music and the virtue of authenticity. Weller's singing on the chorus is augmented by the powerful vocals of Tracie Young. Weller himself also sings impressively, growling and crooning like a classic soul man, yet still admirably refusing to give in to the temptation for American pronunciation. The melody is not only very good but cleverly constructed, necessitating Weller having to respond to himself (overdubbed) in a different key. The instrumentation is dominated by a rumbling piano, with no audible guitar. Majestic brass runs complete the exquisite confection.

Genuinely stirring though his denunciation of 'phonies' and 'fakers' is, Weller's point was slightly undermined by a special radio-play version of the track in which he re-recorded the key line 'Bullshit is bullshit, it just goes by different names' so that 'bullshit' became 'rubbish.' He at least indicated he was aware of the irony/hypocrisy – and did so with some humour – when on the vocal track he laid down for *Top of the Pops* appearances he sang, 'Ballcocks are ballcocks...' There is another issue with the lyric. The title line exhorts the listener to succumber to the beat surrender. Not only is there no such word as 'succumber', but, as the intended 'succumb' means much the same as 'surrender', the expression is a tautology. Remarkably, not a single person pointed out these errors to Weller during the recording process. 'When we're recording, I'm busy on the mixing desk trying to make sure they're playing in time and [that] it's going down nicely onto the tape,' is Wilson's story. 'And anyway, Paul's the lyricist. Unless there's anything seriously out of kilter or racist or whatever that the singer's singing, or some obvious crassness, I wouldn't comment.' Weller's defence? 'That's called poetic licence, mate. We don't have all your fucking semantics and correct grammar in songwriting. We're conveying a message. "Succumber" sounds nice when you're singing it. It's got a *"bah!"* on the end of it.' Wilson, completely independently of Weller, echoes him: 'The "bah" on the end of "succumber" is pivotal to the lyrical rhythm rather than to the meaning.' In fairness, it may indeed only be pedantic journalists who allow themselves to be vexed by these errors. Popular music has a long tradition of indulgence – even celebration – of bad grammar, partly because it's not incongruous in the context of street culture, partly because double negatives and colloquialisms pack more of a punch than textbook English.

It's quite remarkable what a substantial work the extended 'Beat Surrender' package constitutes. At five tracks and nearly twenty minutes it amounts time-wise to half an album, and quality-wise – the preponderance of covers notwithstanding – to one of the best album-sides (that is, album-side equivalents) of the Jam's career. Buckler was acutely aware of the paradox. 'We did try not to release any bummers,' he notes before saying, 'Bruce certainly feels that there was a couple more years, or at least a couple more albums, in us.'

While Wilson expresses enthusiasm for 'Shopping' and 'Stoned Out of My Mind', the producer was less impressed with the main track. 'I think it's too fast,' he says. 'I asked him to slow down when they were doing the backing track and they wouldn't. Partly about getting it done.' As with 'Town Called Malice', the doubts Wilson had about the A-side didn't stop it reaching number one. 'Beat Surrender' may not have been as neat a capstone as Mott the Hoople's final record 'Saturday Gigs' (1974), a moving valedictory and career summary complete with a 'Goodbye' backing chant. However, in contrast to the fact that 'Saturday Gigs' didn't even crack the top 40, 'Beat Surrender' provided, commercially, a perfect closing note. Its high quality was probably not that pertinent to the record's success, however. The same sentimentality that made the Jam's final tour a sell-out ensured 'Beat Surrender' was the third Jam single to debut at the summit. It remained there a fortnight.

Asked if he was surprised by the split, Coppersmith-Heaven shrugs, 'People make changes.' He adds, 'It was clear that Paul wanted a clear change of direction. The other band members were a bit upset about that. Everyone else thought they probably would have gone on for the next twenty years.' He adds, 'It was interesting to see that they split up after I had been dropped from their last album.'

As the man chiefly responsible for putting the Jam on a pedestal, Chris Parry was originally not impressed by them leaving it voluntarily. 'That kind of idea didn't appeal to me, I must admit,' he says. However, asked if the decision has been subsequently vindicated, he responds, 'I would have thought yes.' 'In hindsight, he got it right,' agrees Munday. 'He made the right call.' Bill Smith is in complete agreement with Munday. Says the designer, 'What a clever thing to do to stop when you're at the top because that's what everybody remembers, rather than rehashing old stuff ten years later.' Indeed, around the time of the split a correspondent to the *NME* memorably thanked the Jam for being his generation's Beatles and not being his generation's Rolling Stones. In other words, praised the Jam for bowing out at the top and not spoiling their legacy with a long, slow artistic decline.

'You could argue that,' Buckler concedes. 'But what do you mean by decline? An artist like David Bowie goes in and out of decline all the time. Isn't that just being afraid of failure? We didn't get into the music business just to sell number-one records. We got into it because we wanted to play and we wanted to perform. There was something much stronger at the core of this. I am a bit of a Stones fan and I probably would go and see them given half a chance.' Even though their albums ceased being great three decades ago? 'There's been nothing particularly outstanding there, I agree, but they can still cut it live and they've got a great heritage to do that with. If you actually become a band where you're not liked by anybody, *then* you're in trouble. That's what I would call the decline.'

Foxton agrees with the validity of the Stones still rolling. 'They come up with a corker ever now and again, don't they?' he says. 'And they're still selling out everywhere they're going.' He is insistent that the Jam still had life and good records in them: 'We were riding the top of the charts with album and single, selling out venues, and I certainly didn't think now is the time to call it a day before we start losing our form and start slipping down the charts and out of the charts and playing to one man and his dog. We had a long way to go before we'd have reached that. It's difficult to put a time period on how much longer we had and how much more we had to offer to the public, but I didn't feel that 1982 was the right time. I felt we'd more in us to do, basically.'

Weller feels that the Jam becoming a Stones-like self-parody was almost an inevitability. 'It's hard not to do that, the longer you go on in a band,' he says. 'Maybe it's different with a solo artist, 'cos you can shake things off and twist and turn easier.' Is there not a legitimacy to the idea that the Jam should have continued for a couple more years or albums? 'Not if you're not feeling it and your heart's not in it and you want to be somewhere else. So what are you doing it for? For other people. It doesn't go on like that. [You can't] please other people. You have to be true to yourself, and that does involve being selfish at times. It's just unfortunate. That's the way it is.'

'Beat Surrender' reached the top spot during the Jam's 14-date lap of honour, which started on November 25. On the farewell tour, Colin Graham and Kenny Witton replaced Nichol and Thomas on brass.

'Very confused I suppose,' is how Foxton describes his state of mind during the tour. 'Very emotional time. Here we are at the top of the charts, couldn't get much better and still really enjoying it, but knowing that five days' time or whatever – that is it. The Jam are going to be no more.' As ever, the band allowed fans to watch their soundchecks. This time round, Foxton found the kids permitted access to the inner sanctum approaching him in a state of bewildered aggrievement. 'They would pull you to one side and say, "Why are you splitting up? It's my life, you can't do this." I'm looking at them thinking, "Well, it's mine too. I don't know." Because we didn't really know. Very emotional, very hard to get through.'

The tour kicked off in Glasgow and took in Poole, St Austell, and Port Talbot before settling in at Wembley Arena for the first five days of December. Those triumphant Wembley gigs saw the band perform to an aggregate 50,000 people in less than a week. Parry was invited to what he has a feeling was the final Wembley date. 'We were sitting around a room and Bruce was angry as fuck,' he says. 'Paul had left. I didn't even get to see him. Bruce was just very angry and frustrated. He had left the big stage for the last time and was never going to come back to it and he knew that. It would be a very tough thing for a young man to have to deal with.'

221

'I never particularly cared for the sound at Wembley because it was a bit reverby, but the gigs were good,' says Munday. 'I remember going in the pub up the road, 'cos I would go to the soundcheck, and the fans were in there and they kept coming up to me and saying, "Oh Den, this is terrible. My life's coming to an end" and stuff like that. It's quite touching.' Perhaps some of those fans were at least a little placated by Weller's gruff farewell on the last London date: 'Don't wanna get too sentimental or anything ... but thanks for the last six years.'

From there, the tour travelled to Bridlington, Manchester and Birmingham. A show in Guildford on December 9 was intended as an appropriate end to the tour. In the absence of any venue in Woking, the Civic Hall of the Surrey town six miles southwards was the closest thing to a hometown gig a band of the Jam's stature could now play. 'Even though it was the last gig they were going to play, it was such a good gig,' Munday says. Munday was astonished when the Jam's live career was then prolonged. The tour, and the Jam's life, came to a curious halt with an arbitrary gig at the Brighton Centre two days later. Munday: 'When they said they were going to do Brighton, I said, "What for?" I don't know why they did it, but it was an error.' 'Brighton was a large enough venue close enough to our own town, plus it's got this sort of iconism of fights on the beach and the mod years and a throwback to that,' says Buckler. 'And it is a great venue to play.' 'Monetary reasons' was the rationale for the Brighton gig offered by Alex Ogg in *Our Story*, the Jam biography he wrote with Buckler and Foxton. Certainly, Munday didn't find the Brighton Centre such a great venue that particular night. 'It was a terrible gig,' he says. 'It was just like a wake. It just didn't happen. The atmosphere was sour.' Eyewitness at the concert have reported Foxton and Weller barely communicating on stage and a withdrawn Weller becoming infuriated as he broke a succession of guitar strings. As a goodwill gesture, the doors to the venue had been left open to allow free access to those without tickets. Unfortunately, that also meant that crowds of skinheads – then the sworn enemy of the new mods – were able to get in. Whichever faction was responsible, there was trouble at the gig. At one point, the band left the stage for several minutes after a thrown bottle shattered on Buckler's kit. Munday noted the aggro with some dismay. 'The last two or three years, there was very little violence at their gigs, if any,' he says. The Jam's final number was, rather incongruously for the occasion, an extended version of 'The Gift', that song which took ostentatious joy in life.

Munday adds, 'I stayed in the hotel drinking with Bruce until two or three in the morning ... Paul went home after the gig, he didn't even stay.'

The day after the tour ended came the release of *Dig the New Breed*. This live album was the consequence of the Jam having left their contract uncompleted. 'They owed them two albums,' explains Munday, which suggests that, following the fulfilment of their original four-album deal, the Jam had signed a new contract for the same amount of product. Munday: 'The deal we did was for the live album and the greatest hits, *Snap!*' Could the label have insisted on new studio albums? 'They could, but it would be a waste of time because you could end up with the worst record ever.'

Dig the New Breed's strange title wasn't more of Weller's awkward hipster speak but a quote (albeit apparently apropos of nothing) from James Brown's 'Papa's Got a Brand New Bag'. The elaborate sleeve – designed by Alwyn Clayden – featured a cut-out circle on the front exposing the disc's label. The back carried sleevenotes from all three Jam members. Buckler and Foxton's were commentary on the album, while Weller's was a whistle-stop summary of the Jam's career.

It's a little surprising that *Dig the New Breed* wasn't a double LP:

if any in-concert work might be perceived by a record company as having the potential to rival the phenomenal success of the two-disc *Frampton Comes Alive!* it would surely have been a long-playing capstone to the Jam's oeuvre. The caution, though, was proven wise. As *Dig the New Breed* aesthetically resembled the contractual obligation it was, its actual commercial potential was limited. The album did well but not spectacularly so, peaking at number two and spending 15 weeks in the chart.

The album collects live recordings from across the Jam's career, starting with an 'In the City' from September 1977 at the 100 Club, London and concluding with a 'Private Hell' captured at the Glasgow Apollo in April 1982. Only four of the recordings are from the Seventies. Only one is surprising (a cover of Eddie Floyd's 'Big Bird') and only one ('Ghosts') is particularly inspiring. In some places, the inability of a live three-piece to recreate the Jam's sophisticated latter-day studio fare is glaringly evident: 'Going Underground' sounds pathetically tinny compared to the full-bodied, ferocious original. All in all, hardly a release that lives up to Buckler's oft-stated belief that the Jam's forte was live work. However, two things the album does convey is the sense of occasion at a Jam gig and the depth of the adoration of their audience.

Although in the years between *This is the Modern World* and *Setting Sons* the sales of the Jam's singles had been mediocre and even a source of worry to Polydor, overall the band's chart performance had been so consistent that by the end of their career they had achieved the uncommon feat of eighteen consecutive Top 40 UK hits. In early '83, they went one better. January of that year saw the re-release for the second time of the Jam's entire singles back catalogue, plus the first official UK releases of 'That's Entertainment' and 'Just Who is the Five O'Clock Hero?'. Interestingly, the singles which failed to re-enter the top 75 were the substandard ones of the last part of the Jam's career: 'Funeral

Pyre', 'Absolute Beginners', 'The Bitterest Pill' and 'Just Who is the Five O'Clock Hero?' Four discs re-entered the top forty: 'All Around the World' (number 38), 'Down in the Tube Station at Midnight' (30), 'Going Underground'/'Dreams of Children' (21) and 'News of the World' (39). The fact that by February thirteen of the group's singles were simultaneously sitting in the Top 75 meant that this time the group had outdone even the Beatles. It was a technical knock-out: the Beatles had seventeen singles in the Top 75 in March 1976 when they also benefitted from a posthumous repromotion programme. However, only three of them counted because the official chart in those days was limited to the top fifty places. As someone once said, the law is not always the same as justice: it was the Jam who proceeded to enter *The Guinness Book of Records*.

AN ANTI-MATTER SPLIT

Paul Weller appeared less interested in the Jam being in the record books than in his back pages. He set about constructing his post-Jam musical career with a haste that might be considered unseemly. His next group, the Style Council, released their first record exactly three months after the Jam's final gig, which means they were in the studio only around six weeks after the formal December 31 split.

Weller recruited Mick Talbot to join him in his new musical enterprise. Talbot was burly and lugubrious but also good-natured and possessed of nimble keyboard skills. More importantly, he could write. Talbot got several composing credits on Council records, both on his own and in collaboration with Weller. It was rather lucky for Weller that he was finally in an outfit not completely dependent on his songwriting output. After a laidback first year for the Style Council involving just a scattering of singles and an EP, Weller put himself back on the same album-per-annum treadmill that he (sometimes) claimed to have resented while in the Jam (a volte-face due, some have suggested, to the need to finance Respond Records). There was, though, one crucial difference. Peter Wilson, who continued to be Weller's producer, says, 'He didn't seem under the cosh. He seemed happy in his work.'

It was immediately obvious that the Council were a very different proposition to the Jam. This applied not just to musical style but to set-up and image. Rather than being a conventional group, they were a core of musicians augmented by hired talent as and when necessary. Drummer Steve White was the only other person who could be considered a permanent member. In fact, unbeknownst to the public, the personnel situation was even more basic than that. The impression was given that Talbot was of equal standing to Weller because he (unlike White) appeared in publicity photos and took part in interviews, but Weller was the only one signed to the record company.

This quasi-band (even pseudo-band) devised dramatic, cinematic music-press advertisements for their releases, projected café-culture sophistication and flirted (if always awkwardly) with whimsy, humour and even androgyny. Weller himself threw off the shackles of mod trichology to embrace a bewildering variety of hairstyles. Equally bewildering to Wilson was the loss of the sartorial sure-footedness Weller had hitherto always displayed. 'I did cringe a bit when I saw him on telly in the Style Council wearing vinyl or patent black leather trousers, not playing a guitar but trying to groove as a vocalist,' he says. 'I thought, "This is dreadful, why are you doing this? The music's alright but why do you have to look like that?"'

Lyrically, Style Council product echoed the Jam's in tackling both politics and romance. Its real departure was in its musical forms. The Council tackled jazz, rap, smooth soul, funk, even classical. Just about anything, in fact, except rock. Weller told the *NME* during this period that he 'never particularly liked' Jam favourites like 'Down in the Tube Station at Midnight' and 'Going Underground', observing, 'They're not the sort of things I'd play at home.' Weller even told the *NME* a year after the Council's first release, 'Rock music is shit.' (A response to interviewer X Moore's priceless chide about the lack of guitar on Council records, 'Rock is not *inherently* good, but it *certainly* isn't inherently bad.') Asked if he remembers the comment, Weller says, 'No, I don't at all.' This seems somewhat unlikely, considering that it wasn't a one-off but pretty much a manifesto. In 1983, he told *Flexipop* that he hoped to use Respond Records to 'help towards destroying Rock Music and Rock Culture.' He told X Moore that he had felt rock was shit for 'a good couple of years.' Peter Wilson even recalls being 'hurt slightly' by Weller's anti-rockism, explaining, ''cos I liked Jimi Hendrix. He had no time for Jimi Hendrix or the Rolling Stones at the time.' 'But it fucking was crap,' Weller now says of rock. 'It's improved in recent years.'

227

Weller says he remembers the Style Council overall, 'with great big smiles and love and happiness.' He adds, 'It was just a great time in my life. Some of the music didn't work, but some of it was fucking great. Around '85 time was a peak for me. We really got it together live, a good little band. We used to play all over.'

Had the Style Council flopped, many would have said it proved Weller should never have split up the Jam. Did that knowledge made him feel pressure? 'Yeah, of course,' he says. 'Naturally. But we were very, very successful. At least for the first three years.' Did he feel he inherited the Jam's audience? 'Some people came with me – I couldn't tell you what percentage – and dug it, and then I had a whole lot of new people come to it. A lot more girls, a lot more couples – that kind of vibe. And it wasn't so much blood, sweat and tears. It became something else. It changed. As life should change, people should change.'

Weller used Peter Wilson as producer for the first few years of the Style Council, before taking over production duties himself. 'He was undemonstrative in many ways; he didn't lay on the praise,' says Wilson. 'But clearly he valued my work to ask me to stay on.' Wilson adjudges the Style Council as, 'Definitely a progression or a change.' He adds, 'If you look at the first Style Council album, that's all kinds of diverse styles and pastiches and so on, and some people think it's a bit of a dog's breakfast. It did put a lot of people out. And at the same time, a lot of fans came to him who hadn't liked the Jam particularly. There were a lot of women who went for the Style Council, but didn't like the Jam. The Jam was a bit bloke-ish ... He was listening to Blue Note music, he was a big James Brown fan. He wanted to try stuff, and why shouldn't he? I think we did some great tracks. There were a few experimental things that didn't work out so well, but that's how it is.'

Although they never had a number one single in their home country, the Council had seven UK top-tenners: 'Speak Like A

Child', 'Long Hot Summer', 'My Ever Changing Moods', 'Groovin' (You're The Best Thing)', 'Shout To The Top', 'Walls Come Tumbling Down' and 'It Didn't Matter'. ('Solid Bond In Your Heart', that song he'd withheld from the Jam, made it to number 11, the same position managed by the Council's extraordinary, extended anti-Thatcherism jazz-rap 'Money Go Round'.) The group released four albums between 1984 and 1988, one of which made number one, two of which made number two, and the last number 15.

This commercial success was achieved despite the fact that sometimes it seemed as though Weller was being self-consciously contrary, a prime example being the fact that only six of the thirteen cuts on the Council's first album featured his vocals. Jam fans might have been able to deal with that, but Style Council product was also studiedly quirky, surprisingly middle-of-the-road, increasingly soporific, progressively synthesiser-dominated and ever more pseudo-American. On some of his drowsy, stylised soul numbers, sung in the sort of US accent he had once disdained, Weller seemed on the verge of breaking into a Barry White peroration on love-making. This certainly undermined his dismissal of the Clash's 'Train in Vain'. Weller's political songs lost power in this set-up: the anti-Thatcher messages of the likes of 'The Lodgers' and 'With Everything to Lose' were framed in musical stylings that were the aural equivalent of doilies. Perhaps significantly, the likes of 'Internationalists' and 'Walls Come Tumbling Down' got their fiery power from being rock-oriented. There was also a peculiar dichotomy to Council albums wherein some of the percussion-heavy funk tracks were so gratingly loud as to be impossible to ignore (or tolerate) while other cuts were so smooth as to sound like background music.

What had started as an evolution in sound became almost a complete breach with anything that had once defined Weller. As if to underline this metamorphosis, Weller refused to play Jam songs at Style Council concerts. The only comparable musical transmogrification is, interestingly, that of a Clash member: Mick Jones went from being a true believer in rock 'n' roll into an artist who, in Big Audio Dynamite, embraced clunky, clattering, synth-dominated sounds one could never imagine being of interest to Clash City Rockers.

There is nothing wrong, of course, with an artist spreading his wings, and in fact much to be admired in it. Moreover, Weller's transformation wasn't just admirable for being brave. Sometimes his new music was not just surprising but impressive in unexpected ways. Witness the disarmingly quirky and astonishingly accurate Beach Boys pastiche at the end of 'The Gardener of Eden'. Witness, too, the fact that his Council melodies frequently possessed a soaring quality Weller rarely gave the impression of being capable of in the Jam, where he sometimes deployed technical smoke-and-mirrors to mask deficiencies in that area. The lyrics were often as sophisticated as the melodies and arrangements: those grating malapropisms and examples of fifth-form poetry pretty much disappeared. However, for some this only made it even more of a shame that Weller didn't enable such maturation within the more exciting framework of the Jam. 'Yeah, but I didn't,' shrugs Weller. Has the possibility that he could have recorded more great songs with the Jam never given him cause for regret? 'Not really. Not at all. I never even think about it. My life has not been "what ifs". My life is still going on. I'm still making fucking great records, so it don't enter my orbit.'

His former colleagues watched all this from the sidelines with increasing bewilderment. One can only imagine the disgust of Buckler and Foxton at the plasticky rhythm section Weller employed on 'Long Hot Summer': a Minimoog-generated bass line and a chattering drum machine. *Café Bleu* at least gave Foxton the insight he'd desired on why Weller had split up the Jam. The bassist told thejamfan.net, '...when he came out with the Style

Council album, I understood. I don't think Rick or I would've wanted to go down that path. It was a bit too wimpy for me.' That comment certainly lends credence to one of Weller's main rationales for leaving the Jam.

That the Style Council are not as highly thought-of as the group Weller broke up in order to form them provokes a metaphor, one appropriately involving the Small Faces, the group at whose feet Weller has always worshipped. Steve Marriott left the Small Faces in early 1969 for new musical pastures, but his next group – Humble Pie – never matched the standards of his previous band. The same can surely be said of Weller. Weller made an interesting comment to Paul Lester which goes partway to admitting this: 'In '86, I saw The Smiths at Newcastle, and the power... as soon as they went onstage, it was like the Jam, really … You didn't get that with the Style Council at all.'

Yet when it's suggested to him that there is no Style Council album as highly thought of as *All Mod Cons*, *Setting Sons* or *Sound Affects*, Weller counters, 'It's a matter of opinion. I can think of lots of people who'd tell you different.' His assertion that the Council were 'very, very successful' is less a matter of opinion, but by 1988 the top-20 hits had dried up. The following year, Weller suffered the indignity of the Council's fifth album, *Modernism: A New Decade* – intended to be the finale to the group's career – being refused a release by the record company to which he'd been signed his entire adult life. It was an album of house music. 'Which at the time was fairly cutting edge, was still pretty underground,' says Weller. 'I was digging it. I didn't really care about anything else. That's where my head was at and that's what I'm gonna do.' David Munns, the man who was now Polydor MD, thought such a stylistic departure commercially untenable. 'To take the album, he'd have to pay whatever the money was and he obviously didn't think it was worth the investment,' says Weller. 'So there you go. That's business, innit?'

Back in 1979, Weller had made some interesting comments to Ian Birch: 'We could never get away with doing anything avant-garde, or even vaguely avant-garde … the whole punk thing started because people were alienated by crappy music, obscure lyrics and references and everything. We don't want to get into that … But also we don't want to suppress anything that wants to come through naturally.' He was afflicted by no such inhibitions in the Style Council. 'He just did what he wanted to do,' says Munday. 'My view is with the Style Council he wanted to get away from the Jam and the Jam sound. In the end, he got far away from himself, as well as the Jam, which is why I don't think the Style Council ended that well.' Says Peter Wilson, 'George Michael felt a slave to the record company, and Prince felt a slave to the record company. Paul was able to do what he wanted. Until they dropped him.' Munday: 'The rejected album, the guy was right. After I left, they renegotiated the Style Council's deal and gave them a million pound an album. So by the time that you get to that album, they were well in the red and that record would have had to sell a million copies to get the money back.'

Modernism: A New Decade is sporadically mesmerising, but it is also vocal-light, synth-dominated and feebly propelled by the pattering of drum machines. Even despite the Style Council's extreme eclecticism, it seems unlikely that their fans would have seen this work as possessing any previously established Council attribute and therefore as offering them any reason they should purchase it. Munday adds, 'I've listened to it many times. It's certainly not the finished article. If I was an A&R man, I'd say, "Can you go back and finish it?"' Wilson (by then no longer Council producer) agrees. 'I think they probably did the right thing and played safe,' he says of Polydor. 'It was really weak. I'm not against the style. I think the execution wasn't very good.'

Was this rejection not the culmination of the Style Council's endless, potentially audience-alienating redefinition of their essence? 'Yeah, but why would that stop you from making that type of music?' reasons Weller. 'If you followed what you're saying through, then you'd only make records that your fans want you to make. You'd never progress.'

Munn's refusal to release the album could be posited as the first time in Weller's professional life that someone had said no to him. 'Probably not the first time,' he demurs. 'I'm sure there was a few singles with the Jam Polydor wanted us to [go] back and re-record or whatever. But a whole album? I guess so, yeah. I just thought he was a fucking twat, David Munns. Big fucking twat. Arrogant cunt. He deemed it's gonna kill his career and all that fucking crap, but I thought it was great music for the time. Interesting enough, a few years later they did put the album out anyway.'

That eventuality, though, wouldn't be for nearly a decade, when Weller had finally made himself a viable artist again. Before then came a period where, a has-been at 31, he had to gradually claw his way back to prominence via a solo career that began right at the bottom. During a three-year period at the start of this process, bereft of a record contract or song publishing deal, Weller was nothing more glamorous than a house husband. 'I lost interest in everything,' he told Simon Goddard. 'In doing music. In writing songs. I didn't write at all, or the few attempts I just felt so disassociated and uninspired.' Friends and family became so concerned for him that for a while Weller agreed to go on a psychotherapist's couch. Meanwhile, his reduced circumstances saw him sell Solid Bond, the recording studio he had owned since 1983.

Eventually, he did begin writing again, but even then had to overcome the hurdle that there weren't at that point many people interested in hearing his new songs. 'I was going back to playing much smaller places,' he says. 'Sometimes 300 people or something. It was starting again.' Was this humiliating? 'Maybe it was at the start of it, but after a while I kind of enjoyed it 'cos I thought, "Well, no one's really that interested so I'm free to do whatever I want to do." I didn't know who my audience was anymore, so I could start again musically. Which is what we did on that first album.' Of his eponymous long-playing debut, released in 1992, Weller avers, 'It's got some great songs on it. We just had fun with it: if we wanted to use a fuzzer-bass, if we wanted to use a Moog... There wasn't any market or audience I was aiming at. I just aimed it at me.'

His comeback was fully confirmed with 1995's *Stanley Road*, his third solo album and first to become a UK number one. Some old fans were perplexed by the fact that it unequivocally consisted of the music he had once condemned as 'shit'. Late in life, Weller had broadened his musical horizons. He explained to *Mojo*'s Chris Ingham in 2000, 'I just started to listen to people I'd never listen to before, people I wouldn't have given the time of day to. I dropped that sort of blinkered thing I'd had as a youth, where I wouldn't listen to records made by men with beards … People like Crosby, Stills and Nash, Van Morrison.' Nothing wrong with this change of outlook, of course – rock not being 'inherently bad.' Nor did it matter, that it was all sung in an American accent: as he was no longer writing political songs, and as he was tackling universal themes rather than local issues, delivery in estuary English was hardly a requisite. What did matter was that Weller now seemed to think he sounded like Steve Marriott. He did, but without the rasp that made his Small Faces hero's voice so excitingly imbued with character. The character that had come from Weller's singing was predicated on the refreshing honesty and novelty of it being without artifice or pretension. This lack of vocal character was part of the reason that *Stanley Road*'s twelve tracks all sounded vaguely the same. The other was their unvaryingly mid-tempo nature. Sameyness would also afflict Weller's subsequent offerings: it's difficult to imagine many people being able to hum, or even name, individual cuts from Paul Weller solo albums. Sometimes, it feels that the only positive thing that can be said about his solo music is that its organic grooves are a deliberate rejection of the digital, mechanical sounds of some of the Style Council's offerings. The music is never less than competent, but – like much Style Council output – works best as background music. This is something that could never be said about Jam records.

Weller's lyrics are now restricted to narrow horizons. He has declared in interview that he isn't 'the slightest bit interested' in writing political songs anymore. He has never actually repudiated the Jam's social commentary, but now says that there is no point revisiting that field. He told *Mojo*, 'People say, "Why don't you write any more political songs?" but I would just write exactly the same fucking things I wrote thirty-odd years ago.' He has also come out with comments that indicate writing political songs was partly a function of being forced by lack of life experience to turn his vision outwards. 'I wasn't old enough to write about myself in any detail,' he told Phil Sutcliffe. 'I didn't have the deep backlog of personal emotions, the dark corners. So I observed characters, situations, my class of people who I grew up with.'

Yet Weller's solo releases are consistently successful. Part of the reason for this seems to stem from the inevitable process that results from an artist continuing to be in the public eye as people weaned on his music become opinion formers. Such types bestowed on Weller the worshipful term 'The Modfather' as they sought to remould his image into that of an iconic survivor. That the public have proven receptive to this image-moulding makes it unlikely that in his remaining years as a productive artist the rug will ever again be pulled from under him like it was in '89. 'I suppose I'm fairly secure now, knowing that I'm always gonna do music until the time I don't want to do it anymore,' reflects Weller. 'Whether it's big, small, lots of numbers, small numbers, whatever, I'm always gonna play music 'cos that's what I'm meant to do. I'm far more in tune with that, more comfortable with it. I've also learnt the art of humility over the course of those last twenty years, which is not a bad thing to learn at all, and you're only as good as your last record and you're only as good as your last gig. Whether it's true or not, it's not a bad thing to follow, really.'

It's an arresting fact that, as Weller has been releasing music on his own for a decade and a half, his solo recording career is already considerably longer than those of the Jam and the Style Council combined. Moreover, although – as with all his peers – his productivity is much lower than it was in the Seventies and Eighties, his dozen solo albums still cumulatively outstrip the long-playing product from the first two acts of his public life.

Munday wasn't surprised that Weller clawed his way back. 'I would have thought the opposite if he hadn't have come back,' he states. 'He was always going to, one way or the other. He's one of the most talented songwriters, certainly the most talented of his generation.' Those unimpressed by Weller's recent output might be tempted to scoff at that suggestion, but if we are to measure success by longevity of commercial impact it becomes quickly obvious that Weller is indeed the great survivor of his contemporaries. Outside of the context of the Sex Pistols, Paul Cook, Steve Jones and Glen Matlock did nothing worth writing home about, while Johnny Rotten/John Lydon's achievements are restricted to the occasionally interesting Public Image Ltd. album. The Damned and Buzzcocks made a few great records but recorded nothing spectacular after the first few years, especially when they entered into the merry-go-round of splits and partial reformations. Sham 69 and the Boomtown Rats split up early in the Eighties and their constituent parts went on to no musical glory. Both groups are now – justly or not – ones people feel embarrassed to admit ever having admired. The Clash's Mick Jones made a brace of interesting albums with Big Audio Dynamite before entering into commercial and artistic freefall (one which had a Weller parallel insofar as BAD's demise was precipitated by their last album being rejected by their record company). Before his premature death in 2002, Joe Strummer's post-Clash oeuvre was very slim. This may not have been his fault, but the legal obstacles that led to it being sparse do not account for it also being pitifully uninteresting compared to his often glorious Clash work. Basically, Paul Weller may never have broken out internationally, but – under the banners of the Jam, the Style Council or his own name – he has outlasted and outsold all his generation, punk or otherwise. That he is in the record books with Paul McCartney (as well as Elton John and David Bowie) as the composer of the most self-written hits in UK chart history is not too surprising: it's difficult to think of any other artist who has rivalled Macca's Beatles-Wings-solo feat in being equally successful in three different guises.

Whether as the Jam, Style Council or Paul Weller, his career was guided by his dad right up until 2006. It was only at that point that ill-health forced John Weller to relinquish the managerial reins. He passed away in 2009, aged 77.

Weller states that he never had trouble reconciling the spirit of rock 'n' roll with the careerism intrinsic to being a recording artist. 'I always felt I was in it for the long haul,' he says. 'I didn't know I was going to get to 57 and still be doing it, but then I didn't know I'd still live to 57. Nothing really went beyond 25 years old for me when I was a certain age. I thought it was all over by that time. But I never saw it as just a little flash in the pan. It was all I ever dreamt of wanting to do and I had the chance to do it. I'm thankful that I'm still able to do it and still am doing it.'

'I did want to do a deal for Bruce and Rick, give them a solo deal each,' says Dennis Munday. 'Polydor wouldn't do it. They said, "We got Paul, fuck them." That was their attitude. I would have signed both of them up purely just to see what you could get out of it. The Jam fans liked them. It would be up to them to come up with something.'

Many might have assumed that such a fine rhythm section would forge a joint career as a sort of new-wave Sly and Robbie. Buckler and Foxton did work together several years later in Sharp (a studio project which lasted only as long as one single) and Built Like Stone (a bona fide group which lasted a year but ultimately released no product). However, directly after the Jam, they simply went their separate ways. 'It never actually crossed my mind to keep going with Rick at the time,' says Foxton. He reasons, 'It was the end of the Jam and so that's it. I think if Rick and myself had stayed together ... we would have always been known as from the Jam.'

Exploring his post-Jam career opportunities would for Foxton not involve bed and breakfast proprietorship, nor any other job in the straight world. 'Well, it's all I can really do,' Foxton reasons. 'I didn't want to go back into the print industry, as nice as it was.' The first thing he tried was a career as a solo artist. After turning down a Polydor deal whose numbers he considered insulting (going by Munday's comment, possibly a deliberate ploy by the label), Foxton signed with Arista, who in May 1984 issued his album *Touch Sensitive*. After years of struggling to keep up with Weller's productivity, Foxton managed to write eight songs for it, the same number as all the songs he'd released with the Jam. He also co-wrote two others. Moreover, the album got a fairly encouraging reception, yielding a top-thirty single in the shape of 'Freak'. However, Foxton was quickly dropped by the label.

'I've been dabbling,' Foxton says of his post-Jam career. 'I was in an indie band, the Rhythm Sisters, for a while. They were based up in Leeds. The thing is with any band, to give it a fair shot you've [got] to give it a few years and, whether it's successful or not, time flies. The biggest band I was in was Stiff Little Fingers.' The latter Belfast group formed in 1977 and quickly gained acclaim as a sort of Northern-Irish Clash. 'Ironically, Stiff Little Fingers was a band that kind of escaped me when the Jam were together,' says Foxton. 'I met Jake on the road. Fingers were in town in Germany and the Jam were and we just got chatting at a bar one night and forged a friendship that has lasted thirty years. But I never really knew any of their songs. Jake asked me to join them in 1990. I went to see them at Brixton Academy and it was sold out – 5,000 people.' Although responsible for an indisputable punk classic – 'Alternative Ulster' – Stiff Little Fingers were second-generation punk. Accordingly, some might view Foxton's acceptance of the job offer from band frontman Jake Burns as a master taking employment from an apprentice. 'I wouldn't call them our apprentices at all,' Foxton says. 'They may have been influenced by the Clash or some of the Jam tracks, they weren't maybe as commercially successful, but I still view them as on equal standing. The SLF audience crosses over into the Jam and vice versa.' Foxton remained in the group's ranks for fifteen years, a period that far exceeded the Jam's lifespan. Part of the reason for this long tenure is presumably a sense of fulfilment stemming from having the opportunity to compose. 'Over the years, we've contributed a few songs together for three or four albums,' says Foxton of Burns. 'He was good to work with. I thought that I would be with Fingers until I couldn't play anymore.'

What changed matters for Foxton was that by 2005 he was involved in another band, Casbah Club, for whom things were taking off. Foxton: 'It was getting tricky because Casbah Club were getting a lot more work and that was exciting for me. It was new material. I still love SLF, but I was getting a little bit bored with the set. I had this new project on the go and it was going to come to a crunch. So we parted Christmas 2005.'

It was in that same year that Foxton came into a totally unexpected but very welcome Jam-related windfall. BBC television began broadcasting a current affairs comedy panel show called *Mock the Week*. It used 'News of the World', the Jam's only Foxton-written A-side, as its title theme. 'Good edit job they did on it as well,' says the 'very pleased' Foxton. At the time of writing, the show is still using his song despite the fact that the newspaper referenced in it ceased to exist in 2011.

Rick Buckler says he 'knocked around the music industry after the Jam.' His first project was a group called Time UK, whose promising line-up included former Tom Robinson Band guitarist Danny Kustow. However, the group never really got going, despite one of their singles being produced by the celebrated Tony Visconti. After three singles spread over two years and a brace of labels, the band gave up the ghost.

'Then I had a recording studio for a couple years,' says Buckler. 'I did some management work. I did all sorts of things.' However, during the Eighties, Buckler became disenchanted with the business. 'Things seemed to be changing a great deal,' he laments. 'The whole music industry, the onus didn't really seem to be on the band, it seemed to be on the image and electronics. I just really did feel very much out of place during that period. So I decided I would spend a couple years indulging myself in something else, which led me into the cabinet-making side of things. I did it for twelve years, which was ten years longer than I really originally planned.'

Fans who attended Jam soundchecks would be mesmerised when Buckler rehearsed patterns. To such people, it will seem tragic that one of the finest sticks-wielders of his era should have dropped out of the business in favour of carpentry. Did trying to acquire session work not appeal to him? 'No, it didn't really. I'm pretty much in control of what I do, so therefore if I don't fancy doing something I simply won't do it. I always thought I would get back into playing, but the opportunity just didn't seem to arise.'

The public explanations that Weller had given for the Jam's dissolution might have been more noble than his real motivations,

240

but as nobody except the inner circle knew this he reaped the PR benefits of the fact that the Jam falling on their swords was perceived as the final confirmation of the cast-iron integrity for which they had been long celebrated. Weller's early Style Council songs ramped up his righteous image further in being even more outspoken than his Jam work about inequality, unemployment and the nuclear threat. Yet Weller's personal behaviour toward his ex-colleagues following the Jam's split displayed none of the honourable ideals he espoused.

With no fallings-out having occurred, Weller cut Buckler and Foxton out of his life completely. Three times, Buckler popped into Solid Bond Studios only to find that Weller wouldn't see him. Weller's office also flatly refused Buckler's request for a list of Jam fan-club members to enable the drummer to send out information on Time UK. Foxton, meanwhile, found that Weller wouldn't come to the phone to speak to him when Munday called his ex-colleague in his presence. Foxton told the *West Sussex Gazette* in 2007, 'Rick and myself sent various birthday cards and Christmas cards to Paul, but when you don't get a response after a few years, you just think "Well, the guy doesn't really want to keep in touch" – which I was very sad about. The band was finished and he just wanted to sever all ties.' It was almost like an anti-matter rock group split: the estrangement coming after the dissolution rather than before it.

Weller's post-Jam 'Rock music is shit' credo was part of a pattern whereby he downplayed his former group. Foxton notes, 'It always puzzled me in the early days where he would almost deny that he was ever part of the Jam. That I found kind of ridiculous. I suppose he wanted to talk about the Style Council, he didn't want to talk about the Jam. But he'll always be known [as] Paul Weller from the Jam. He's still a very successful songwriter and performer and I take my hat off to him for that. But in the early days he seemed almost ashamed of the Jam, which I couldn't understand, because without the Jam and Rick and myself he wouldn't have got where he is today. It's probably just [being] young and immature. Now he's playing Jam songs in his set and I think he realises that the Jam gave him the leg-up he needed.' Munday offers, 'I just think that because people were ramming it in his face about, "Are you going to get the Jam back together?" it pisses him off. It's like divorce. It did get a bit silly after. It's typical record business bullshit. Bands do that.'

Dismissing the Jam was one thing, but more hurtful were the comments Buckler and Foxton found Weller making about them personally. Anyone reading Weller interviews in the 1980s would be forgiven for concluding that the three Jam members had never exchanged a friendly word. Foxton says, 'Although he has said we weren't the best of mates, I think he was very close to Rick.' Buckler: 'I find that all a bit disconcerting when Paul says things like, "Oh, we were never mates, anyway." You think, "Well that's not exactly the way that myself and Bruce remember things." I don't know why he says that sort of stuff really.' 'He's a knob,' Weller says of Buckler. 'I don't really like him. Mutual thing, really. I don't remember us ever getting on. I've seen him say about me saying we were never friends, but I don't remember being fucking buddies. We're chalk and cheese. But let's not dwell on these things, 'cos they're pointless and meaningless.'

Psychologists will no doubt have a theory about what insecurity motivates Weller to deem figures from his past not merely irrelevant but some sort of danger that needs to be shut out. Buckler and Foxton were suffering the same fate that many of Weller's friends and colleagues have suffered from Steve Brookes onwards: being made a non-person.

Then again, there might have been a more sinister reason for Weller not wanting to speak to his ex-colleagues. *The Jam: Our Story*, the book on which Buckler and Foxton collaborated with journalist Alex Ogg, appeared in 1993. Despite the title, it was disappointingly devoid of the rhythm section's perspectives, being more a bog-standard recounting of the group's career. Its real impetus was to help pay for legal action that Buckler and Foxton were proceeding with against their former colleague and former manager.

Although plaintiffs Paul Richard Buckler and Bruce Douglas Foxton launched their case against defendants Paul Weller and John Weller in late 1992, it was one that had been on the cards for a decade, ever since the moment in early 1983 when Buckler contacted John Weller to ask him why the bank account of the Jam partnership had been emptied. The partnership consisted of the three group members and their manager. The sum that had been mysteriously cleared from its account was over £400,000, not £139,618, as has been widely stated. The latter figure, equating to one third of the sum involved, was simply a best-guess starting point for the legal claim, essentially the figure then not in doubt. A considerable degree of the said doubt had been created by Weller Sr's lack of cooperation in clarifying financial details. Buckler noticed the movement of money because he, like all the partnership members, received copies of the bank statements, something Weller Sr hadn't seemed to realise.

Buckler found John Weller evasive, but at the time had no concrete reason to disbelieve his vague reassurances that the money was set aside for such things as tax and outstanding debts. As Buckler says of the whole saga that would unravel, 'At the time I felt that this sort of thing only happened to other people, and … I could not quite believe that John and Paul would act in such a way towards Bruce and myself, as we were very much as instrumental in the Jam's success. Paul's reluctance to speak about the Jam in interviews and avoidance [of] myself and Bruce in the following years was very telling.'

Buckler and Foxton were shown no documents to substantiate Weller Sr.'s explanations. Moreover, whenever over the next few years Buckler and/or Foxton tried to arrange meetings with Weller Sr to discuss Jam monetary matters, the latter always found a reason to defer them. The further the rhythm section delved into the issue of Jam monies, the more concerned they became. Royalties had continued flowing from the likes of Polydor, merchandisers, publishing companies and the performance rights society Phonographic Performance Limited. As before, they had been sent to the band's manager. John Weller was unable to deposit them in the Jam's partnership account like he had previously because, once emptied, that account had been closed. Weller Sr instead put the money into his own bank account. To facilitate this, he crossed through the words 'The Jam' in the cheques' payee fields and substituted them with his own name. Buckler and Foxton were shocked to discover that Weller Sr's bank branch had accepted these cheques.

Buckler and Foxton were only able to retrieve their share of record royalties via an elaborate system whereby at the end of each accounting period they asked the record company what figures had been paid to Weller Sr and then invoiced the latter. They would then wait for the payments, most of which were continually more than nine months overdue. With the pair having to pay VAT to HM Revenue & Customs on all invoices raised – as opposed to paid – this consistently left them out of pocket.

More issues came to light, such as the non-payment of publishing and performing rights monies. With all the different income streams and companies involved, getting a clear picture of sums due became very complicated, expensive and time-consuming. Buckler and Foxton's legal claim initially estimated that they had been deprived of £17,237 each regarding publishing on 'Funeral Pyre' and £14,480 each from merchandise and fan club profits.

The years ground on with no satisfactory response from the Wellers to Foxton and Buckler's 1992 writ. As these events were taking place some years before the introduction of Conditional Fee Agreements ('no win, no fee' cases), the litigants suspected that Weller Sr was gambling on the probability that sooner or later they would run out of funds and have to drop the action, especially if – as was also suspected – he was fighting Buckler and Foxton with their own money. Certainly, in Buckler's case he was forced into a lamentable Hobson's choice, selling off his gold discs and other treasured Jam mementoes in order to keep paying the lawyers.

In late 1995, it seemed clear to Buckler and Foxton that a full court hearing was their only option. Buckler publicly commented, 'We have tried to resolve this amicably but have never had any response from Paul or his dad. There is too much money involved for us to let it go. It's a shame it had to end up like this.' A spokesman for Buckler and Foxton's management company noted, 'It really is silly that it has gone on for so long. The legal costs must have far outweighed the claim a long, long time ago.'

The case was finally settled in the litigants' favour in February 1996, when it was adjudged that the Jam partnership was still in existence because the legal requirement to fully wind down such a partnership – the complete and proper disposal of all its assets – had not been effected. As part of the settlement, it was ordered that John Weller stop collecting any royalties on Buckler and Foxton's behalf and that royalties should henceforth be paid direct from source – an implicit acknowledgment that Weller Sr had failed in his legal responsibility to pass on income due to individuals he represented.

There was one final financial upshot of the court case. Two separate record companies had recently heard recordings the group had made before they were signed to Polydor. As both companies considered them to have a value, they formally became an asset of the Jam partnership. Rights to these recordings were promptly bought from Buckler and Foxton by John and Paul Weller to prevent them being released. (This purchase may be the cause of erroneous reports that Buckler and Foxton agreed to a deal whereby they accepted a lump sum in settlement of their case in lieu of royalties on future Jam product.)

Paul Weller can count himself extremely fortunate that the famous Jam taciturnity and lack of drama has ensured that the court case has received little media attention down the years. The Alex Ogg book had been lacking in meat because, at the time, the pair had not wanted to aggravate the legal dispute with the Wellers. However, even in victory the rhythm section have been too gentlemanly to publicly criticise John and Paul Weller much about the matter, frequently coming up with formulae of words about how they don't want to get the knives out or rake over old coals. There is nothing about the case in Buckler's subsequent book *That's Entertainment*. One also suspects that Buckler and Foxton were unsettled by the fact that the long, grisly process caused them for the very first time to doubt the unsullied integrity of John Weller. Paul Weller has also benefitted from a rather sycophantic attitude from journalists, with some chroniclers of the band seeming illogically determined to draw a moral equivalence between Weller and Buckler & Foxton in the matter. The less credulous type of Jam fan has been heard to suggest that the behaviour revealed by the case undermines and devalues everything for which the Jam ever stood.

If Weller did not know about his father's conduct, its unravelling and exposing must have been painful for him. However, this hardly seems to justify the tone of injury in his 2002 comment to *The Guardian*'s Adam Sweeting about Buckler and Foxton: 'I never felt we were best of friends, and best friends don't take each other to court.'

Says Buckler, 'The court case was a sensitive issue, especially embarrassing for John and Paul Weller. It left me feeling very disappointed with Paul and John, after all we had achieved together.'

In the mid-Noughties, Buckler decided that he missed performing. To that end, he got together with Russell Hastings and Dave Moore to form the band the Gift. 'I wanted to revisit the Jam songs,' he says. In May 2006, Foxton's Casbah Club played support to the Gift at Guildford University. Buckler recalls, 'We asked them to jump up. Did a couple of numbers. That went really, really well. The response was fantastic and we did it a few more times during the year and basically by the end of the year we decided that we'd do something a bit more concrete with it.' The ex-colleagues joined forces in From the Jam, a group whose *raison d'etre* was to bring the group's songs back to a live audience. Munday says, 'I've seen From the Jam and they're fantastic.' The groups' success on the nostalgia circuit served to prove, a quarter-century too late, that the pair might have been wise to stick together back in '82.

Buckler's only sighting of Weller post-Jam occurred in 1983. 'I bumped into him when I went to one of Bruce's solo concerts,' he reveals. 'Paul was at the back. Just happened to walk past him really and that was the last time that I actually saw him, which is a long time ago.'

The situation is slightly different with Foxton. Although Weller and the bassist didn't speak for nearly a quarter of a century, they are now on friendly terms. In 2006, London's Hyde Park was hosting a concert by the Who. As Foxton's Casbah Club was fronted by Simon Townshend, brother of the Who's Pete, they were able to secure a slot as one of the day's support acts. Recalls Foxton, 'Casbah had a Portakabin and Ocean Colour Scene were opposite in their Portakabin. It was a glorious sunny day. Myself and the band and family and friends were outside and Ocean Colour Scene were doing similar opposite. Lo and behold, Paul showed up, 'cos he came to see them, amongst other acts. And it was those awkward glances across twenty yards of grass or whatever. All my friends and family: "Go and say hi. It's a good opportunity to break the ice." I was really nervous about our show anyway, because we were due to go on in twenty minutes, and I was thinking, "Oh, shall I or shan't I, what's he going to say?" I was quite nervous really [about] how he would be. Would he blank me or would he give me the time of day? In the end, it came about naturally. I needed to go to the loo just before our show and Paul came in right behind me. I don't know if he was waiting for that moment or just needed to go for a pee as well, but he just gave us a big hug and said, "Oh, it's been too long man, great to see ya and I love ya." And I said, "Well, likewise, it has been too long." It was really nice, but it was so brief. It was probably thirty seconds, a minute at the most, and then, I said semi-jokingly, "Well we'd better kind of leave it at that, because people will start talking about us in the toilets." It was a great moment for me, that he was so friendly.'

Tragedy turned this brief reunion into a full-blown reconnection. In 2008, Weller, having received word that Foxton's wife Pat was ill with breast cancer, took the trouble to telephone her. Sadly, Pat's condition worsened and she died the following year, but the bond between the two men was now fully repaired. Foxton played on a couple of tracks on Weller's 2010 album *Wake Up the Nation* and joined him onstage at his birthday concert at the Royal Albert Hall in 2010. Weller returned the favour by appearing on three tracks on *Back in the Room*, Foxton's second solo album, a crowd-funded affair released in 2012. It was recorded at Black Barn, the studio now owned by Weller and located near Woking.

By then, ironically, Foxton and Buckler were incommunicado. The drummer quit From the Jam by email in 2009. In 2012, Foxton told David Owens of Wales Online, 'We had management issues at the time Rick left ... Whether he disagreed with ... wanting to part company with the management or not I don't know, but it was weird because he never actually fully explained the reason why.' Buckler's version of events, told to Barry Rutter, was, 'I just got fed up with it, it wasn't going anywhere … it ran its course.' Foxton continued From the Jam with Russell Hastings. Buckler formed a new group and worked in artist management. He also runs Jam website thejamfan.net.

Weller's kindness to Foxton is a touching story, but his newfound loyalty to the bassist also brought out his imperious side. Following a telephone interview with the present author designed to tie in with the Jam exhibition About The Young Idea, Weller instructed his PR to contact the magazine for which the interview was conducted to request that it not be printed. He was said to be unhappy with the interview and to consider the questions contentious. The interview in fact was perfectly friendly, so much so that Weller allowed it to run for an hour more than its intended length. Judging by the fact that Weller communicated that he felt compelled to ring Foxton straight after the interview, it would seem he had misgivings about the frankness of some of his comments, possibly his blunt dismissal of Foxton's claim that he and Buckler could be said to have co-written many Jam songs attributed to Weller alone. The magazine – a small proposition dependent on music-company advertising – acquiesced to Weller's request. Leaving aside how over-anxious was his behaviour, it didn't seem to occur to Weller that his actions would cost money to a blameless journalist of far less means than he.

I subsequently informed Weller's representatives that to compensate me for the financial loss his actions had caused me I would be publishing the interview material in a Jam biography. His response was to contact his lawyer, who across the course of two months issued threats of injunctions before going quiet after I pointed out that there were no grounds to prevent publication. This response on the part of Weller was made all the more shocking by the fact that I had offered to let him read the interview transcript before publication to put his mind at rest about its contents and further offered to allow him to append clarifying comments if he felt he had misrepresented himself. I had become yet another individual whose personal experience of Weller called into question his Man of the People image.

THE LEGACY

While the Jam dissolved in an orgy of worshipful eulogies, their bookends/rivals/enemies headed further into the realms of farce.

The Clash's return in 1982 after a year-and-a-half without long-playing product was hardly a triumphant one, at least at first. With ticket sales for the UK tour to promote new album *Combat Rock* transpiring to be very poor, they had to resort to a publicity stunt involving Strummer faking his disappearance. While this worked in raising their profile and drumming up sales, *Combat Rock* was unimpressive. Despite its occasional charms, it spurned their trademark anthemic rebel rock for inexpert exploration of musical arcana, while addressing the social ills of several countries but never, recognisably, Britain's. Paradoxically, this artistic nadir became an international success. With the Clash now acceding to the type of shameless marketing tactics they had once ostentatiously rejected – including gimmicky gifts with records, playing support to rock aristos in stadia, refusing magazine interviews without the guarantee of featuring on the cover – the album very lucratively climbed into the US top ten. Just when they had clawed their way back to the top, though, the Clash snatched defeat from the jaws of victory by sacking Mick Jones. While the guitarist's prima-donna airs were doubtlessly irritating, he was the group's musical director. The result of his dismissal was no less shocking for it being predictable. Three-and-a-half years after *Combat Rock* had achieved a platinum disc in the States, *Cut the Crap* – its belated, cringe-making follow-up – failed to chart there. The Clash split up even before its release. That this sub-standard swansong sullied the reputation of a great band could be argued to have almost instantly validated Weller's decision to wind up the Jam before they became a joke.

Yet it can't be denied that that situation changed quite profoundly over the following decades. While the Clash's reputation posthumously soared, the Jam's somehow deflated. As the Eighties progressed, the Jam seemed to fall off the radar in a way that many other defunct but celebrated groups have not: there was little discussion in the music press about them, few references to them as influences in artist interviews, few appearances of their works in polls to determine history's best albums, a scant presence on radio even as the 'gold' broadcast format became ever more prevalent. At the time they were extant, especially the second half of their career, it was universally accepted, at least in the UK, that the Jam were titans who deserved to be mentioned in the same breath as the Beatles, the Rolling Stones, Bob Dylan and all the other fixtures of the popular-music pantheon. Although their body of work is certainly not viewed as discredited, it has subsequently settled into a much lower place in the hierarchy of public respect.

Part of the reason was their local appeal. Fans in their homeland had loved the Jam precisely because they stayed in touch with the nation and its concerns. Yet that also made them parochial: they wrote songs for a section of a small island. That they were a big fish in a small pond can't, however, be the whole explanation for the fading of the Jam's allure. The Clash might have thrown more traditional rock 'n' roll shapes in both image and music, and might have ultimately ranged further for subject matter, but overall their songs were no less suffused with British slang and cultural references than the Jam's.

One part of the explanation is that the Jam were less commercially successful and therefore less visible in other countries, particularly the United States. The Jam admitted to Chris Salewicz in 1981 – a point where they were one of the biggest bands in Britain – that outside of the shores of the UK they had large followings only in Sweden and Japan. The Jam have suffered from what we might call Small Faces Syndrome: there are many Americans who genuinely know a lot about rock history but who the brilliance of the Small Faces' music has bypassed simply because that ensemble never 'broke' their country.

Even then, that is not sufficient as an explanation, particularly for the group's lower standing in the UK. The simple truth is that – although during their respective lifetimes the two bands seemed very similar in hinterland, outlook, approach and aesthetic achievement – when the dust settled the Clash were revealed as the superior artists. It was hard to see it at the time because once past their honeymoon period (essentially their early singles and first album), the UK music press so often and so consistently ridiculed the Clash. The difficulty in such an atmosphere of evaluating the quality of their work is demonstrated by *London Calling*. Weller's contemporaneous scathing view of an album now revered as a classic is documented earlier in this text. It's also interesting to note that, in his 1980 Jam retrospective in *Sounds*, Phil Sutcliffe gleaned these comments on the record from Jam fan 'Norman': 'I couldn't see the Jam doing anything like *London Calling*. I think Weller would rather die than give up his ideals like that.' Once removed from disgust at their posturing, broken promises about giving their riches away, alleged desertion of their fans and arguable Americanisation, the only thing that mattered was the quality of the Clash's music. The consensus is that their albums *The Clash* and *London Calling* and standalone singles 'Complete Control' and '(White Man) in Hammersmith Palais' are all-time classics. Jam peaks like *Setting Sons* or *Sound Affects*, meanwhile, remain highly respected, but are not revered. They are footnotes, cropping up only in the lower reaches of critics' greatest-album polls (if at all), including UK ballots. The way the Jam consistently swept the board in the *NME* end-of-year poll now seems a distant memory from a time of different values, as does the fact that 'Going Underground''s success prompted people to rush out to buy their back catalogue like Beatlemania had taken a new form.

In the Jam-Clash battle of the bands, the Clash belatedly and unexpectedly won.

Commerce was also triumphant. The Clash proceeded to turn rebellion into money more assiduously than the Jam had ever managed. The CD version of their first proper compilation, *The Story of the Clash Volume 1,* was shockingly over-priced (£22.99 for two discs – in 1988) and dismayingly conventional (it spurned the perfect opportunity to mop up their many hard-to-obtain non-album tracks). Their 1991 box set *Clash on Broadway* was cynically exploitative and hypocritically American-oriented.

The Jam could be said to be no better. The first Jam compilation was *Snap!,* a double album released in October 1983. Compiled by Munday, it featured all the band's A-sides, some B-sides and selected album tracks. Munday was pleased with the result: 'When you look at that, you think, "Well, what a great band."' However, while it was undeniably a good listen and additionally useful for the way it rounded up so many tracks not available on Jam albums (which included some A-sides slightly different to LP versions), *Snap!* was overall a collection not for the dedicated fan but the casual purchaser. It was understandable that a trade-off had to be effected between satisfying the purist, who would have preferred a set exclusively devoted to non-album tracks, and pleasing the wider public, who wanted the hits, regardless of whether they'd also appeared on LPs. However, the inclusion of rarities – a demo of 'That's Entertainment', a remix of 'Funeral Pyre' and (initially) a free EP of live Wembley Arena tracks – was clearly a means of acquiring the custom of people who already had everything else on the set. Having not yet been split a year, the Jam were already allowing their fans to be exploited. There would be several further Jam compilations down the decades, each seeming progressively more pointless.

In 1997 came a Jam compilation with a difference, the five-CD box set *Direction Reaction Creation.* It was admirable in being designed to be all-encompassing, but lamentable in failing to be such. It sought to represent every different song the Jam released during their lifetime, but only once. It was the album versions that were uniformly deemed by compiler Munday the ones worthy of inclusion. Some suggested that the whole point of a box set is comprehensiveness, regardless of song repetition, and in any case why was an exception made for 'Smithers-Jones'? Moreover, the album sequencings were broken up to facilitate a tracklisting that cleaved to chronological order, so that for instance 'The Eton Rifles' preceded the remainder of *Setting Sons* because it had appeared as a single before the LP's release.

Nonetheless, the set was very popular. It climbed to number eight in the UK chart like it was a regular best-of rather than a deluxe product. 'I was surprised how many it sold,' says Munday. 'The company only expected to sell fifteen to twenty thousand and it sold over fifty.' Munday doubts that only the old fans bought it: 'I think they've got a new generation of fans, every generation. They're a band that are about a young generation. If you're eighteen, nineteen now, you can relate to what they're saying.'

Some felt the deluxe format and hefty price tag of *Direction Reaction Creation* to not be in the spirit of punk. 'It's a box set, innit?' shrugs Weller. 'It was a box set with the complete recordings as far as I remember. That's what box sets with complete recordings do, really. You can't please 'em all.' This air of nuffin-to-do-wiv-me-guv seems a little disingenuous if we are to believe the claims Munday has made that the project was Weller's idea, and that furthermore Weller didn't want the set to include disc five, a collection of mostly unreleased tracks that would be just about the only part of its contents that the average Jam fan didn't already own.

Subsequent Deluxe and Super Deluxe reissues of Jam albums feature previously unheard demos and alternate takes. There have also been several compilations of live Jam material and a dedicated collection of radio sessions. All serve to create the slightly ridiculous state of affairs of the Jam's original legacy being dwarfed by ephemera, yet at the same time they demonstrate the loyalty and hunger generated by that original legacy's excellence.

This is no more something to lose sleep over than the use of Jam music in TV dramas and movies, a broadly harmless and handy new revenue stream in a day and age of diminishing income from what used to be called records. A different issue is the granting of permission to use Jam songs in commercials. In 2014, the breathy-voiced Whinnie Williams sang 'That's Entertainment' in a television advertisement for the Renault Zoe. The chaotic urban scenes outside the insulated calm of the car interior presumably accounted for the choice of song, but no discernible logic could be read into the soundtrack of a 2017 advert for financial services comparison website confused.com in which rotund actor James Corden persuaded a herd of sheep to step out of the way of approaching cars on a country lane to the sonic backdrop of 'Town Called Malice'. This time, the music used was not a cover version but the hallowed original recording. Even leaving aside the fatuousness issue, it can't be denied that songs such as these – which mean so much to so many in terms way beyond the good memories routinely invoked by the average pop song – are left cheapened by such usage. 'Sell out' was a term deployed all too often in the era of punk, but few veterans of that period would argue that it would be unfair to use it in this instance.

Asked if there are some fans who want him even after all this time to reassemble the Jam, Weller says, 'There must be, 'cos Bruce is still out there playing and stuff.'

Indeed. Many people found risible the Gift and From the Jam because of the Paul Weller-sized hole in their line-ups, yet the success of those ensembles proves that people are willing to pay to hear Jam songs from a group which contains merely the band's rhythm section, or even just half of it. A fully reassembled Jam fronted by the man who was by far the most important member of the group would logically, therefore, have concert promoters and music labels beating a path to the door with chequebooks in perspiring hands. Yet even in Weller's darkest days, he seems never to have countenanced a Jam reunion. Although the blow of his early-Nineties nadir was softened by the financial stability he had built up – and although he doubtlessly loved the company of his new son – unemployment and house-husbandry must have been crushing for somebody used to activity and adoration. Yet there was never the slightest whiff of an inclination to reactivate the Jam, even though such an act would have given him back his lost audience at a stroke. It's not surprising, then, that Weller hasn't changed his attitude since.

During the early days of From the Jam, Weller's former colleagues made overtures to him. 'His office didn't get back to us,' says Foxton, 'but we just had to say via the press, "The door is always open and if you care to join us, it would be fantastic" and that's the best we could do. Couldn't actually get to speak to him.' However, those approaches were clearly half-hearted and anticipating either silence or refusal. 'Paul doesn't want to get involved and it's not going to happen,' Buckler admits of the possibility of a revival of the Jam.

Asked about the prospect of a reunion in the *About the Young Idea* documentary, Weller said, 'Absolutely, categorically, fucking no. To me it would be against everything we ever stood for.' If those words seem strong, they are as nothing compared to his comments in a 2006 interview with BBC 6 Music in which he said, 'That will never, ever happen. Me and my children would have to be destitute and starving in the gutter before I'd even consider that ... I think it's a great thing that the Jam's music has endured over the years and people still love it and still play it. It still means something to people and a lot of that's because we stopped at the right time. It didn't go on and become embarrassing.'

Those who suggested that 'embarrassing' was the right description for Buckler and Foxton's From the Jam venture received a fair-enough response from Buckler, who told *Edinburgh News*, 'Paul Weller still does Jam songs and no one dares call him a tribute band. Bruce Foxton and I were two thirds of the original Jam line-up...' Buckler was shocked by an assumption he felt emanating from his former colleague's direction that, if Weller took no part in From the Jam, it would never get off the ground. 'There is a view that he thinks he was the Jam,' says the drummer. 'Maybe he started to believe his own press.' Buckler's point is not completely undermined by the fact that when he left From the Jam he gave as an explanation to Barry Rutter, 'We were in grave danger of turning into a tribute band to ourselves. When I read that Paul had turned round and criticised it, I thought maybe he has a point!'

For the record, the rhythm section's comments on the possibility of a reunion given in the *About the Young Idea* documentary – recorded after the interviews for this book – are as follows. Buckler: 'I don't know whether it would be the wisest thing to do in actual fact.' Foxton: 'There's too much time and too much water under the bridge and it's best probably left there.'

While few could applaud Weller's aloofness, even callousness, toward his ex-bandmates, even fewer would dispute his wisdom in not acceding to calls for a reunion. From the Byrds to the Animals to the Small Faces, popular music is littered with reunions which seem only to prove that alchemy cannot be recreated. Despite punk having been explicitly opposed to veneration of idols past their peak, graduates of the class of '77 have proven no more immune to exploiting the nostalgia market than any other generation of musicians. Their reunions are commensurately more embarrassing, even where the reunion is deliberately designed not to sully a corpus by being restricted to live events, e.g., the Sex Pistols. Raddled, greying, middle-aged men reviving songs of teenage disaffection was categorically not on punk's original agenda. 'Some bands split up and then ten or fifteen years later they re-form 'cos they need the money,' notes Peter Wilson. 'Then all these people in their forties and fifties go and see them 'cos they knew them when they were adolescents. There's something slightly strange about it that makes me feel a bit uneasy, especially when they're charging 150 quid a ticket.'

The Jam recorded many classic songs. They fulfilled the dreams and promises of punk by securing hit records of frequently exquisite quality and often acute social commentary, suffused with an additional cultural authenticity. They then bowed out at the top, a feat even more impressive than the early dissolutions of the Beatles, Mott the Hoople and the Smiths because done (whatever the background machinations) in an orderly and clean manner. This is a remarkable legacy. It's one best served by never being tampered with.

'It was great fun while it lasted,' says Bruce Foxton. 'That's kind of throwaway comment now, but we have left a fantastic legacy there.' Which raises the question: what exactly is the Jam's legacy? 'We were an important part of the punk movement and overall stuck to the principles of that.' The bassist adds, 'It's very contemporary to this day. When they play a Jam song on the radio it invariably sounds fantastic, to my ears anyway.'

When Rick Buckler began playing gigs again in the mid-Noughties, it brought on a peculiar feeling. 'Being outside of the business for a while and living a fairly quiet life for twelve years, coming back and finding there's all this interest, I suddenly found myself being regarded as being a part of the old-age pension of rock 'n' roll. It was a bit of a strange one to confront, because I never really regarded myself like that. All of a sudden, there's a lot of people citing the Jam as being their influence and whatever. It's very satisfying to hear other musicians have got something from something that you've done, apart from all the enjoyment that obviously the fans had as well.' And the legacy? 'We probably refreshed up the idea of the great British single and the song. Things had gone a little bit glitzy and [a] little showbizzy as far as the pop industry had gone, and it was either that or it was going into the mega, the sort of bloated.' Buckler also says, 'We knew what our identity was and we knew what we wanted to sound like and that's just down to being quite focused in what you're doing and not necessarily being influenced too much by the wrong things, for instance having to change a sound just because you want to go and tour the States. It's being true to yourself musically.' He is also impressed by the feedback he has had from Jam fans about what they feel the band's legacy constitutes: 'They do like that, when you look at the collection of albums, there was a definite change happening and there was definitely musical exploration going on. We were always looking for a new way of doing something and I think that does show in the progression. They're all very much different from each other and, depending on what you happen to feel in the mood for, you'll find it there.'

The *About the Young Idea* exhibition served to confirm that, however relatively diminished, the Jam's legacy both existed and was substantial. It was the concept of Jam collector Den Davis. The exhibition was curated by Weller's sister Nicky, who ran not only the Jam's fan club, but later her brother's recording studio. She was assisted by Tory Turk and Russell Reader with additional advice from Gary Crowley. Originally running from June 26 to September 27, 2015, it featured artefacts and memorabilia provided by fans and all three Jam members. Exhibits included handwritten lyrics, personal photographs, home film footage, promotional films/videos, letters, postcards, posters, fanzines, stage outfits and instruments. Although it might be said that historical building Somerset House was an incongruously grand setting for an exhibition devoted to a socially conscious, proudly working-class band like the Jam, Bill Smith felt *About the Young Idea* was less successful when the following year it transferred to the Cunard Building in Liverpool. 'The one in Liverpool, although it was much, much bigger and there was much more in it, it felt a bit more glamorous,' he says. 'The one in Somerset House was a bit more personal, because they were quite small rooms and everything was nicely encapsulated.'

Smith and Mankowitz were invited to display at the exhibition their never-seen 'Absolute Beginners' video. Smith also got to recreate his first and most iconic piece of Jam design. 'We created the tiled wall and I re-sprayed the logo for the exhibition at Somerset House,' he says. 'Literally everybody wanted to have their picture taken with that behind.'

Considering his past ambivalence about the group, some were surprised both by how enthusiastically Paul Weller promoted the exhibition and his attendant statements that he was proud of the Jam. 'Why wouldn't I be, though?' he says. 'Of course I'm proud of my old work and the band and what we created and our legacy. I'd have to be a fucking idiot to not be proud of that. We're talking about 35 years later and people are still interested in seeing an exhibition and people are still talking about the band. That's a great testament to any band, innit? That you stand the test of time. People are still playing Jam records on the radio after God knows how many decades, so there's no reason to not [think] when I'm dead and gone they'll still be playing them. What more could you ask for, really? We meant something to people. The young people now I see at my gigs who know the words to the songs, they would have got into it through the parents or I don't know whatever method. That's a great testament to our legacy.' As to the specific qualities of that legacy, Weller says, 'Great songs was our achievement. Songs that meant something to people. The best of it stood the test of time and is still relevant. That's my greatest achievement as a songwriter, as well.'

Weller has one more thing to say about the Jam, something which can perhaps serve as a little bit of an antidote to the bad feelings that have tended to overshadow the band since their dissolution. 'We had a good time doing it,' he avers. 'There's lots of laughs in that band. We had loads of great times, 'specially the early days. It was fun. When you're fifteen, sixteen, playing on Friday and Saturday night, getting paid a bit of money for it, getting pissed as well – does it get any better at that age?'

THE JAM: SELECTED DISCOGRAPHY

Note: listed releases are from the Jam's lifespan only.

29 April 1977
A: In the City
B: Takin' My Love
Chart: 40

20 May 1977
IN THE CITY
Side One
Art School
I've Changed My Address
Slow Down
I Got By In Time
Away from the Numbers
Batman Theme
Side Two
In the City
Sounds from the Street
Non-Stop Dancing
Time for Truth
Takin' My Love
Bricks and Mortar
Chart: 20

15 July 1977
A: All Around the World
B: Carnaby Street
Chart: 13

28 October 1977
A: The Modern World
B: Sweet Soul Music/Back in My Arms Again/Bricks and Mortar
Note: B-side tracks are live recordings.
Chart: 36

18 November 1977
THIS IS THE MODERN WORLD
Side One
The Modern World
London Traffic
Standards
Life from a Window
The Combine
Don't Tell Them You're Sane
Side Two
In the Street Today
London Girl
I Need You (For Someone)
Here Comes the Weekend
Tonight at Noon
In the Midnight Hour
Chart: 22

3 March 1978
A: News of the World
B: Aunties and Uncles (Impulsive Youths)
B: Innocent Man
Chart: 27

18 August 1978
A: David Watts
A: "A" Bomb in Wardour Street
Chart: 25

13 October 1978
A: Down in the Tube Station at Midnight
B: So Sad About Us
B: The Night
Chart: 15

3 November 1978
ALL MOD CONS
Side One
All Mod Cons
To Be Someone (Didn't We Have a Nice Time)
Mr. Clean
David Watts
English Rose
In the Crowd
Side Two
Billy Hunt
It's Too Bad
Fly
The Place I Love
"A" Bomb in Wardour Street
Down in the Tube Station at Midnight
Chart: 6

9 March 1979
A: Strange Town
B: The Butterfly Collector
Chart: 15

17 August 1979
A: When You're Young
B: Smithers-Jones
Chart: 17

26 October 1979
A: The Eton Rifles
B: See-Saw
Chart: 3

16 November 1979
SETTING SONS
Side One
Girl on the Phone
Thick as Thieves
Private Hell
Little Boy Soldiers
Wasteland
Side Two
Burning Sky
Smithers-Jones
Saturday's Kids
The Eton Rifles
Heat Wave
Chart: 4

14 March 1980
A: Going Underground
A: The Dreams of Children
Chart: 1 (aggregated with other editions of release)

14 March 1980
A: Going Underground
A: The Dreams of Children
B: Away from the Numbers
B: The Modern World
B: Down in the Tube Station at Midnight
Note: seven-inch double-pack; tracks on second disc are live recordings.
Chart: 1 (aggregated with other editions of release)

15 August 1980
A: Start!
B: Liza Radley
Chart: 1

28 November 1980
SOUND AFFECTS
Side One
Pretty Green
Monday
But I'm Different Now
Set the House Ablaze
Start!
That's Entertainment
Side Two
Dream Time
Man in the Corner Shop
Music for the Last Couple
Boy About Town
Scrape Away
Chart: 2

December 1980
A: Boy About Town/Pop Art Poem
Note: flexidisc given away with *Flexipop* magazine; Boy About Town is an alternate version.
Chart: n/a

December 1980
A: When You're Young
Note: flexidisc mailed out to Jam fan club members; live version.
Chart: n/a

February 1981
A: That's Entertainment
B: Down in the Tube Station at Midnight (Live Version)
Note: import.
Chart: 21

29 May 1981
A: Funeral Pyre
B: Disguises
Chart: 4

16 October 1981
A: Absolute Beginners
B: Tales From the Riverbank
Chart: 4

December 1981
Tales from the Riverbank
Note: flexidisc mailed out to Jam fan club members; alternate version.
Chart: n/a

29 January 1982
A: Town Called Malice
A: Precious
Chart: 1 (aggregated with other editions of release)

29 January 1982
A: Town Called Malice
A: Precious (Extended Version)
Note: twelve-inch single; Town Called Malice is live version.
Chart: 1 (aggregated with other editions of release)

12 March 1982
THE GIFT
Side One
Happy Together
Ghosts
Precious
Just Who Is the 5 O'Clock Hero?
"Trans-Global Express"
Side Two
Running on the Spot
Circus
The Planner's Dream Goes Wrong
Carnation
Town Called Malice
The Gift
Chart: 1

11 June 1982
A: Just Who is the Five O'Clock Hero?
B: The Great Depression
Note: import (disputed).
Chart: 8 (aggregated with other editions of release)

June 1982
A: Just Who is the Five O'Clock Hero?
B: War
B: The Great Depression
Note: import (disputed); twelve-inch single.
Chart: 8 (aggregated with other editions of release)

6 September 1982
A: The Bitterest Pill (I Ever Had to Swallow)
B: Pity Poor Alfie/Fever
Chart: 2

22 November 1982
A: Beat Surrender
B: Shopping
Chart: 1 (aggregated with other editions of release)

A: Beat Surrender
A: Shopping
B: Stoned Out of My Mind
B: Move on Up
B: War
Note: twelve-inch single.
Chart: 1 (aggregated with other editions of release)

A: Beat Surrender
B: Shopping
B: Stoned Out of My Mind
B: Move on Up
B: War
Note: seven-inch double-pack.
Chart: 1 (aggregated with other editions of release)

10 December 1982
DIG THE NEW BREED
Side One
In the City
All Mod Cons
To Be Someone (Didn't We Have a Nice Time)
It's Too Bad
Start!
Big Bird
Set the House Ablaze
Side Two
Ghosts
Standards
In the Crowd
Going Underground
Dreams of Children
That's Entertainment
Private Hell
Note: live recordings.
Chart: 2

18 December 1982
A: Move on Up
Note: flexidisc given away with *Melody Maker* magazine; live version.
Chart: n/a

BIBLIOGRAPHY

BOOKS

The Jam: Our Story; Rick Buckler, Bruce Foxton; Castle Communications; 1993

That's Entertainment; Rick Buckler; Omnibus Press; 2015

The Dead Straight Guide to The Jam;   Rick Buckler, Ian Snowball; Red Planet; 2017

Boy About Town; Tony Fletcher; Windmill Books; 2014

British Hit Albums; Paul Gambaccini, Tim Rice, Jonathan Rice; Guinness Publishing; 1990

British Hit Singles; Paul Gambaccini, Tim Rice, Jonathan Rice; Guinness Publishing; 1993

The Jam: A Beat Concerto; Paolo Hewitt; Omnibus Press; 1983

Paul Weller: The Changing Man; Paolo Hewitt; Transworld; 2008

The Jam: The Modern World by Numbers; Paul Honeyford; Eel Pie; 1980

Shout to the Top: The Jam and Paul Weller; Dennis Munday; Omnibus Press; 2008

The Complete Guide to the Music of Paul Weller & the Jam; John Reed; Omnibus Press; 1999

Paul Weller: My Ever Changing Moods; John Reed; Omnibus Press; 2005

The Jam: Sounds from the Street; Graham Willmott; Reynolds & Hearn; 2003

WEBSITES

en.wikipedia.org
thejam.org.uk
www.45cat.com
www.bankofengland.co.uk
www.bbc.co.uk
www.discogs.com

www.officialcharts.com
www.rocklistmusic.co.uk
www.somersethouse.org.uk
www.thejamfan.net
www.thejamofficial.com

ACKNOWLEDGMENTS

My grateful thanks are extended to the following people for providing me interviews: Rick Buckler, Vic Coppersmith-Heaven, Bruce Foxton, Dennis Munday, Chris Parry, Bill Smith, Tony Taverner, Paul Weller and Peter Wilson.

THE GUYS WHO WROTE 'EM

SONGWRITING GENIUSES OF ROCK AND POP

The untold story of popular music

SEAN EGAN

ALSO FROM ASKILL PUBLISHING

UPDATED AND EXPANDED

animal tracks

The Story of The Animals:
Newcastle's Rising Sons

Sean Egan

ALSO FROM ASKILL PUBLISHING

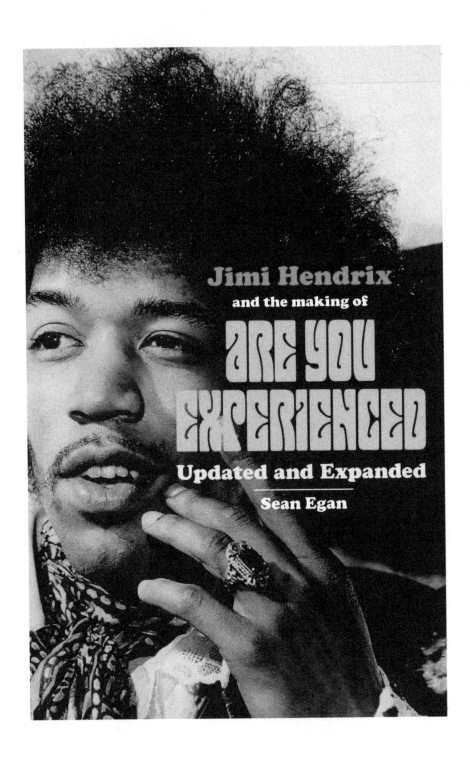

Jimi Hendrix
and the making of

are you
experienced

Updated and Expanded

Sean Egan

ALSO FROM ASKILL PUBLISHING

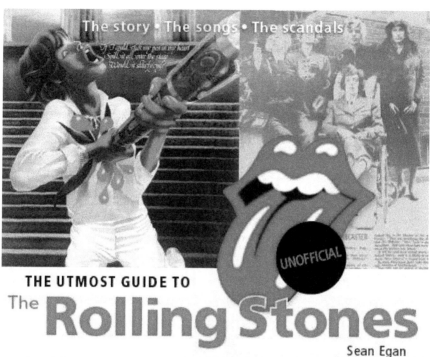

The story • The songs • The scandals

UNOFFICIAL

THE UTMOST GUIDE TO

The Rolling Stones

Sean Egan

THE ESSENTIAL STONES COMPANION

UPDATED

The Rolling Stones are still going strong after five decades. *The Utmost Guide to The Rolling Stones* leaves no stone unturned in exploring all aspects of the tumultuous career of The Greatest Rock 'n' Roll Band in the World.

The Story: From the blues clubs of 60s West London to the world tours and millionaire mansions

The Music: 50 essential songs and the stories behind them, plus the albums, bootlegs, soundtracks and solo projects

The Entourage: The girlfriends, managers and musicians, from Jerry Hall and Marianne Faithfull to Andrew Loog Oldham and Nicky Hopkins

The Rolling Review: The movies, books and websites — all the Stones info you'll ever need

Originally published as *The Rough Guide to The Rolling Stones*, this improved publication comes with larger pages and is in beautiful full colour. An afterword updates the band's story.

"Author Egan does a fine job of freshening well-trodden facts and busting myths... He also nicely steers clear of sycophancy... All in all, a perfect introduction for the wannabe Stoner"
— *Guitar & Bass*

"...illuminating to newcomers, as well as those who imagine that they know it all" — *Record Collector*

ASKILL PUBLISHING

ISBN 978-0-9545750-9-1

ALSO FROM ASKILL PUBLISHING

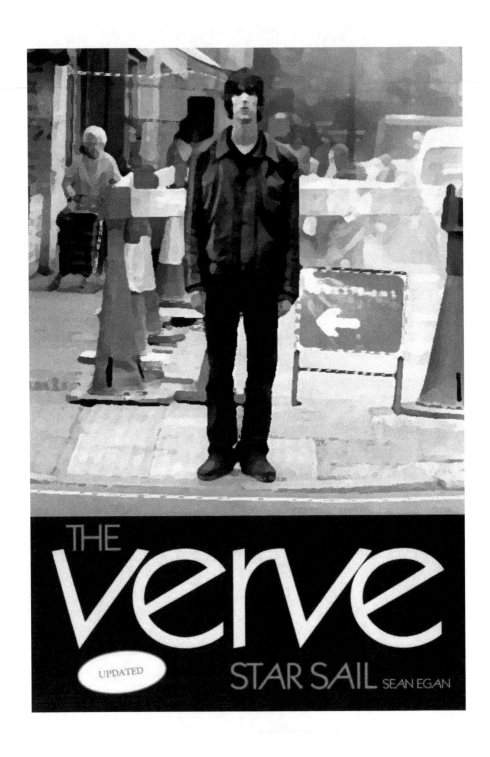

THE verve

UPDATED

STAR SAIL SEAN EGAN

ALSO FROM ASKILL PUBLISHING

CPSIA information can be obtained
at www.ICGtesting.com
Printed in the USA
FSHW04n1947190418
47228FS